EARLY ORIGINS OF
AMERICAN BANKING

Printed and bound by
Antony Rowe Ltd., Chippenham, Wiltshire

THE HISTORY OF BANKING
IN AMERICA

James William Gilbart

ROUTLEDGE/THOEMMES PRESS

This edition published by Routledge/Thoemmes Press, 1996

Routledge/Thoemmes Press
11 New Fetter Lane
London EC4P 4EE

Early Origins of American Banking
7 Volumes : ISBN 0 415 14450 7

This is a reprint of the 1837 edition

Routledge / Thoemmes Press is a joint imprint
of Routledge and Thoemmes Antiquarian Books Ltd.

British Library Cataloguing-in-Publication Data
A CIP record of this set is available from the British Library

Publisher's Note

The publisher has gone to great lengths to ensure the
quality of this reprint but points out that some
imperfections in the original book may be apparent.

THE

HISTORY OF BANKING

IN

AMERICA:

WITH

AN INQUIRY HOW FAR THE BANKING INSTITUTIONS OF
AMERICA ARE ADAPTED TO THIS COUNTRY;

AND

A REVIEW OF THE CAUSES OF THE RECENT PRESSURE ON
THE MONEY MARKET.

BY

JAMES WILLIAM GILBART,

GENERAL MANAGER OF THE LONDON AND WESTMINSTER BANK.

LONDON:

LONGMAN, REES, ORME, BROWN, GREEN, & LONGMAN.

MDCCCXXXVII.

E. JUSTINS AND SON, PRINTERS,
MARK LANE.

PREFACE.

THE " History of Banking in America" was not
written for Americans, nor for persons well acquainted
with American Banking, but for those who know but
little about it, and who have not time to read lengthy
publications on the subject. To give an outline of
the progress of Banking in America—to point out
the principal features in which it differs from English
Banking—to present a summary of the condition of
the Banks in the respective States—and to notice the
opinions with reference to Banking of some of the
leading men in America, is all that has been attempted
in this portion of the work.

The inquiry how far the Banking Institutions of
America are adapted to this country, will point out
more forcibly to the general reader the difference
between the two systems of Banking; while it will
suggest some matters for consideration to those who
feel an interest in the improvement of our Banking
Institutions.

Here this work was intended to close, but the publication of Mr. Horsley Palmer's Pamphlet upon the " Causes and Consequences of the Pressure on the Money Market," and the discussions it occasioned, induced me to write two additional Sections. My chief object in doing this has been to repel the charges brought against the Joint Stock Banks. In noticing the other causes to which the recent pressure has been assigned, I have contented myself with transcribing the sentiments of other writers.

As the publication of Mr. Horsley Palmer has been " looked upon as a sort of official document, embodying the views and opinions of the directors generally," it may be proper to inform the reader, that the work now before him conveys only the individual opinions of the author.

J. W. G.

38, THROGMORTON STREET,
May 1, 1837.

CONTENTS.

SECTION I.

THE RISE AND PROGRESS OF AMERICAN BANKING.

SECTION II.

THE BANK OF THE UNITED STATES.

SECTION III.

THE STATE BANKS.

SECTION IV.

AN INQUIRY HOW FAR THE BANKING INSTITUTIONS OF AMERICA ARE ADAPTED TO THIS COUNTRY.

❖

SECTION V.

A COMPARISON BETWEEN THE ENGLISH AND THE AMERICAN
SYSTEMS OF BANKING, WITH REFERENCE TO THE CUR-
RENCY AND TO THE FOREIGN EXCHANGES.

❖

SECTION VI.

AN INQUIRY INTO THE CAUSES OF THE RECENT PRESSURE ON
THE MONEY MARKET.

APPENDIX.

WORKS

PUBLISHED BY THE SAME AUTHOR.

---

1. THE HISTORY AND PRINCIPLES OF BANKING.

Third Edition.

" A work likely to be extensively useful at this period has just appeared, entitled, " The History and Principles of Banking." By *James William Gilbart.* The author's object has not been to advance any new theories of his own, but to make the reader acquainted with the facts and principles of the question, as deduced from the existing practice. In this, his long experience must make him a very competent guide. The numerous claims on our crowded columns prevent our giving a full notice of the work: the recommendation of which may be summed up in his own phrase—that it is a " Grammar of banking."—*Times, Feb.* 20, 1834.

" This work may be advantageously consulted for a practical knowledge of banking in all shapes from the Bank of England down to loan banks, and the new law to facilitate the purchase of small annuities. It should also be added, that a variety of tables are contained in the volume, not mere transcripts from official documents, but intelligible recasts by a man of business. So far as we are able to judge by inspection, they seem to have the rare merit of containing what is wanted, and nothing more."—*Spectator. Feb.* 15, 1834.

"Combining a clear appreciation of the science of banking, with the best practical knowledge of his business, we have seen no work on this subject which better deserves to be consulted and studied than Mr. Gilbart's volume."—*Literary Gazette, Feb.* 22, 1834.

"Mr. Gilbart claims for his book that it contains both features (theory and practice), and is a scientific work written by a practical man. His claims appear to be fully borne out by the perspicuity of his views, and the analytical spirit with which he treats the subject. He is fully master of the details, and ascends with equal ease to the examination of the elementary principles. His account of the nature of joint stock banks, of branch banks, of deposit, remittance, circulation, and discount, of cash credit, loan and savings banks, will be found by men of business to be of considerable value for reference." —*Atlas, Feb.* 24, 1834.

"We have been highly pleased with its agreeable and instructive character, and we think that no man connected with trade should be without this book."—*Monthly Review, May,* 1834.

"As the author most truly says in his preface, the aim of this book is to impart useful knowledge. Those who are ignorant of the art, or rather science of banking, (for banking may be considered as a science in political economy) will here obtain a knowledge of facts and principles which will sufficiently enlighten their minds on the subject, and they will have the good fortune of not having principles instilled which may lead them into error. The question of currency, cash payments, &c. which have been such a source of labyrinthic litigation are not mooted. It is a clear and well written work, and must have been written by a person endowed with a lucid head and an impartial mind."—*Metropolitan Magazine, August,* 1834.

" A more complete and accurate work, with less irrelevant matter, we never read."—*Gentleman's Magazine, October,* 1834.

" We have before us a most interesting work from the pen of Mr. Gilbart, entitled " The History and Principles of Banking." This subject, which is generally considered abstruse and recondite, has been, by the pen of Mr. Gilbart, rendered so plain, that the most ordinary capacity may easily comprehend it. It requires such a man as the manager of the London and Westminster Bank to produce this work. A speculative theorist, no matter how acute his intellect, must have failed in presenting us with those forcible details which belong only to the practical man, whilst to the mere man of business, that power of combination and mastery of language must have been wanting, which the literary abilities of Mr. Gilbart have enabled him to bring to bear upon the subject. The peculiar interest which it possesses, is owing, as the author truly states in his preface, to the circumstance of its being a scientific work, written by a practical man. The subject of banking, at all times of such importance to a mercantile country, possesses paramount claims to attention at the present moment, when two fresh bodies of *Argentarii* have come into the field to bear away whatever spoil may have escaped the hands of the vetéran campaigners. " The History and Principles of Banking" should be in the hands of every man, who wishes to be acquainted with the manner in which the money transactions of this great country are carried on."—*Waterford Chronicle, June* 9, 1836.

---

2. THE HISTORY OF BANKING IN IRELAND.

" It affords a succinct view of the acts of parliament, through which the banking operations of Ireland were affected from the time of Henry VI. to the present day, shewing briefly the main features of the monetary system in that country."—*Atlas, June* 19, 1836.

" It is a valuable statistical work, and a desirable appendix to his " History and Principles of Banking."—*Gentleman's Magazine, July,* 1836.

" It gives a very clever and succinct account of the History of Banking in Ireland."—*Monthly Review, July,* 1835.

" It is a useful book for those who are anxious for practical information, touching the money matters of the sister kingdom ; or who wish, by investigating her banking system, to track her slow and late progress in commerce and civilization."—*Spectator, July,* 1836.

---

3. A PRACTICAL TREATISE ON BANKING.

Fourth Edition.

" A valuable and useful little work."—*Mr. M'Cullock's Smith's Wealth of Nations."*

THE

HISTORY OF BANKING

IN

AMERICA.

SECTION I.

THE RISE AND PROGRESS OF AMERICAN BANKING.

THE first settlers in America had not a sufficient
quantity of gold and silver to serve as a circulating
medium. Hence other materials, such as tobacco or
corn, were in some of the States occasionally employed as money. In the year 1618, Governor
Argall, of Virginia,* ordered " that all goods should
be sold at an advance of twenty-five per cent., and
tobacco taken in payment at three shillings per pound,
and not more or less, on the penalty of three years
servitude to the Colony." In 1641, the General
Court of Massachusetts " made orders about payment
of debts, setting CORN at the usual price, and making
it payable for all debts which should arise after a time
prefixed." In 1643, the same General Court ordered
that WAMPOMPEAG (an article of traffic with the
Indians) should pass current in the payment of debts
to the amount of forty shillings, the white at eight a
penny, the black at four a penny, except for county
rates. In Virginia, the value of a wife even was
estimated in tobacco. The following extract is taken
from Holmes' American Annals:

---

* See " A Short History of Paper Money and Banking in the
United States," published by William M. Gouge, at Philadelphia, 1833.

B

" The enterprizing colonists being generally des-
titute of families, Sir Edward Sandys, the treasurer,
proposed to the Virginia Company to send over a
freight of young women to become wives for the
planters. The proposal was applauded, and ninety
girls, ' young and uncorrupt,' were sent over in the
ships that arrived this year (1620,) and the year
following, sixty more, handsome and well recommended to the company for their virtuous education
and demeanor. The price of a wife at the first was
one hundred pounds of tobacco; but as the number
became scarce, the price was increased to *one hundred
and fifty pounds;* the value of which in money was
three shillings per pound. This debt for wives it was
ordered should have the precedency of all other debts,
and be first recoverable."

The Rev. Mr. Weems, a Virginian writer, intimates
that it would have done a man's heart good to see the
gallant young Virginians hastening to the water side,
when a vessel arrived from London, each carrying a
bundle of the best tobacco under his arm, and taking
back with him a beautiful and virtuous young wife.

So late as in the year 1732, an act was passed at
Maryland, making tobacco a legal tender at one penny
a pound, and Indian corn at twenty-pence a bushel.

Afterwards gold and silver became more plentiful.
In 1652, a mint was established in New England, for
coining shillings, sixpences, and three-penny pieces.
In 1645, Virginia prohibited dealings by barter, and
established the Spanish piece of eight, as six shillings,
as the standard currency of that colony. In all the
colonies the money of account was the same nominally
as in England, but the coin was chiefly Spanish and
Portugueze. But different colonies affixed various
values to the dollar. In South Carolina, the dollar
was estimated at 4s. 8d.—in Virginia and New England,
at 6s.—in Pennsylvania, New Jersey, and Maryland,
at 7s. 6d.—and in New York and North Carolina, at 8s.

Paper money was first issued by the State of Massachusetts in 1690. A public bank was established

in South Carolina in 1702, and issued £48,000 in
bank bills, to be lent at interest, and sunk at the rate
of £4,000 a year. Pennsylvania first issued paper
money in 1723. The province of Virginia does not appear to have issued any paper money previous to the
revolutionary war.

At the commencement of that war, paper money
was issued upon the authority of Congress. This
money was called continental money. The first issue
was dated May 10, 1775, but the notes were not
actually in circulation until the following August.

" The paper money issued by Congress during the war of the American independence, experienced no sensible depreciation before the
year 1776, and so long as the amount did not exceed nine millions of
dollars. A paper currency, equal in value to that sum in gold and
silver, could therefore be sustained so long as confidence was preserved.
The issues were gradually increased during the ensuing years, and in
April, 1778, amounted to thirty millions. A depreciation was the
natural consequence; but had the value of the paper depended solely
on its amount, the whole quantity in circulation would have still been
equal in value to nine millions, and the depreciation should not have
been more than 3⅓ to 1 ; instead of which, it was then at the rate of
six dollars in paper for one silver dollar, and the whole amount of the
paper in circulation was worth only five millions in silver.

" It is obvious that the difference was due to lessened confidence. The
capture of Burgoyne's army was followed by the alliance with France,
and her becoming a party to the war against England. The result of the
war was no longer considered as doubtful, and sanguine expectations
were formed of its speedy termination. The paper accordingly rose in
value; and in June, 1778, although the issues had been increased to
more than forty-five millions, the depreciation was at the rate of only
four to one. From the end of April of that year, to the month of
February, 1779, although the issues had been increased from thirty-
five to one hundred and fifteen millions, the average value in
silver of the whole amount of paper in circulation exceeded ten millions,
and it was at one time nearly thirteen millions, or considerably more
than that which could be sustained at the outset of the hostilities.
But when it was discovered that the war would be of longer continuance, confidence in the redemption of a paper money daily increasing in amount was again suddenly lessened.

" The depreciation was increased from the rate of six to that of
thirty to one in nine months.

" The average value in silver of the whole amount of paper in circulation, from April to September, 1779, was about six millions, and it
sunk below five during the end of the year. The total amount of the
paper was at that time 200,000,000 ; and although no farther issues
took place, and a portion was absorbed by the loan offices and by

taxes, the depreciation still increased, and was at the end of the year 1780, at the rate of eighty dollars in paper for one in silver. The value in silver of the paper currency was then less than two and a half millions of dollars; and when Congress, in March following, acknowledged the depreciation, and offered to exchange the old for new paper, at the rate of forty for one, the old sunk in one day to nothing, and the new shared the same fate."—*Considerations on the Currency and Banking System of the United States, by Albert Gallatin, Philadelphia,* 1831.

According to an estimate by the register of the treasury in 1790, the issues of continental money were as follows :—

	OLD EMISSION.		NEW EMISSION.	
	Dollars.	90th.	Dollars.	90th.
In 1776.........	20,064,464	66	—	
1777.........	26,426,333	1	—	
1778.........	66,965,269	34	—	
1779.........	149,703,856	77	—	
1780.........	82,908,320	47	891,236	80
1781.........	11,408,095	—	1,179,249	—
	357,476,541	45	2,070,485	80

On the 31st May, 1781, the continental notes ceased to circulate as money, but they were afterwards bought on speculation at various prices, from 400 for one, up to 1,000 for one.

In the year 1781, the Congress granted a charter to be called the " Bank of North America." It was accordingly established in Philadelphia, and commenced business on Jan. 7, 1782. It obtained a charter of incorporation upon the ground that it would offer assistance to the States in carrying on the war. So profitable was the business that the early dividends were at the rate of 12 to 16 per cent. per annum. Upon an allegation that the bank had produced evil effects, its charter was repealed in Sept. 1785, by the state government of Pennsylvania; but it continued its business, claiming the right to do so under the act of Congress. In 1787, the bank was re-incorporated, and has been continued to the present day. Its operations are confined however to the state of Pennsylvania.

After the conclusion of the war it was provided by the constitution of the United States, that no state should coin money, emit bills of credit, make any thing but gold and silver coin a tender in payment of debts, or pass any law impairing the obligation of contracts; and the power to coin money, and to regulate the value thereof, was vested exclusively in Congress.

This article of the constitution has given rise to considerable discussion, as it involves the question whether Congress has the power to constitute a national bank. The following summary of the arguments on both sides is taken from Mr. Justice Story's " Commentaries on the Constitution of the United States."

" One of the earliest and most important measures, which gave rise to a question of constitutional power, was the act chartering the Bank of the United States in 1791. That question has often since been discussed ; and though the measure has been repeatedly sanctioned by Congress, by the executive, and by the judiciary, and has obtained the like favour in the great majority of the States, yet it is, up to this very hour, still debated upon constitutional grounds, as if it were still new and untried. It is impossible, at this time, to treat it as an open question, unless the constitution is for ever to remain an unsettled text, possessing no permanent attributes, and incapable of having any ascertained sense; varying with every change of doctrine and of party, and delivered over to interminable doubts.

" The reasoning, upon which the constitutionality of a national bank is denied, turns upon the strict interpretation of the clause, giving auxiliary powers necessary and proper to execute the other enumerated powers. It is to the following effect. The power to incorporate a bank is not among those enumerated in the constitution. In the next place, all the enumerated powers can be carried into execution without a bank. A bank therefore is not *necessary*, and consequently not authorized by this clause of the constitution. It is urged that a bank will give great facility or convenience to the collection of taxes. If this were true, yet the constitution allows only the means which are *necessary*, and not merely those which are *convenient* for effecting the enumerated powers. If such a latitude of construction were allowed, as to consider convenience as justifying the use of such means, it would swallow up all the enumerated powers. Therefore, the constitution restrains Congress to those means, without which the power would be nugatory.

" The reasoning by which the constitutionality of the national bank is sustained is, in part, contained in the following summary. The powers confided to the national government are unquestionably, so far as they exist, sovereign and supreme. It is not, and cannot be disputed, that the power of creating a corporation is one belonging to sovereignty. But so are all other legislative powers; for the original power of giving the law on any subject whatever is a sovereign power. If the erecting of a corporation be an incident to sovereignty, and it is not prohibited, it must belong to the national government in relation to the objects entrusted to it. The true difference is this : where the authority of a government is general, it can create corporations in all cases ; when it is confined to certain branches of legislation, it can create corporations only as to those cases. It cannot be denied, that implied powers may be delegated as well as express. It follows that a power to erect corporations may as well be implied, as any other thing, if it be an instrument, or means of carrying into execution any specified power.

" It is true, that among the enumerated powers we do not find that of establishing a bank or creating a corporation. But we do find there the great powers to lay and collect taxes, to borrow money, to regulate commerce, to declare and conduct war, and to raise and support navies. Now if a bank be a fit means to execute any or all of these powers, it is just as much implied as any other means. If it be 'necessary and proper' for any of them, how is it possible to deny the authority to create it for such purposes ? There is no more propriety in giving this power in express terms, than in giving any other incidental power or means in express terms.

" That a national bank is an appropriate means to carry into effect some of the enumerated powers of the government, and that this can be best done by erecting it into a corporation, may be established by the most satisfactory reasoning. It has a relation, more or less direct, to the power of collecting taxes, to that of borrowing money, to that of regulating trade between states, and to those of raising and maintaining fleets and armies. And it may be added, that it has a most important bearing upon the regulation of currency between the States. It is an instrument, which has been applied by governments, in the administration of their fiscal and financial operations ; and in the present times it can hardly require argument to prove, that it is a convenient, a useful, and an essential instrument in the fiscal operations of the United States."

The constitution of the United States was adopted in 1789, and shortly after the government was organized. On the 14th of December, 1790, the then secretary of the treasury, (General Hamilton) reported to Congress the plan of a bank. In February, 1791, the bill passed, and was presented to General Washington for his approval. In the progress of the bill it was opposed by Mr. Madison, (subsequently president) Mr. Giles, and others, on the ground that the States had not delegated the power to create such an institution, and therefore that it was unconstitutional. It was supported by Mr. Ames, Mr. Boudinot, &c., who were members of what was termed, in those days, the high-toned federal party.

The president, (General Washington) previous to signing the bill, consulted his cabinet ministers. Thomas Jefferson, secretary of state, and Edmund Randolph, attorney-general of the United States, were opposed to his signing it. Alexander Hamilton, secretary of the treasury, and General Knox, secretary of war, were in favour of it. At that time there was no secretary of the Navy. On the 25th of February, 1791, the president approved of the bill, and it became a law.

The following account of this bank is taken from the American almanack of 1835.

" The idea of this institution was conceived immediately after the adoption of the constitution, by Alexander Hamilton, the founder of the American system of finance, when secretary of the treasury ; the plan of it was submitted to Congress Dec. 13, 1790; and it was incorporated by act of Congress, and approved Feb. 1791, in the first term of Washington's administration. Its continuance was limited by the charter to the 4th of March, 1811, at which time it expired, as Congress refused to renew the charter.

" The capital was limited to $10,000,000, divided into 25,000 shares, of $400 each, payable one-fourth in gold and silver, and three-fourths in public securities bearing an interest of six and three per cent. The corporation were restricted from contracting debts beyond the amount of their capital, and from holding property, exceeding the value of $15,000,000, or real estate more than necessary for the convenient transacting of their business. The affairs of the bank were to be managed by twenty-four directors, to be elected by the stockholders, without any interference on the part of the government in the election ; but the government reserved the right of inspecting of the affairs of the bank ; and for this purpose the secretary of the treasury was authorized to demand of the president and directors a statement of its concerns as often as he might see fit.

" The subscriptions were filled as soon as opened.

The government, conformably to the right reserved in the charter, subscribed for 5,000 shares, equal to $2,000,000 ; and the bank went into immediate operation. Its stock, a great portion of which was held in Europe, soon rose considerably above par ; and the institution proved always convenient, on some occasions eminently useful to the government, and not less beneficial to the public at large. The dividends were made semi-annually ; and, during the twenty years' continuance of the charter, the average annual dividend amounted to $8\frac{1}{3}$ per cent.

" The bank was not merely or principally a commercial establishment, but was essentially and mainly of a finanical and political character ; and it was on this ground that its constitutionality was defended ; the right of Congress to grant such a charter being maintained chiefly upon the strength of that clause of the constitution, which gives to it the power necessary for carrying into execution the powers enumerated, and expressly invested in that body. At the time of its establishment, it was opposed on the ground of its presumed unconstitutionality, by the political party, then in the minority, of which Mr. Jefferson was regarded as the leader ; and before the termination of the charter, this party having come into power, the renewal of the charter was refused, and the institution was dissolved."

In June, 1812, war was declared against England ; and by August and Sept. 1814, all the banks south and west of New England, had suspended their specie payments. This suspension of cash payments in America is ascribed by Mr. Gallatin to the following causes :—

" It has always been found difficult to ascertain with precision the causes which, in each special case, produce an extraordinary drain of specie, and compel a bank to suspend its payments.

" Although it clearly appears, that very large and unforeseen advances to government were the immediate cause of the suspension of the payments of the Bank of England in the year 1797, it would seem, at this distance of time, to have been easy to prevent that occurrence. The bills of exchange from abroad on government, or any other floating debt, from the payment of which the bank was required to make those advances, might with facility have been converted into funded debt.

And when we find that in less than seven months after the suspension, the bank declared, by a solemn resolution, that it was enabled to issue specie, and could with safety resume its accustomed functions, if the political circumstances of the country did not render it inexpedient, it is hardly possible to doubt that the suspension, in its origin, as in its continuance, was a voluntary act on the part of the government. Opinions are however divided to this day on that subject ; and some distinguished English writers ascribe that event to some unaccountable panic. There can be no doubt that there was a great and continued run on the bank for specie prior to the suspension ; and what renders the transaction still more inexplicable is, that almost immediately, and during some years after the suspension had actually taken place, the bank notes, though no longer convertible into specie, were at par.

" The question is not free of difficulty as respects the similar event in the United States.

" The following reasons were assigned by the directors of the chartered banks of Philadelphia, in an address to their fellow-citizens, dated the 30th of August, 1813.

" ' From the moment when the rigorous blockade of the ports of the United States prevented the exportation of our produce, foreign supplies could be paid for in specie only ; and as the importation of foreign goods in the eastern states has been very large, it has for many months past occasioned a continual drain from the banks. This drain has been much increased by a trade in British government bills of exchange, which has been extensively carried on, and has caused very large sums to be exported from the United States.

" ' To meet this great demand for specie, the course of trade did, for a considerable time, enable us to draw large supplies from the Southern States, but the unhappy situation of affairs there, having deprived us of that resource, and circumstances having occurred, which have in a considerable degree occasioned alarm and distrust ; it became a serious consideration, whether the banks should continue their exertions to draw within their vaults the specie capital of the country, and thus facilitate the means of exporting it from the United States ; or whether they should suspend the payment of specie, before their means were exhausted.'

" The great drain from the east, alluded to by the Philadelphia banks, is proved by the comparative view of the specie in the vaults of the banks of Massachusetts, in June 1814, immediately before the suspension of payments, and on the same days of the preceding and succeeding years.

This amounted on June 1, 1811 to $1,709,000
    ,,   1812   3,915,000
    ,,   1813   6,171,000
    ,,   1814   7,326,000
    ,,   1815   3,915,000
    ,,   1816   1,270,000

And the fact that a large amount of British government bills was sent to this country from Canada in the years 1812—1814, and sold at twenty and twenty-two per cent. discount, is corroborated by authentic information from several quarters. Other causes, however, concurred in producing the suspension of specie payments.

" 1. The circulating capital of the United States, which must supply the loans required in time of war, is concentrated in the large cities, and principally north of the Potomac. The war was unpopular in the Eastern States; they contributed less than from their wealth might have been anticipated; and the burthen fell on the Middle States. The proceeds of loans, (exclusively of treasury notes, and temporary loans) paid into the treasury from the commencement of the war to the end of the year 1814, amounted to forty-one millions ten thousand dollars. Of that sum the

Eastern States lent	$2,900,000
New York, Pennsylvania, Maryland and Columbia	35,790,000
The Southern and Western States...	2,320,000

" The floating debt, consisting of outstanding treasury notes, and temporary loans unpaid, amounted on January 1st, 1815, to eleven millions two hundred and fifty thousand dollars, about four-fifths of which were also due to the Middle States. Almost the whole of the large amount advanced to government in those States, was loaned by the cities of New York, Philadelphia, and Baltimore, and by the district. The banks made advances beyond their resources, either by their own subscriptions, or by enlarging their discounts in favour of the subscribers. They, as well as several wealthy and patriotic citizens, displayed great zeal in sustaining government at a critical moment; and the banks were for that purpose compelled to enlarge their issues.

" 2. The dissolution of the bank of the United States deprived the country of a foreign capital of more than seven millions of dollars, vested in the stock of that institution, and which was accordingly remitted abroad during the year that preceded the war. At the same time, the state banks, had taken up a considerable part of the paper formerly discounted by that of the United States. As the amount of this exceeded fifteen millions, their aid in that respect was absolutely necessary, in order to prevent the great distress which must otherwise have attended such diminution of the usual accommodations.

" 3. The creation of new state banks, in order to fill the chasm, was a natural consequence of the dissolution of the bank of the United States. And, as is usual under such circumstances, the expectation of great profits gave birth to a much greater number than was wanted. They were extended through the interior parts of the country, created no new capital, and withdrew that which might have been otherwise lent to government, or as profitably employed. From the 1st January, 1811, to the 1st January, 1815, not less than one hundred and twenty new banks were chartered and went into operation, with a capital of about forty, and making an addition to the banking capital of the country of near thirty millions of dollars. That increase took place on the eve of, and during a war which did nearly annihilate the exports, and both the foreign and coasting trade. And as the salutary regulating power of the bank of the United States no longer existed, the issues were accordingly increased much beyond what the other circumstances already mentioned rendered necessary."

In February, 1815, peace was proclaimed with England, and it was expected that the bank would immediately return to cash payments. Bank notes accordingly rose in value, but as this expectation was not realized they again sunk in value.

The suspension of cash payments in the United States differed from that of England in two particulars; first, it did not take place throughout the country. Secondly, as each bank was independent, there was a different scale of depreciation for each county and each town. The following is the scale of depreciation per cent. at Baltimore, Philadelphia, and New York.

	Balti-more.	Phila-delphia.	New York.		Balti-more.	Phila-delphia.	New York.
1814. Sept.	20		10	1815. Dec.	18	14	12⅔
Oct.	15		10	1816. Jan.	15	14	12½
Nov.	10		11	Feb.	13	14	9
Dec.	14		11	March	18	12½	12½
1815. Jan.	20		15	April	23	14½	10
Feb.	5		2	May	20	14	12½
March	5		5	June	20	17	12½
April	10		5½	July	15	15	6
May	14	5	5	Aug.	12	10	5
June	16	9	11½	Sept.	10	7½	3
July	20	11	14	Oct.	8	9½	2
Aug.	19	11	12½	Nov.	9	7	1¾
Sept.	20		13	Dec.	9	7	2¼
Oct.	21½	15	16	1817. Jan.	3	4½	2½
Nov.	15	16	12½	Feb.	2½	4	2½

SECTION II.

THE BANK OF THE UNITED STATES.

The state banks having suspended cash payments, the treasury was compelled to receive the taxes in the local currencies of the various districts. All notes

which circulated at par were received, but those
which were at a discount were rejected. The
banks which did not suspend cash payments very
much restricted their issues; and hence there was
such a scarcity of money in those States that the
taxes could not be collected. To meet this emergency, the government issued treasury notes, somewhat resembling our exchequer bills, which bore
interest at six per cent.

Another difficulty which the government experienced from the condition of the banks was in the
transmission of money from one State to another.
The money which was collected at one place was
required to be expended at another. But the banks
of one State had no connexion with those of the
others. Hence the government had great difficulty
in paying any sum of money either for supplies or
services at any particular place, where the party to
whom the money was due might happen to reside.

Another inconvenience was, that the government
was obliged to employ as agents for receiving the
taxes, a vast number of banks. Had there been one
national bank, with a branch in each state, the collectors would have lodged the taxes at the various
branches, and the head office would have accounted
for the whole to the government. But the country
was studded with a great number of banks totally
independent of each other, and refusing to take each
others' notes. The greater part of these banks had
also stopped payment, though their notes still circulated at a discount. At the same time there was
a risk in having large sums of money in the hands
of the collectors. The collectors were therefore in-
structed to lodge the taxes in the banks of their
respective districts; and thus the treasury had
accounts open at no fewer than ninety-four banks.
The sums lodged in these banks were usually composed of—1. Notes of the bank in which the taxes were
deposited—2. Notes of other banks—3. Treasury
notes bearing interest—4. Small treasury notes not

bearing interest. As to coin, that was out of the question.

The confusion thus introduced into the public accounts, as well as into private transactions, led to the formation of the second Bank of the United States. The act of incorporation was passed in the session of 1816.

By this act a Bank of the United States of America was to be established, with a capital of 35,000,000 dollars, to be divided into 350,000 shares of 100 dollars each—70,000 shares or 7,000,000 dollars to be subscribed and paid for by the government of the United States.

The payments of the subscriptions to be made by instalments, one-fourth in gold or silver coin, the remainder in like coin or funded debt of the United States.

It was declared lawful for the United States to redeem the funded debt subscribed, and for the bank to sell the same for gold and silver, provided that it shall not sell more than 2,000,000 dollars thereof in any one year, nor any part without giving notice to the secretary of the treasury, and offering it to the United States at the current price.

The management of the affairs of the bank was committed to twenty-five directors, five of whom being stockholders to be appointed annually by the President of the United States and the Senate; not more than three of whom to be residents of any one State, and twenty of whom to be annually elected by the qualified stockholders.

The corporation was restricted from contracting debts exceeding the sum of 35,000,000 dollars, unless authorized by law. Not to make any loan to the United States, exceeding 500,000 dollars, nor to any particular State exceeding 50,000 dollars, nor to any foreign State, unless authorized by law. The dividends to be paid half-yearly; a statement of the affairs of the bank to be laid before the stockholders every three years. The secretary was authorized to call upon the

bank for a statement, not exceeding a weekly one of
its concerns.   No stockholder unless he be a citizen
of the United States to vote in the choice of directors.
In case they suspended payments in specie, the corporation was made chargeable with interest at the
rate of twelve per cent. per annum.   The notes of
the bank were to be received in all payments to the
government ; and on the other hand, the bank was
bound to receive and transmit the public revenue free
of charge.   Congress to establish no other bank except in the district of Colombia.

The bank commenced business at Philadelphia,
January 1, 1817.

In the latter end of the same month a meeting of
delegates from the banks of New York, Philadelphia,
Baltimore, and Virginia, took place at Philadelphia,
with a view to a general and simultaneous resumption
of cash payments.   In consequence of a compact
between them and the Bank of the United States,
sanctioned by the secretary of the treasury, cash
payments were resumed.   To facilitate this object,
the Bank of the United States imported from abroad
seven millions of dollars in specie, and agreed to
afford reasonable assistance to such of the State banks
as might require it.   The resumption of cash payments was now general throughout the union.

The year 1819 was one of great commercial difficulty in America.   This distress was attributed to
those measures which it had been found necessary to
adopt in order to effect a return to cash payments.
To accomplish this object, the State banks had been
compelled to restrict their issues by limiting their
discounts.   Many of those banks which were formed
at the dissolution of the first bank of the United
States now failed.   And the new bank of the United
States, which had in the first instance made very
liberal advances to the Western States, were obliged
to resort to measures for compelling the repayment
of their loans.   Those too who had contracted debts
either to the banks or to private parties in the de-

preciated currency, sustained great loss when required to discharge their obligations in a currency convertible into gold.

The Bank of the United States established a branch or office in each state. At each branch deposits were received, bills and notes of hand discounted, and letters of credit granted payable on demand upon all the other branches. Their notes were legally payable at the respective branches where they were issued, but were often paid as matter of courtesy at the other branches. The *five dollar notes*, the lowest issued by any branch were made legally payable at every branch.

Average Amount for the years 1819—1829, *of the principal items of the Situation of the Bank of the United States.*

	Discounts.	Domestic Bills.	Funded Debt.	Total on Interest.	Real Estate.	Specie.	Deposits.	Gross am. of Notes.*
1819	32,211,674	336,760	7,236,153	39,784,587		2,743,834	5,734,682	5,056,829
1820	28,808,267	1,526,600	8,258,701	38,593,568		5,214,773	6,581,628	4,410,332
1821	27,099,050	1,598,473	11,859,296	40,556,619	245,846	6,469,224	6,990,073	5,609,220
1822	28,574,893	2,394,688	13,116,004	44,085,785	579,152	3,711,145	6,365,570	3,562,335
1823	30,584,919	2,588,245	10,911,700	44,084,864	736,370	4,899,686	10,401,786	4,671,271
1824	29,478,255	2,563,672	13,373,095	45,415,022	1,393,193	5,909,351	12,918,108	5,935,496
1825	29,327,219	3,270,699	19,807,665	52,405,583	1,566,728	4,686,557	12,885,829	8,836,646
1826	29,592,102	3,592,145	17,885,210	51,069,458	1,745,566	5,174,643	12,578,523	10,235,528
1827	27,948,592	4,568,297	17,724,192	50,244,081	2,118,560	6,327,758	13,727,274	10,808,244
1828	30,820,944	6,018,784	17,127,077	53,966,805	2,298,352	6,205,107	14,454,169	12,414,390
1289	32,703,280	8,417,021	13,925,701	55,046,002	2,474,750	6,411,998	15,172,164	15,011,352

* The actual amount of circulation is generally four-fifths of the gross amount, the rest being notes *in transitu,* or accumulated in offices where they are not payable.

Actual Circulation of the Bank of the United States in September, 1830, *and Places where the Notes were payable.*

Where payable.	Notes in circulation.	Where payable.	Notes in circulation
	Dollars.		Dollars.
Bank United States	1,367,180	Amount brought forward...	7,190,095
Portland	79,280	Mobile	940,825
Portsmouth	101,985	New Orleans	2,623,320
Boston	271,180	St. Louis	228,700
Providence	113,920	Nashville	1,235,275
Hartford	171,532	Louisville	662,375
New York	834,733	Lexington	908,625
Baltimore	528,638	Cincinnati	647,240
Washington	647,602	Pittsburg	554,102
Richmond	469,440	Buffalo	258,130
Norfolk	532,400	Burlington	96,595
Fayetteville	713,760	Agencies Cincinati and Chillicothe	2,375
Charleston	835,840		
Savannah	522,605		
Amount carried forward	7,190,095		15,347,657

In the year 1831, Mr. Albert Gallatin thus speaks of the advantages derived from the Bank of the United States:

" Experience, however, has since confirmed the great utility and importance of a Bank of the United States, in its connexion with the treasury. The first great advantage derived from it, consists in the safe keeping of the public monies ; securing, in the first instance, the immediate payment of those received by the principal collectors, and affording a constant check on all their transactions; and afterwards rendering a defalcation in the monies once paid, and whilst nominally in the treasury, absolutely impossible. The next, and not less important benefit is to be ¡found in the perfect facility with which all the public payments are made by the cheques or treasury drafts, payable. at any place where the bank has an office ; all those who have demands against government are paid in the place most convenient to them ; and the public monies are transferred, through our extensive territory, at a moment's warning, without any risk or expense, to the places most remote from those of collection, and wherever public exigencies may require. From the year 1791 to this day, the operations of the treasury have, without interruption, been carried on through the medium of banks ; during the years 1811 to 1816 through the State banks ; before and since, through the bank of the United States. Every individual who has been at the head of that department, and, as we believe, every officer connected with it, has been made sensible of the great difficulties that must be encountered without the assistance of those institutions; and of the comparative ease, and great additional security to the public, with which their public duties are performed through the means of the banks. To insist that the operations of the treasury may be carried on with equal facility and safety, through the aid of the State banks, without the interposition of a bank of the United States, would be contrary to fact and experience.

" The uniformity of duties and taxes of every description, whether internal or external, direct or indirect, is an essential and fundamental principle of the constitution. It is self-evident, that that uniformity cannot be carried into effect without a corresponding uniformity of currency. Without laws to this effect, it is absolutely impossible that the taxes and duties should be uniform, as the constitution prescribes : such laws are therefore necessary and proper, in the most strict sense of the words. There are but two means of effecting the object, a metallic, or a uniform paper currency. Congress has the option of either ; and either of the two, which may appear most eligible, will be strictly constitutional, because strictly necessary and proper for carrying into effect the object. If a currency exclusively metallic is preferred, the object will be attained by laying prohibitory stamp duties on bank notes of every description, and without exception. If it is deemed more eligible, under existing circumstances instead of subverting the whole banking system in the United States, and depriving the community of the accommodation which bank loans afford to resort to less harsh means; recourse must be had to such, as will ensure a currency sound and uniform itself, and at the same time check and regulate that which will continue to constitute the greater part of the currency of the country.

" Both those advantages were anticipated in the establishment of the bank of the United States; and it appears to us, that the bank fulfils both those conditions. As respects the past, it is a matter of fact, that specie payments were restored, and have been maintained, through the instrumentality of that institution. It gives a complete guarantee, that under any circumstances, its notes will preserve the same uniformity which they now possess.

" Placed under the control of the general government, relying for its existence on the correctness, prudence, and skill with which it shall be administered, perpetually watched, and occasionally checked by both the treasury department and rival institutions; and without a monopoly, yet with a capital and resources adequate to the object for which it was established. The bank also affords the strongest security which can be given with respect to paper, not only for its ultimate solvency, but also for the uninterrupted soundness of its currency. The statements we have given of its progressive and present situation, show how far those expectations have heretofore been realized. Those statements also show that the bank of the United States wherever its operations have been extended, has effectually checked excessive issues on the part of the state banks; if not in every instance, certainly in the aggregate. They had been reduced before the year 1820 from sixty-six to less than forty millions. At that time those of the bank of the United States fell short of four millions. The increased amount required, by the increase of population and wealth during the ten ensuing years, has been supplied in a much greater proportion by that bank, than by those of the States. With a treble capital, they have added little more than eight millions to their issues. Those of the bank of the United States were nominally twelve, in reality about eleven millions greater in November, 1829, than in November, 1819. The whole amount of the paper currency has, during those ten years, increased about forty-five, and that portion which is issued by the state banks only twenty-two and a half per cent. We have indeed a proof, not very acceptable perhaps to the bank, but conclusive of the fact, that it has performed the office required of it in that respect. The general complaints on the part of many of the state banks, that they are checked and controlled in their operations by the bank of the United States, that, to use a common expression, it operates as a screw, is the best evidence that its general operation is such as had been intended. It was for that very purpose that the bank was established. We are not however, aware, that a single solvent bank has been injured by that of the United States, though many have been undoubtedly restrained in their operations much more than was desirable to them. This is certainly inconvenient to some of the banks, but in its general effects is a public benefit to the community. The best way to judge whether, in performing that unpopular duty, the bank of the United States has checked the operations of the state banks more than was necessary, and has abused, in order to enrich itself

C

at their expense, the power which was given for another purpose, is to compare their respective situations in the aggregate. In order to avoid any erroneous inference, we will put out of question those banks of which we could only make an estimate, and compare, with that of the United States, those only of which we have actual returns. The profits of banks, beyond the interest on their own capital, consists, in that which they receive on the difference between the aggregate of their deposits and notes in circulation and the amount of specie in their vaults. We have given the aggregate situation for the end of the year 1829 of two hundred and eighty-one banks, with a capital of 95,003,557 dollars, the deposits and circulating notes of which

Amounted together to $71,706,033
Deduct specie in their vaults........ 11,989,643

Leaves for difference 59,716,390
Or sixty-two and one-eighth per cent. on their capital.

" The notes in circulation of the bank of the United States (adding one million for its drafts in circulation) amounted in November, 1829, to $14,042,984; and together

With the deposits to................. $28,827,793
Deducting specie 7,175,274

Leaves for the difference 21,652,519
Or sixty-one and one-eighth per cent. on its capital.

" It is clear that those state banks, taken in the aggregate, have no just reason to complain, since that of the United States imposes no greater restraints on them than on itself. It will also be perceived, that it had in specie more than one-fifth part of the aggregate of its notes in circulation and deposits ; whilst the state banks, had little more than one-sixth, and the bank of the United States had in addition a fund of about one million of dollars in Europe. The difference would have been more striking, had we taken a view of the situation of all the state banks, including those on estimate ; for the difference between the aggregate of their notes and deposits and their specie is sixty-seven and a quarter on their capital.

" The manner in which the bank checks the issues of the state banks, is equally simple and obvious. It consists in receiving the notes, of all those which are solvent, and requiring payment from time to time, without suffering the balance due by any to become too large. Those notes on hand, taking the average of the last three years and a half, amount always to about one million and a half of dollars; and the balances due by the banks in account current (deducting balances due to some) to about $900,000.

" We think that we may say, that on this operation, which requires particular attention and vigilance, and must be carried on with great firmness and due forbearance, depends almost exclusively the stability of the currency of the country.

" The principal advantages derived from the bank of the United

States, which no state bank, and as it appears to us, no bank established on different principles could afford, are, therefore ; first and principally, securing with certainty an uniform, and as far as paper can, a sound currency: secondly, the complete security, and great facility it affords to government in its fiscal operations : thirdly, the great convenience and benefit accruing to the community, from its extensive transactions in domestic bills of exchange and inland drafts. We have not adverted to the aid which may be expected from that institution in time of war, and which should, we think, be confined to two objects.

" First. The experience of the last war has sufficiently proved, that an efficient revenue must be provided, before, or immediately after that event takes place. Resort must be had for that purpose to a system of internal taxation, not engrafted on taxes previously existing, but which must be at once created.

" The utmost diligence and skill cannot render such new taxes productive before twelve or eighteen months. The estimated amount must be anticipated ; and advances to that extent, including at least the estimated proceeds of one year, of all the additional taxes laid during the war, may justly be expected from the bank of the United States.

" Secondly. It will also be expected, that it will powerfully assist in raising the necessary loans, not by taking up, on its own account, any sum beyond what may be entirely convenient and consistent, with the safety and primary object of the institution, but by affording facilities to the money lenders. Those who, in the first instance, subscribe to a public loan, do not intend to keep the whole, but expect to distribute it gradually, with a reasonable profit. The greatest inducements, in order to obtain loans on moderate terms, consists in the probability that, if that distribution proceeds slower than had been anticipated, the subscribers will not be compelled, in order to pay their instalments, to sell the stock, and by glutting the market, to sell it at a loss ; and the assistance expected from the bank is to advance, on a deposit of the scrip, after the two first instalments have been paid, such portions of each succeeding payment, as may enable the subscribers to hold the stock a reasonable length of time. As this operation may be renewed annually on each successive loan, whilst the war continues, the aid afforded in that manner is far more useful than large direct advances to government, which always cripple the resources, and may endanger the safety of a bank."

In 1832 a law passed both houses of Congress for a renewal of the charter of the bank of the United States ; but the president, General Jackson, refused to ratify it. This power is conferred upon the President by the following article of the constitution of the United States :

" Every bill that shall have passed the House of Representatives and the Senate, shall before it become a law be presented to the President of the United States. If he approves, he shall sign it ; but if not, he shall return it, with his objections, to that House in which it shall have originated, who shall enter the objections at large on their journal, and proceed to reconsider it. If after such reconsideration two-thirds of that House shall agree to pass the bill, it shall be sent, together with the objections, to the other House, by which it shall likewise be reconsidered ; and if approved by two-thirds of that House, it shall become a law. But in all such cases, the votes of both Houses shall be determined by yeas and nays; and the names of the persons voting for and against the bill, shall be entered on the journal of each House respectively."

The President returned the bill to the Senate, with a very long message stating his objections. The following are extracts :

"The bill "to modify and continue" the act entitled "an act to incorporate the subscribers to the bank of the United States," was presented to me on the 4th July inst. Having considered it with that solemn regard to the principles of the constitution, which the day was calculated to inspire, and come to the conclusion that it ought not to become a law, I herewith return it to the Senate, in which it originated, with my objections.

"A bank of the United States is, in many respects, convenient for the government, and useful to the people. Entertaining this opinion, and deeply impressed with the belief that some of the powers and privileges possessed by the existing bank, are unauthorised by the constitution, subversive of the rights of the States, and dangerous to the liberties of the people, I felt it my duty, at an early period of my administration, to call the attention of Congress to the practicability of organizing an institution, combining all its advantages, and obviating these objections. I sincerely regret that, in the act before me, I can perceive none of those modifications of the bank charter which are necessary, in my opinion, to make it compatible with justice, with sound policy, or with the constitution of our country.

"The present corporate body, denominated the president, directors, and company of the bank of the United States, will have existed, at the time this act is intended to take effect, twenty years. It enjoys an exclusive privilege of banking under the authority of the general government, a monopoly of its favor and support, and, as a necessary consequence, almost a monopoly of the foreign and domestic exchange. The powers, privileges, and favors bestowed upon it in the original charter, by increasing the value of the stock far above its par value, operated as a gratuity of many millions to the stockholders.

"The modifications of the existing charter, proposed by this act, are not such, in my view, as make it consistent with the rights of the States, or the liberties of the people. The qualification of the right of the bank to hold real estate, the limitation of its power to establish branches, the power reserved to Congress to forbid the circulation of small notes, are restrictions comparatively of little value or importance.

All the objectionable principles of the existing corporation, and most of its odious features, are retained without alleviation.

" By documents submitted to Congress, at the present session, it appears, that on 1st of January, 1832, of the twenty millions of private stock in the corporation, $8,405,500 were held by foreigners, mostly of Great Britain. The amount of stock held in the nine Western States is $140,200, and in the four Southern States is $5,623,100, and in the Eastern and middle States about $13,522,000. The profits of the bank in 1831, as shown in a statement to Congress, were about $3,455,598 : of this there accrued in the nine Western States, about $1,640,048 ; in the four Southern States about $352,507 ; and in the middle and Eastern States, about $1,463,041. As little stock is held in the West, it is obvious that the debt of the people in that section to the bank is principally a debt to the Eastern and foreign stockholders ; that the interest they pay upon it, is carried into the Eastern States and into Europe ; and that it is a burden upon their industry, and a drain of their currency, which no country can bear without inconvenience, and occasional distress. To meet this burden, and equalize the exchange operations of the bank, the amount of specie drawn from those States, through its branches, within the last two years, as shown by its official reports, was about $6,000,000. More than half a million of this amount does not stop in the Eastern States, but passes on to Europe, to pay the dividends to the foreign stockholders. In the principle of taxation recognized by this act, the Western States find no adequate compensation for this perpetual burden on their industry, and drain upon their currency. The branch bank at Mobile made last year $95,140; yet, under the provisions of this act, the State of Alabama can raise no revenue from these profitable operations, because not a share of the stock is held by any of her citizens. Mississippi and Missouri are in the same condition in relation to the branches at Natches and St. Louis, and such, in a greater or less degree, is the condition of every Western State. The tendency of the plan of taxation which this act proposes, will be to place the whole United States in the same relation to foreign countries which the Western States bear to the Eastern. When, by a tax on resident stockholders, the stock of this bank is made worth ten or fifteen per cent. more to foreigners than to residents, most of it will inevitably leave the country.

" Thus will this provision, in its practical effect, deprive the Eastern as well as the Southern and Western States, of the means of raising a revenue from the extension of business and the great profits of this institution. It will make the American people debtors to aliens in nearly the whole amount due to this bank, and send across the Atlantic from two to five millions of specie every year, to pay the bank dividends.

" In another of its bearings this provision is fraught with danger. Of the twenty-five directors of this bank, five are chosen by the government, and twenty by the citizen stockholders. From all voices in these elections the foreign stockholders are excluded by the charter. In proportion, therefore, as the stock is transferred to foreign holders, the extent of suffrage in the choice of directors is curtailed. Already is almost a third of the stock in foreign hands, and not represented in elections. It is constantly passing out of the country, and this act will accelerate its departure. The entire control of the institution would necessarily fall into the hands of a few citizen stockholders, and the ease with which the object would be accomplished, would be a temptation to designing men to secure that control in their own hands by monopolising the remaining stocks. There is danger that a president and directors would then be able to elect themselves from year to year, and without responsibility or control manage the whole concerns of the bank during the existence of its charter. It is easy to conceive that great evils to our country and its institutions might flow from such a concentration of power in the hands of a few men irresponsible to the people.

" If we must have a bank with private stockholders, every consideration of sound policy, and every impulse of American feeling, admonishes that it should be purely American. Its stockholders should be composed exclusively of our own citizens, who at least ought to be friendly to our government, and willing to support it in times of difficulty and danger. So abundant is domestic capital, that competition in subscribing for the stock of local banks has recently led almost to riots. To a bank exclusively of American stockholders, possessing the powers and privileges granted by this act, subscriptions for two hundred millions of dollars could be readily obtained. Instead of sending abroad the stock of the bank, in which the government must deposit its funds, and on which it must rely to sustain its credit in times of emergency, it would rather seem to be expedient to prohibit its sale to aliens, under penalty of absolute forfeiture.

" The government of the United States have no constitutional power to purchase lands within the States, except " for the erection of forts, magazines, arsenals, dock yards, and other needful buildings," and even for these objects only " by the consent of the legislature of the State, in which the same shall be." By making themselves stockholders in the bank, and granting to the corporation the power to purchase lands for other purposes, they assume a power not granted in the constitution, and grant to others what they do not themselves possess. It is not necessary to the receiving, safe-keeping, or transmission of the funds of the government, that the bank should possess this power, and it is not proper that Congress should thus enlarge the powers delegated to them in the constitution.

The old bank of the United States possessed a capital of only eleven millions of dollars, which was found fully sufficient to enable it, with despatch and safety, to perform all the functions required of it by the government. The capital of the present bank is thirty-five millions of dollars, at least twenty-four more than experience has proved to be necessary to enable a bank to perform its public functions. The public debt which existed during the period of the old bank and on the establishment of the new has been nearly paid off, and our revenue will soon be reduced. This increase of capital is, therefore, not for public, but for private purposes.

" That a bank of the United States, competent to all duties which may be required by the government, might be so organized as not to infringe on our own delegated powers, or the reserved rights of the States, I do not entertain a doubt. Had the executive been called upon to furnish the project of such an institution, the duty would have been cheerfully performed. In the absence of such a call, it is obviously proper that he should confine himself to pointing out those prominent features in the act presented, which, in his opinion, make it incompatible with the constitution and sound policy. A general discussion will now take place eliciting new light, and settling important principles; and a new Congress, elected in the midst of such discussion, and furnishing an equal representation of the people according to the last census, will bear to the capitol the verdict of public opinion, and, I doubt not, bring this important question to a satisfactory result."

1833. General Jackson removed the government deposits from the bank of the United States. By an article of the act which established the bank in 1816 it was ordered, " that the deposits of public money be made into that bank and its branches, in places in which the said bank and its branches may be established, unless the secretary of the treasury shall otherwise order and direct, in which event the secretary of the treasury is required to give his reasons to Congress." The President considered himself justified by this clause in directing the secretary of the treasury to remove the deposits, usually amounting to eleven or twelve million dollars from the bank of the United States. The Secretary, Mr. Duane, refused to do so, alleged it would not be legal, unless the bank were in danger of becoming insolvent; and even in that case, the secretary was not under the direction of the President, but should report to Congress. Mr. Duane was consequently removed from his office, and another secretary appointed, who immediately carried the President's orders into effect. The deposits were accordingly removed from the bank of the United States, and placed in the different State Banks. The bank of the United States was accordingly compelled to limit its discounts and advances, and this produced considerable distress. The bank was accused by its opponents of reducing its accommodation more than was necessary in order to raise a popular outcry against the President. At the same time, the President seemed anxious to introduce a metallic currency, and the mint was worked with unusual activity.

OPERATIONS OF THE MINT IN 1833.

The coinage effected within the year 1833, amounted to $3,765,710; comprising $978,550 in gold coins, $2,759,000 in silver, $28,160 in copper, and consisting of 10,307,790 pieces of coin, viz.

				Dollars.
Half Eagles.........	193,630	pieces, making	......	968,510
Quarter Eagles ...	4,160	do.	do.	10,400
Half Dollars	5,206,000	do.	do.	2,603,000
Quarter Dollars ...	156,000	do.	do.	39,000
Dimes..............	485,000	do.	do.	48,500
Half Dimes.........	1,370,000	do.	do.	68,500
Cents	2,739,000	do.	do.	27,390
Half Cents	154,000	do.	do.	770

Total no. of pieces 10,307,790   *Total value* . 3,765,710

Of the amount of gold coined within the year, about $85,500 were derived from Mexico, South America, and the West Indies; $12,000 from Africa; $868,000 from the gold region of the United States; and about 13,000 dollars from sources not ascertained.

A great part of the session of 1834 was occupied in debates connected with the removal of the public deposits from the bank of the United States, and upon the embarrassments produced by the consequent pressure upon the money market. The senate took the side of the bank, and March 26 passed two resolutions. 1. That the reasons assigned by the secretary of the treasury for the removal of the money of the United States, deposited in the bank of the United States and its branches, communicated to Congress on the 4th of December, 1833, are unsatisfactory and insufficient." 2. " That the President in the late executive proceedings in relation to the public revenue has assumed upon himself authority and powers not conferred by the constitution and laws, but in derogation of both." The House of Representatives took the side of the President, and on April 4, passed

the following resolutions. 1. " That the bank of the
United States ought not to be re-chartered." 2.
" That the public deposits ought not to be restored to
the bank of the United States."

The following bills relating to gold and silver coins
were passed in June, 1834.

1. *A Bill concerning the Gold Coins of the United States, and for other
purposes.*

" Be it enacted by the Senate and House of Representatives of the
United States of America, in Congress assembled, that the gold coins
of the United States shall contain the following quantities of metal;
that is to say, each eagle shall contain two hundred and thirty-two
grains fine gold and two hundred and fifty-eight grains standard gold;
each half eagle one hundred and sixteen grains fine gold, and one hundred and twenty-nine grains standard gold; each quarter eagle shall
contain fifty-eight grains fine gold and $64\frac{1}{2}$ grains standard gold; every
such eagle shall be of the value of ten dollars; every such half eagle
shall be of the value of five dollars; and every such quarter eagle
shall be of the value of two dollars and fifty cents; and the said gold
coins shall be receivable in all payments, when of such weight, according to their said respective values; and when of less than such weight,
at less values, proportioned to their respective actual weights.

" *Sec.* 2. And be it further enacted, that all standard gold and silver
deposits for coinage, after the 31st day of July next, shall be paid for in
coin, under the direction of the secretary of the treasury, within five
days from the making such deposit, deducting from the amount of said
deposit of gold and silver one half of one per centum; provided, that
no deduction shall be made unless said advance be required by such
depositor within forty days.

" *Sec.* 3. And be it further enacted, that all gold coins of the United
States, minted anterior to the 31st day of July next, shall be receivable
in all payments at the rate of ninety-four and eight-tenths of a cent. per
pennyweight.

" *Sec.* 4. And be it further enacted, that this act shall be in force
from and after the 31st day of July, in the year one thousand eight
hundred and thirty-four."

2. *An Act, regulating the value of certain Foreign Gold Coins, within
the United States.*

" Be it enacted, &c. that from and after the 31st day of July
next, the following gold coins shall pass current as money, within the
United States, and be receivable in all payments, by weight, for the
payment of all debts and demands, at the rates following; that is to say,
the gold coins of Great Britain, Portugal, and Brazil, of not less than
twenty-two carats fine, at the rate of 94 cents. and 8-10ths of a cent.
per pennyweight; the gold coins of France, 9-10ths fine, at the rate of

93 cents. and 1-10th of a cent. per pennyweight; and the gold coins of Spain, Mexico, and Colombia, of the fineness of 20 carats, 3 grains, and 7-16ths of a grain, at the rate of 89 cents. and 9-10ths of a cent. per pennyweight.

" *Sec.* 2. And be it further enacted, that it shall be the duty of the secretary of the treasury to cause assays of the aforesaid gold coins made current by this act, to be had at the mint of the United States, at least once in every year, and to make report of the result thereof to Congress."

3. *An Act, regulating the value of certain Foreign Silver Coins within the United States.*

" Be it enacted by the Senate and House of Representatives of the United States of America, in Congress assembled, that from and after the passage of this act, the following silver coins shall be of the legal value, and shall pass current as money within the United States, by tale, for the payment of all debts and demands, at the rate of one hundred cents. the dollar; that is to say, the dollars of Mexico, Peru, Chili, and Central America, of not less weight than four hundred and fifteen grains each, and those restamped in Brazil of the like weight, of not less fineness than ten ounces fifteen pennyweights of pure silver in the troy pound of twelve ounces of standard silver; and the five-franc pieces of France, when of not less fineness than ten ounces and sixteen pennyweights, in twelve ounces troy weight of standard silver, and weighing not less than three hundred and eighty-four grains each, at the rate of ninety-three cents. each.

" *Sec.* 2. And be it further enacted, that it shall be the duty of the secretary of the treasury to cause assays of the aforesaid silver coins, made current by this act, to be had at the mint of the United States, at least once in every year, and to make report of the result thereof to Congress."

Mr. Gallatin had some years before recommended a new coinage, and pointed out its effects in preventing the exportation of the gold coins.

" We have already adverted to the erroneous value assigned to gold coins by the laws which regulate the mint of the United States. The relative value of that metal to silver was, by the law of 1790, fixed at the rate of 15 to 1. In England it was at that time at the rate of 15,2 to 1; and it had in France, after an investigation respecting the market price of both metals, been established at the rate of $15\frac{1}{2}$ to 1, as early as the year 1785. From that to this time, gold coins have never been below par in that country, and have generally commanded a premium, varying from one-fifth to one per cent.; but which, on an average, has been rather less than one-half per cent. This ratio in all those instances is that of gold to silver coins, but the difference is greater between gold and silver bullion.

" It is evident that our gold coins are under-rated at least four per cent. The necessary consequence is the disappearance of gold coins, and their exportation to Europe whenever the exchange will admit of it. According to that regulation a ten dollar gold coin, or eagle, contains 270 grains of standard gold ; and as the twenty shillings sterling gold coin, or sovereign, contains $123 \frac{171}{623}$ grains of gold of the same standard, about $4,56 in gold coin of the United States, contains a quantity of pure gold equal to that contained in a sovereign. Allowing one per cent. for charges and transportation, our gold coins may commence to be exported to England as soon as the exchange rises to $4,61 per pound sterling, which rate corresponds with nearly $3\frac{3}{4}$ per cent. above the nominal, and three per cent. below the true par, calculating this at the ratio of near 15,6 to 1, or $4,75 per pound sterling. We find by the tables of exchange annexed to the report of the secretary of the treasury, that, with the exception of the year of the embargo, unless incidentally for a few days, the exchange on London from 1795 to 1811, never rose to $4,62 per pound sterling, or about four per cent. above the nominal par ; or in other words, that during the whole of that period, the exchange was constantly favourable to the United States, having never been higher, with the exception aforesaid, than two per cent. below the true par. This is the reason why our gold coins, though underrated, were not exported till the year 1821 ; when the exchange rose from $4,60 to $4,98 per pound sterling ; and our gold coins began to be exported, a premium of one-half per cent. upon them being given, when the premium on the nominal par of exchange was five per cent., corresponding to an exchange of near $4,67 per pound sterling. From that time to the end of the year 1829, the exchanges have, with few short exceptions, been unfavourable to the United States ; and the exportation has continued, not only during that period, but also during the last nine months, though the exchange has this year been but little, if any, above the true par. It is perfectly clear, that, whilst our gold coins are thus underrated, they will be exported, whenever the exchange rises above $4,61 to $4,64 per pound sterling ; and that if rated according to the true or approximate relative value of gold to silver, they would not be exported to England till the exchange had risen to at least $4,80 to $4,83, or more than one per cent. above the true par.

" The importance of preserving a permanent standard of value is the leading principle which we have tried to enforce in this paper ; and it is for that express purpose that we consider an alteration in the mint regulations, which alone can bring gold into circulation, as absolutely necessary. The rate heretofore adopted had its origin in a mistake, and was not at all intended for the purpose of excluding gold. It did not produce that effect for thirty years, on account of the favourable rate of exchanges. To persist in it, now that experience has shewn the evils it produces, and amongst others the undeniable exportation of gold, and of gold coins, at a time when the exchanges may be three per cent. under the true par, instead of being adherence to the original plan, is an obvious deviation from its avowed object."

Condition of the bank of the United States, Nov. 1,
1834.

LIABILITIES.

	Dollars.	
Notes in circulation	15,968,731	90
Deposit to the credit of the Treasury	429,465	07
Do. Public Offices	1,837,168	66
Private Deposits	6,741,752	24
Capital Stock	35,000,000	00
Total liabilities............	59,977,117	87

RESOURCES.

To meet the foregoing, the bank has the following resources,
  viz :—

	Dollars.	
Discounts	34,667,828	24
Mortgages	87,591	29
Domestic Bills	11,086,373	07
Foreign Bills	2,727,782	11
Real Estate....................................	3,024,788	45
Due from State Banks	427,102	89
Specie...	15,910,045	31
Total resources	67,931,511	36
Showing a surplus of resources over liabilities of	7,954,393	49

In his address to Congress, delivered Dec. 1, 1834,
General Jackson referred to the bank of the United
States in the following terms :

" Circumstances make it my duty to call the attention of Congress
to the bank of the United States. Created for the convenience of
the government, that institution has become the scourge of the people.
Its interference to postpone the payment of a portion of the national
debt, that it might retain the public money appropriated for that
purpose to strengthen it in a political contest—the extraordinary
extension and contraction of its accommodations to the community—
its corrupt and partisan loans—its exclusion of the public directors
from a knowledge of its most important proceedings—the unlimited
authority conferred on the President to expend its funds in hiring
writers and procuring the execution of printing, and the use made of
that authority—the retention of the pension money and books, after
the selection of new agents—the groundless claim to heavy damages,

in consequence of the protest of the bill drawn on the French government, have, through various channels, been laid before Congress. Immediately after the close of the last session, the bank, through its president, announced its ability and readiness to abandon the system of unparalleled excitement, and the interruption of domestic exchanges, which it had practised upon from the 1st of August, 1833, to the 30th of June, 1834, and to extend its accommodations to the community. The grounds assumed in this annunciation amounted to an acknowledgment that the curtailment, in the extent to which it had been carried, was not necessary to the safety of the bank, and had been persisted in merely to induce Congress to grant the prayer of the bank in its memorial relative to the removal of the deposits, and to give it a new charter. They were substantially a confession that all the real distresses which individuals and the country had endured for the preceding six or eight months had been needlessly produced by it, with the view of effecting, through the sufferings of the people, the legislative action of Congress. It is a subject of congratulation that Congress and the country had the virtue and firmness to bear the infliction; that the energies of our people soon found relief from this wanton tyranny in vast importations of the precious metals from almost every part of the world; and that at the close of this tremendous effort to control our government the bank found itself powerless, and no longer able to loan out its surplus means. The community had learned to manage its affairs without its assistance, and trade had already found new auxiliaries; so that on the 1st of October last the extraordinary spectacle was presented of a national bank, more than one-half of whose capital was either lying unproductive in its vaults, or in the hands of foreign bankers. To the needless distresses brought on the country during the last session of Congress has been added the open seizure of the dividends on the public stock, to the amount of 170,041 dollars, under pretence of paying damages, costs, and interests upon the protested French bill. This sum constituted a portion of the estimated revenues for the year 1834, upon which the appropriations made by Congress were based. It would as soon have been expected that our collectors would seize on the customs, or the receivers of our land offices on the monies arising from the sale of public lands, under pretences of claims against the United States, as the bank would have retained the dividends.

" That the money had not technically been paid into the treasury does not affect the principle intended to be established by the constitution. The executive and judiciary have as little right to appropriate and expend the public money without authority of law, before it is placed to the credit of the treasurer, as to take it from the treasury. In the annual report of the secretary of the treasury, and in his correspondence with the president of the bank, and the opinion of the attorney-general accompanying it, you will find a further examination of the claims of the bank, and the course it has pursued.

" It seems due to the safety of the public funds remaining in that bank, and to the honour of the American people, that measures be taken to separate the government entirely from an institution so mischievous to the public prosperity, and so regardless to the constitution and laws. By transferring the public deposits, by appointing other pension agents, as far as it had the power, by ordering the discontinuance of the receipt of bank checks in payment of the public dues after the first day of January next, the executive has exerted all its lawful authority to sever the connection between the government and this faithless corporation. The high-handed career of this institution imposes upon the constitutional functionaries of this government duties of the gravest and most imperative character—duties which they cannot avoid, and from which I trust there will be no inclination on the part of any of them to shrink. My own sense of them is most clear, as is also my readiness to discharge those which may rightfully fall on me. To continue any business relations with the bank of the United States that may be avoided without a violation of the national faith, after that institution has set at open defiance the conceded right of the government to examine its affairs,—after it has done all in its power to deride the public authority in other respects, and to bring it into disrepute at home and abroad,—after it has attempted to defeat the clearly expressed will of the people by turning against them the immense power entrusted to its hands, and by involving a country otherwise peaceful, flourishing, and happy, in dissention, embarrassment, and distress, would make the nation itself a party to the degradation so sedulously prepared for its public agents, and do much to destroy the confidence of mankind in popular governments, and to bring into contempt their authority and efficiency. In guarding against an evil of such magnitude, considerations of temporary convenience should be thrown out of the question, and we should be influenced by such motives only as look to the honor and preservation of the republican system. Deeply and solemnly impressed with the justice of these views, I feel it to be my duty to recommend to you, that a law be passed authorizing the sale of the public stock : that the provision of the charter requiring the receipt of notes of the bank in payment of public dues shall, in accordance with the power reserved to Congress in the 14th section of the charter, be suspended until the bank pays to the treasury the dividend withheld ; and that all laws connecting the government or its officers with the bank, directly or indirectly, be repealed ; and that the institution be left hereafter to its own resources and means. Events have satisfied my mind, and I think the minds of the American people, that the mischiefs and dangers which flow from a national bank far overbalance all its advantages. The bold effort the present bank has made to control the government, the distresses it has wantonly produced, the violence of which it has been the occasion in one of our cities famed for its observance of law and order, are but premonitions of the fate which awaits the American people should they be deluded into a perpetuation of this institution, or the establishment of another like it. It is fervently hoped that, thus admonished, those who have heretofore favoured the establishment of a substitute for the present bank will be induced to abandon it, as it is evidently better to incur any inconvenience that may be reasonably expected, than to concentrate the whole monied power of the republic in any form whatsoever, or under any restrictions. Happily, it is already illustrated that the agency of such an institution is not necessary to the fiscal operations of the government. The state banks are found fully adequate to the performance of all services which were required of the bank of the United States, quite as promptly, and with the same cheapness. They have maintained themselves, and discharged all these duties, while the bank of the United States was still powerful, and in the field as an open enemy : it is not possible to conceive that they will find greater difficulties in their operations when that enemy shall cease to exist.

" The attention of Congress is invited to the regulation of deposits in the state banks by law. Although the power exercised by the executive department in this behalf is only such as was uniformly exerted through every administration from the origin of the government up to the establishment of the present bank, yet it is one which is susceptible of regulation by law, and therefore ought so to be regulated. The power of Congress to direct in what places the treasurer shall keep the monies in the treasury, and to impose restrictions upon the executive authority in relation to their custody and removal is unlimited, and its exercise will rather be courted than discouraged by those public officers and agents on whom rests the responsibility for their safety. It is desirable that as little power as possible should be left to the president or secretary of the treasury over those institutions—which, being thus freed from executive influence, and without a common head to direct their operations, would have neither the temptation nor the ability to interfere in the political conflicts of the country. Not deriving their charters from the national authorities, they would never have those inducements to meddle in general elections which have led the bank of the United States to agitate and convulse the country for upwards of two years. The progress of our gold coinage is creditable to the officers of the mint, and promises in a short period to furnish the country with a sound and portable currency, which will much diminish the inconvenience to travellers of a want of a general paper currency, should the state banks be incapable of furnishing it. Those institutions have already shown themselves competent to purchase and furnish domestic exchange for the convenience of trade at reasonable rates, and not a doubt is entertained that in a short period all the wants of the country in bank accommodations and exchange will be supplied as promptly and cheaply as they have heretofore been by the bank of the United States. If the several states shall be induced gradually to reform their banking systems, and prohibit the issue of all small notes, we shall in a few years have a currency as sound, and as little liable to fluctuations, as any other commercial country."

OPERATIONS OF THE MINT IN 1834.

According to the Report of Samuel Moore, the late Director, dated January 1, 1835.

" The coinage effected within that period [1834] amounts to 7,388,423 dollars; comprising 3,954,270 dollars in gold coins; 3,415,002 dollars in silver; 19,151 dollars in copper; and consisting of 11,637,643 pieces of coin, viz.

				Dollars.
Half Eagles	732,169	pieces,	making	3,660,845
Quarter Eagles	117,370	do.	do.	293,425
Half Dollars	6,412,004	do.	do.	3,206,006
Quarter Dollars	286,000	do.	do.	71,500
Dimes	635,000	do.	do.	63,500
Half Dimes	1,480,000	do.	do.	74,000
Cents....................	1,855,100	do.	do.	18,551
Half Cents	120,000	do.	do.	600
	11,637,643			7,388,423

" The deposits of gold within the past year have amounted, in round numbers, to 4,389,000 dollars; of which about 1,067,000 dollars consisted of coins of the United States, issued previously to the act of 28th of June, establishing a new ratio of gold and silver: about 898,000 dollars were derived from the gold regions of the United States; 225,000 dollars from Mexico, South America, and the West Indies; 2,180,000 dollars from Europe; 12,000 dollars from Africa; and 9,008 from sources not ascertained. Of the amount received from Europe, about four-fifths were in foreign coins.

" The coinage of gold under the new ratio commenced on the 1st day of August, the earliest period permitted by the act. In anticipation, however, of a change in the legal valuation of gold, it had been considered proper to suspend the coinage of all deposits received after the 1st of June. Previously to this period, the sum of $383,545 had been coined, so that of the above amount of the gold coinage for the past year, $3,570,725 consist of coins of the new standard. This amount, however, is the result of the operations of the mint, during only five months of the year, corresponding to an amount, for a full year, of about 8½ millions in gold. Within the same period, the coinage of silver was regularly maintained at the average rate of the whole year, making a general result of both gold and silver corresponding to a yearly coinage of nearly $12,000,000.

" The amount in gold in the vaults of the mint on the 1st of August, was $468,500: the amount now remaining in the mint uncoined is $435,000; no part of which was deposited earlier than the 9th of December. The amount of silver remaining in our vaults for coinage, is, in round numbers, $475,000; no part of which was deposited earlier than the 20th of November.

" The amount of silver coined within the past year, it is satisfactory to state, has exceeded by about a quarter of a million the silver coinage of any previous year; while the gold coinage has exceeded the aggregate coinage of gold during the nine preceding years, from 1825 to 1833, inclusive.

" The influx of silver during the past year having very considerably exceeded the amount contemplated in the estimates for the year, occasioned, during a large portion of that period, an unusual retardation in the delivery of coins; and the amount of deposits has no doubt been restrained, to some extent, by this consideration.

OPERATIONS OF THE MINT IN 1835.

" The coinage executed during the year 1835, has amounted to $5,668,667, comprising $2,186,175 in gold coins, $3,443,003 in silver, and $39,489 in copper; and composed of 15,996,342 pieces of coin, viz.

			Dollars.
Half Eagles	371,534 pieces, making		1,857,670
Quarter Eagles	131,402	do. do.	328,505
Half Dollars	5,352,006	do. do.	2,676,003
Quarter Dollars	1,952,000	do. do.	488,000
Dimes	1,410,000	do. do.	141,000
Half Dimes	2,760,000	do. do.	138,000
Cents....................	3,878,400	do. do.	38,784
Half Cents	141,000	do. do.	705
	15,996,342		5,668,667

" The deposits of gold within the year have amounted, in round numbers, to $1,845,000, of which $698,000 was from bullion derived from the gold mines in the United States.

" The amount of gold bullion in the vaults of the mint at the end of the year, was $77,880, all of which was deposited in December. The amount of silver bullion in the vaults was $780,600, all of which was deposited in November and December.

" The amount of gold coinage is less than that of 1834 by $1,768,095. This difference has arisen, in part, from the recoinage of American gold of the former ratio, which amounted, in 1834, to $1,067,000, and in 1835, to only $160,000.

" The silver and the copper coinages are greater than in any former year, and the whole number of pieces struck exceeds that in any former year by more than four millions.

" In consequence of an unusual demand for small silver coins, the amount of this coinage, for the last year, has been so great as nearly to equal the whole of that for the four years preceding.

" Measures have been taken recently, and are now in progress, for introducing improvements in the processes and machinery of the mint, by which it is believed that the efficiency of the establishment may be much increased. Heretofore the milling and coining have been done exclusively by human labour. New machines are nearly completed by which these operations will be executed with steam power. The humid assay for silver has been successfully introduced, and new arrangements for the assay by fire are about to be commenced.

" *Amount of Gold received annually from the Gold Region of the United States, from* 1824 *to* 1835, *inclusive.*

Years.	Virginia.	N. Carolina.	S. Carolina.	Georgia.	Tennessee.	Alabama.	Not ascertained.	Total.
	Dollars.	Dollars.	Dollars.	Dollars.	Dollars.	Dollars.	Dollars.	Dollars.
1824	—	5,000	—	—	—	—	—	5,000
1825	—	17,000	—	—	—	—	—	17,000
1826	—	20,000	—	—	—	—	—	20,000
1827	—	21,000	—	—	—	—	—	21,000
1828	—	46,000	—	—	—	—	—	46,000
1829	2,500	134,000	3,500	—	—	—	—	140,000
1830	24,000	204,000	26,000	212,000	—	—	—	466,000
1831	26,00 0	294,000	22,000	176,000	1,000	1,000	—	520,000
1832	34,000	458,000	45,000	140,000	1,000	—	—	678,000
1833	.04,000	475,000	66,000	216,000	7,000	—	—	868,000
1834	62,000	380,000	38,000	415,000	3,000	—	—	898,000
1835	60,400	263,500	42,400	319,900	100	—	12,200	698,500
	312,900	2,317,500	242,900	1,478,900	12,100	1,000	12,200	4,377,500

" *American Almanack,* 1837."

1836. The charter of the Bank of the United States expired in this year. A new charter was however obtained from the State of Pennsylvania, authorizing the bank to carry on business in that state. The bank also obtained permission to continue their agencies in some of the other states. Though it retains the title of " Bank of the United States," yet it is not chartered by Congress, it is no longer the bank of the government; it has no longer the power to establish branches in the various states without their consent, and it must be subject to such laws or taxes as the respective states may impose.

The following are stated in an American paper, to be the terms on which the bank obtained its charter from the State of Pennsylvania.

" It is proposed to say a few words about the Bank of the United States, and the efforts which certain persons are making to disturb the country about it. The whole matter is simply this :—

" There was a bank called the Bank of the United States, chartered by Congress, but fixed in Pennsylvania, and managed principally by Pennsylvanians. The charter was about to expire on the 4th of March, 1836, and the directors had nearly completed their arrangements for closing its concerns.

" They made no application to the legislature of Pennsylvania or to any other legislature for the re-charter of the bank.

" But while they were going on quietly winding up the institution, an official application was made by the Legislature of Pennsylvania to the bank, to know whether the stockholders of the bank would accept a charter from Pennsylvania. A joint letter from the committee on banks, and the committee of ways and means of the House of Representatives of Pennsylvania, was addressed to the President of the bank, inquiring whether the stockholders of the bank would agree to a re-charter by Pennsylvania.

" The answer was, that upon certain terms it would be accepted. The legislature and the governor accordingly passed a bill for re-chartering the bank, on payment of certain sums.

ı " This was sent to the stockholders to know whether they would take it. They agreed to take it, and there—both contracting parties having bound themselves—the matter was closed.

" The state acted very wisely in all this. It made a good bargain. It made what in common life is called a hard bargain.

It gained a bonus of	$4,500,000
Subscriptions to internal improvement	675,000
To which the bank has voluntarily added ...	560,000
And a privilege of obliging the bank to make loans always of 6,000,000 at 4 per cent., and 1,000,000 at 5 per cent., making a gain equal to..	620,000
Making a total of	$6,355,000

Besides retaining within the state, loans from the bank which at present amount to nearly $20,000,000, employed in advancing every branch of its home industry.

" The stockholders would not have accepted the charter but for two reasons. First, they had reserved funds out of their old earnings which went far to pay these heavy charges ; and second, they were themselves Pennsylvanians, and they were anxious to give to their state the advantage and the credit of converting to its own benefit the mass of capital about to be dispersed.

" The advantage of the contract was to the state, not to the bank. The favour, if there was any, was done to the state by the bank—not to the bank by the state.

" For all these benefits the state in return gave absolutely nothing.

They merely furnished what is called a charter; that is, they said that these stockholders should be called the bank of the United States, and be able to sue for their debts—a convenience this in managing their capital, but adding not a dollar of advantage to that capital, any more than the mere piece of tape which is used to tie up a bundle of notes gives value to the notes.

" The remarkable part of it is, that the charter is not at this moment worth the money paid for it. If the state would refund that money, a charter just as good could be had for one-fourth of the sum in other states—and the funds withdrawn from Pennsylvania might be much more profitably employed elsewhere.

" But the bank has made the bargain, and will stand by it. The state too, the honest, sober part of the community, are perfectly satisfied."

In his farewell address to Congress, delivered Dec. 6, 1836, the President thus adverts to the bank of the United States:

" It was in view of these evils, together with the dangerous power wielded by the bank of the United States, and its repugnance to our constitution, that I was induced to exert the power conferred upon me by the American people, to prevent the continuance of that institution. But, although various dangers to our republican institutions have been obviated by the failure of that bank to extort from the government a renewal of its charter, it is obvious that little has been accomplished, except a salutary change of public opinion, towards restoring to the country the sound currency provided for in the constitution. In the acts of several of the states prohibiting the circulation of small notes, and the auxiliary enactments of Congress at the last session forbidding their reception or payment on public account, the true policy of the country has been advanced, and a larger portion of the precious metals infused into our circulating medium. These measures will probably be followed up in due time by the enactment of state laws, banishing from circulation bank notes of still higher denominations; and the object may be materially promoted by further acts of Congress, forbidding the employment, as fiscal agents, of such banks as continue to issue notes of low denominations, and throw impediments in the way of the circulation of gold and silver.

" Experience continues to realize the expectations entertained as to the capacity of the states' banks to perform the duties of fiscal agents of the government; at the time of the removal of the deposits it was alleged by the advocates of the bank of the United States, that the state banks, whatever might be the regulations of the treasury department, could not make the transfers required by the government, or negotiate the domestic exchanges of the country. It is now well ascertained that the real domestic exchanges performed through discounts, by the United States' Bank and its twenty-five branches, were at least one-third less than those of the deposit banks for an equal period of time; and if a comparison be instituted between the

amounts of service rendered by these institutions, on the broader basis
which has been used by the advocates of the United States' Bank, in
estimating what they consider the domestic exchanges transacted by it,
the result will be still more favourable to the deposit banks.

" The whole amount of public money transferred by the bank of
the United States in 1832, was 16,000,000 dollars. The amount
transferred and actually paid by the deposit banks in the year ending
the first of October last, was 39,319,899 dollars; the amount transferred and paid between that period and the 6th of November
5,399,090 dollars, and the amount of transfer warrants outstanding on
that day, was 14,450,000 dollars; making an aggregate of 59,168,895
dollars. These enormous sums of money first mentioned have been
transferred with the greatest promptitude and regularity, and the rates
at which the exchange have been negotiated previously to the passage
of the deposit act, were generally below those charged by the Bank of
the United States. Independent of these services, which are far
greater than those rendered by the United States Bank, and its twenty
five branches, a number of the deposit banks have, with a commen-
dable zeal to aid in the improvement of the currency, imported from
abroad, at their own expense, large sums of the precious metals for
coinage and circulation.

" It will be seen by the report of the secretary of the treasury and
the accompanying documents, that the bank of the United States has
made no payment on account of the stock held by the government in
that institution, although urged to pay any portion which might suit
its convenience, and that it has given no information when payment
may be expected. Nor, although repeatedly requested, has it furnished
the information in relation to its condition, which Congress authorised
the secretary to collect at their last session; such measures as are
within the power of the executive have been taken to ascertain the
value of the stock, and procure the payment as early as possible.

" The conduct and present condition of that bank, and the great
amount of capital vested in it by the United States, require your
careful attention. Its charter expired on the third day of March last,
and it has now no power but that given in the twenty-first section, " to
use the corporate name, style, and capacity, for the purpose of suits
for the final settlement and liquidation of the affairs and accounts of
the corporation, and for the sale and disposition of their estate, real,
personal, and mixed, but not for any other purpose, or in any other
manner whatsoever, nor for a period exceeding two years after the
expiration of the said term of incorporation." Before the expiration
of the charter the stockholders of the bank obtained an act of incorporation from the legislature of Pennsylvania, excluding only the United
States. Instead of proceeding to wind up their concerns, and pay over
to the United States the amount due on account of the stock held by
them, the president and directors of the old bank appeared to have
transferred the books, papers, notes, obligations, and most of all of its
property to this new corporation, which entered upon business as a
continuation of the old concern. Among other acts of questionable
validity, the notes of the expired corporation are known to have been

used as its own, and again put in circulation. That the old bank had no right to issue or re-issue its notes after the expiration of its charter, cannot be denied, and that it could not confer any such right on its substitute, any more than exercise it itself, is equally plain. In law and honesty, the notes of the bank in circulation, at the expiation of its charter, should have been called in by public advertisement, paid up as presented, and, together with these on hand, cancelled and destroyed. Their re-issue is sanctioned by no law, and warranted by no necessity. If the United States be responsible in their stock for the payment of those notes, their re-issue by the new corporation, for their own profit, is a fraud on the government. If the United States is not responsible, then there is no legal responsibily in any quarter, and it is a fraud on the country. They are the redeemed notes of a dissolved partnership, but, contrary to the wishes of the retiring partner, and without his consent, are again re-issued and circulated."

The establishment of a National Bank being a strong party question in America, it naturally became connected with the contest for the office of President; and a letter was written by the Hon. Martin Van Buren, the successful candidate, upon the subject. The following are extracts:

" You next ask, whether I will sign and approve (if it becomes necessary to secure and save from depreciation, the revenue and finances of the nation, and to afford a sound uniform currency to the people of the United States) a bill (with proper modifications and restrictions) chartering a bank of the United States.

" In the published letter of Mr. Butler to Mr. Garland, which has already been referred to, he thus states my opinions upon the subject of the bank :—" Mr. Van Buren's opinions in regard to the Bank of the United States, were expressed in the Senate of the United States in 1828 ; repeated in his letter to the Shocco-Springs committee, whilst a candidate for the Vice-Presidency, and have been so freely uttered by him, that there cannot, I think, be occasion to say much upon the subject. But to close the door to cavil, I state,—1st. That he holds that Congress does not possess the power to establish a national bank in any of the states of the union, nor to establish, in such states, the branch of any bank located in the district of Colombia ; and, 2nd. That he is therefore decidedly opposed to the establishment of a national bank in any of the states ; and is also opposed to the establishment of any such bank in the district of Colombia, as unnecessary and inexpedient, and as liable to a great proportion of the abuses which have, in his opinion, been practised by the existing bank."

" But whilst I so confidently entertain, and so readily promulgate these sentiments, in regard to the want of power to establish in any of the states a national bank, I am at the same time equally desirous that it should be fully understood that I am decidedly opposed to the creation of any such institution in the district of Colombia. I do not

BANKING IN AMERICA.   39

believe that any national bank, there or elsewhere, is necessary to secure either of the advantages to which your question has reference. The principal grounds relied upon by the advocates for a bank, to establish its utility and necessity, as I understand them, are,—

" 1st. That such an institution is necessary for the transmission and safe keeping of the public monies.

" 2nd. To secure a safe, cheap, and convenient system of domestic exchange ; and

" 3rd. To make and preserve a sound currency.

" The limits of this letter will not admit of a full discussion of these points, but I cannot refrain from referring to a few of the facts which belong to them.

" The official reports of the secretary of the treasury shew first, that the average amount of money annually transferred by the Bank of the United States from 1820 to 1823, was from ten to fifteen millions of dollars ; and the amount transferred by the deposit banks, from June 1835 to April 1836, or about ten months, over seventeen millions of dollars. In both cases the operation has been without loss, failure, or expense. And it farther appears, from the same source, that at no previous period has the safety of the public monies been more carefully or securely provided for. An examination of the official documents will, I am well satisfied, fully sustain these positions. What foundation, then, was there for the assumptions, upon this part of the subject, which were put forth with so much solemnity, and insisted upon with so much earnestness, in the early discussion upon the subject of the bank ? If so much has been done in this respect, whilst the substituted agency has had to contend with the most powerful opposition that was ever made upon any branch of the public service, what may we not expect from it now, when it has received legislative sanction—and if there be not gross dereliction of faith and duty—when it must also receive the support of all parties.

" In regard to domestic exchanges, the following facts are established by the same authentic source, namely, that the amount of domestic exchanges, performed at the last returns by the deposit banks, exceed thirty-five millions of dollars, and at no return, for many months, has it been less than twenty-five millions ; which, at an average of thirty millions at each return, would be in a year one hundred and eighty millions, if each bill of exchange run on an average sixty days. On the contrary, the amount of domestic exchanges performed by the United States Bank, did not for many years equal twenty millions at any one return, and seldom exceeded it ; being quite one-third less than what is now done by the deposit banks. It further appears that these exchanges have in many cases been effected at lower rates by the deposit banks than by the United States Bank. Indeed, can it be doubted that even if there was not a single bank, state or national, in the country, it would nevertheless be quite easy to place its domestic exchanges upon an advantageous and safe footing, so long as there is a sufficiency of solid capital to be employed in the business. From the nature of the thing itself, and from the experience of Europe, we may be assured that the profit and necessities of trade would invite and obtain ample facilities for the business of exchange from other sources, so long as the commercial community, with one accord, desire to see it successfully carried on, and assist in good faith in effecting it.

" Lastly, the currency. The proportion of our whole circulating medium that was composed of the notes of the bank of the United States, during the existence of that institution, was much smaller than was generally supposed. The calculation of the United States Bank, as I am informed, ranged, for some years before it expired, at about twenty millions, often below that amount, which was not over one-fourth of the paper circulation of the United States. Some think it has been less than one-fifth. The great mass of the business of the country was therefore even carried on, so far as money was employed in it, by means of the notes of state banks and specie. The beneficial effects that were claimed to be rendered by that institution in respect to the currency, consisted,—

" 1st. In supplying bills that were current throughout the Union ; and

" 2nd. The salutary effects of its supervision over the state banks, in preventing over-issues, and compelling them to keep on hand larger supplies of specie for the redemption of their notes.

" The transactions in which it became necessary, or was usual, to carry bank notes from one state to another, were very limited in their amounts—large sums being then, as they are now, and ever will be, transmitted through the medium of bills of exchange. It will not even now, I think, be seriously denied, that the increase of the gold coinage, and the facilities of getting that species of coin, together with the large denomination of notes issued by the leading state banks, are abundantly sufficient for those purposes, and that they can be quite as conveniently employed in them.

" As to the benefits alleged to have been rendered by the bank of the United States, in checking excessive issues by the state banks, and compelling them to maintain an adequate supply of specie,—whilst by no means disposed to undervalue them, I yet think the same objects can be accomplished, not only without the agency of any such institution, but to a much greater and more useful extent without than with it :—provided a proper policy be pursued by the federal and state governments ; by the former, through the mint and treasury depart-ment ; by the latter, by suppressing small bills, by discouraging the extension of the paper system, and by subjecting existing banks to wholesome restraints and to a rigid supervision.

" Three additional mints have been established, and the President is authorized by the deposit bill to keep them amply supplied with bullion ; and the secretary of the treasury is empowered to require an increase of specie in any deposit bank, and is restricted from employing, as an agent for the government, any state bank which issues bills under the denomination of five dollars. By another general law, the notes of such banks are prohibited from being received for debts due to the United States of any description ; and it has also been provided by law, that no note shall hereafter be offered in payment by the United States or post office department of a less denomination than ten dollars, and after the third day of March next of a less denomination than twenty dollars, nor any note of any denomination, which is not payable and paid on demand in gold and silver at the place where issued, and which should not be equivalent to specie at the place where offered, and convertible upon the spot into gold and silver, at the will of the holder, and without loss or delay to him. Nor have the states lagged behind in their efforts to improve the currency by infusing into it a greater proportion of the precious metals. Already are the issuing of bills under the denomination of five dollars prohibited by the states of Pennsylvania, Maryland, Virginia, Georgia, Tennessee, Louisiana, North Carolina, Indiana, Kentucky, Maine, New York, New Jersey, and Alabama, and of one and two dollars by Connecticut. That this policy will become general, and gradually extended, cannot be doubted. To what precise extent it may be carried with advantage to the country, will be decided by time, experience, and judicious observation. Evasions of it may for a season take place, and some slight inconveniences arise from the change, but they will both be temporary. The union committee of the city of New York, confessedly combining some of the best business talents of our great commercial emporium, regarded it as an improvement of the currency of great importance to all classes of the people. Legislative bodies have shewn great unanimity in its favour. It is approved by the people, and must prevail.

" Sincerely believing, for the reasons which have just been stated, that the public funds may be as safely and conveniently transmitted from one portion of the Union to another, that domestic exchange can be as successfully and as cheaply effected, and the currency be rendered at least as sound under the existing system, as those objects could be accomplished by means of a national bank, I would not seek a remedy for the evils to which you allude, should they unfortunately occur, through such a medium, even if the constitutional objection were not in the way."

By a report recently made by the auditor-general to the Pennsylvanian legislature, the following are the principal items in the condition of the new bank of the United States.

	Dollars.
Capital	35,000,000
Notes in circulation	36,620,420
Deposits	2,194,231
Notes of other banks	19,078,796
Specie	5,079,460
Debts owng by other banks	31,553,035
Bills discounted	56,389,253
Unclaimed dividends	241,900
Contingent Fund	1,695,105
Real Estate	315,214
Due to other banks	30,755,561

SECTION III.

THE STATE BANKS.

The Bank of the United States was founded by
Congress, but all the other banks derived their charter from the government of the states in which they
are established.   They are all joint-stock companies,
as no private banking is allowed.   The chartered
banks are subject to various restrictions, according to
the enactments of the different states ; and their restrictions are often such as are unknown in this country.   Generally no shareholder is answerable for the
debts of the bank beyond the proportionate amount
of his shares.   In some cases the government retains
the option of subscribing an additional number of
shares, and of appointing a corresponding number
of directors.   And in others, the banks are under
obligation to advance a certain sum to the government whenever required.   Some states have laid a
tax of ten per cent. on the dividends paid on the
stock of each bank.   The banks are sometimes restricted not to incur debts beyond a certain proportion
to their capital ; and in all the states the banks are
now required to make periodical returns to the
government.

I. The business of the States Banks.

" The business of all those banks consists, in receiving money on
deposit, in issuing bank notes, and in discounting notes of hand or bills
of exchange.   A portion of the capital is sometimes vested in public
stocks, but this is not obligatory, and in this they differ essentially
from the Bank of England.

" Whenever therefore an American bank is in full operation, its
debts generally consist, 1st. to the stockholders of the capital; 2nd.
to the community, of the notes in circulation, and of the credits in
account current, commonly called deposits ; and its credits, 1st. of discounted notes or bills of exchange, and occasionally of public stocks.
2. Of the specie in its vaults, and of the notes of, and balances due by,
other banks.   3. Of its real estate, either used for banking purposes
or taken in payment of debts.   Some other incidental items may sometimes be introduced ; a part of the capital is occasionally invested in
road, canal, and bridge stocks, and the debts secured on judgments,
or bonds and mortgages, are generally distinguished in the official
returns of the banks."—*Gallatin.*

II. The following is a list of all the State Banks in operation on the 1st of January, 1830.—*(From Mr. Galatin.)*

MASSACHUSETTS.	Capital.		Capital
Massachusetts - -	800,000	Falmouth - - -	100,000
Union - - -	800,000	Farmers - - -	100,000
Phœnix - - -	200,000	Franklin, (Boston) -	100,000
Gloucester - -	120,000	Franklin, (Greenfield)-	100,000
Newburyport - -	210,000	Globe - - -	1,000,000
Beverly - - -	100,000	Hampden - - -	100,000
Boston - - -	900,000	Hampshire Man. -	100,000
Salem - - -	250,000	Housatonic - -	100,000
Plymouth - - -	100,000	Leicester - - -	100,000
Worcester - -	200,000	Lowell - - -	100,000
Marblehead - -	120,000	Man. & Mech.'s (Nantucket) - -	100,000
Pacific - - -	200,000	Mendon - - -	100,000
State - - -	1,800,000	Mercantile - -	200,000
Mechanics - - -	200,000	Mercht. (New-Bedford)	250,000
Merchants, (Salem) -	400,000	Millbury - - -	100,000
Taunton - - -	175,000	Norfolk - - -	200,000
New-England - -	1,000,000	North Bank - -	750,000
Hampshire - -	100,000	Oxford - - -	100,000
Dedham - - -	100,000	Sunderland - -	100,000
Manuf.&Mech's.(Boston)	750,000	Sutton - - -	75,000
Springfield - -	250,000	Washington - -	500,000
Lynn Mechanics -	100,000		
Merrimack - -	150,000	66 Banks	20,420,000
Pawtucket - -	100,000		
Suffolk - - -	750,000	MAINE.	
Commercial, Salem -	300,000	Portland - - -	200,000
Bedford Commercial -	250,000	Saco - - -	100,000
Agricultural - -	100,000	Cumberland - -	200,000
American - - -	750,000	Bath - - -	100,000
Andover - - -	100,000	Lincoln - - -	100,000
Asiatic - - -	350,000	Augusta - - -	100,000
Atlantic - - -	500,000	Kennebunk - -	100,000
Barnstable - -	100,000	Gardiner - - -	100,000
Blackstone - -	100,000	Waterville - -	50,000
Brighton - - -	150,000	Bangor - - -	50,000
Bunker Hill - -	150,000	Casco - - -	200,000
Cambridge - -	150,000	Canal - - -	300,000
Central - - -	50,000	Manufacturers - -	100,000
City - - -	1,000,000	Merchants - -	150,000
Columbian - -	500,000	South Berwick -	50,000
Commonwealth - -	500,000	Thomaston - -	50,000
Danvers - - -	120,000	Union - - -	50,000
Eagle - - -	500,000	Vassalborough - -	50,000
Exchange - - -	300,000		
Fall River - - -	200,000	18 Banks	2,000,000

Capital.

NEW-HAMPSHIRE.

	Capital
Union - - -	150,000
Concord, (Lower) -	80,000
Portsmouth - -	100,000
Exeter - - -	100,000
Strafford - - -	100,000
Cheshire - - -	100,000
New-Hampshire -	165,500
Rockingham -	100,000
Commercial - -	100,000
Piscataqua - -	150,000
Dover - - -	128,070
Merrimack Co. - -	100,000
Farmers - - -	65,000
Winnepisogee - -	83,100
Pemigewasset - -	50,000
Grafton - - -	100,000
Claremont -	60,000
Connecticut River -	60,000
18 Banks	**1,791,670**

VERMONT.

Burlington - -	63,000
Windsor - - -	80,000
Brattleborough - -	50,000
Rutland - - -	60,000
Montpelier - .	30,000
St. Albans -	20,000
Caledonia - - -	30,000
Vergennes - -	30,000
Orange County - -	29,625
Bennington - -	40,000
10 Banks	**432,625**

RHODE ISLAND.

Providence - -	500,000
Rhode Island - -	100,000
Exchange - - -	500,000
Bristol - - -	150,000
Washington - -	75,000
Warren - - -	105,350
Smithfield Union	60,000
Newport - - -	120,000
Roger Williams - -	499,950
Rhode Island Union -	200,000
Narragansett - -	50,000
Commercial (Bristol) -	150,000
Manufacturers - -	220,000

Capital.

Union (Providence) -	500,000
Pautuxet - - -	87,858
Burrillville (Agric. and Mang.) - - -	37,360
Cranston - - -	25,000
Eagle (Providence) -	300,000
Eagle (Bristol) - -	50,000
Franklin - - -	38,000
Freeman's - - -	67,000
Kent - - -	20,000
Landholders - -	50,000
Merchants (Newport)-	50,000
Merchants (Providence)	500,000
N. E. Commercial (Newport) - -	75,000
Phœnix (Westerly) -	42,000
R. I. Central - -	66,275
Scituate - - -	15,660
Warwick - - -	20,000
Bank of N. America -	100,000
Mechanics - - -	394,600
Mechanics and Mang. (Prov.) - - -	103,990
High St. Bank - -	70,000
Smithfield Exchange -	60,000
Village Bank - -	40,000
Smithfield Lime Rock -	100,100
Cumberland - -	65,750
R. I. Agricultural -	50,000
Mount Vernon - -	40,000
N. E. Pacific - -	83,750
Union (Bristol) - -	40,000
Hope (Warren) - -	100,000
North Kingston - -	44,485
Centreville - -	25,000
Woonsocket Falls -	51,269
Mount Hope (Bristol)-	75,000
47 Banks	**6,158,397**

CONNECTICUT.

New London - -	146,437
Norwich	150,000
Hartford - - -	1,252,900
Phœnix - - -	1,218,500
Bridgeport - -	100,000
Union (New-London -	100,000
Windham Co. -	104,390
Thames - - -	153,500

	Capital.
Fairfield Co. - -	133,000
Mechanics of N. Haven	333,350
Middletown - -	400,000
New Haven - -	339,600
Stonington - -	53,000
13 Banks	**4,485,177**

NEW-YORK.

	Capital.
State Bank at Albany -	369,000
Geneva - - -	400,000
Utica - - -	500,000
Mech's and Farmers, Albany - - -	312,000
Catskill - - -	110,000
Phœnix - - -	500,000
New-York - -	1,000,000
Merchants - -	1,490,000
Mechanics - -	2,000,000
Farmers, (Troy) -	278,000
Albany - - -	240,000
Mohawk - - -	165,000
Union - - -	1,000,000
America - - -	2,031,200
City Bank - -	1,000,000
Troy - - -	352,000
Ontario - - -	500,000
Chenango - - -	100,000
Middle District -	406,153
Auburn - - -	184,000
Central (Cherry Valley)	86,000
Jefferson County -	74,000
Tradesmens - -	480,000
Dry Dock Co. - -	200,000
North River - -	500,000
Commercial - -	225,000
Duchess County - -	75,000
Rochester - -	250,000
Long Island - -	300,000
Franklin - · -	510,000
Newburgh - -	120,000
Orange County - -	106,000
Lansingburgh - -	220,000
Manhattan Co. -	2,050,000
Delaware and Hudson -	700,000
Fulton - - -	750,000
Chemical - - -	500,000
37 Banks	**20,083,353**

NEW-JERSEY.

	Capital.
State Bank Camden -	266,050
„ New Brunswick	71,984
„ Elizabeth Town	132,550
„ Newark - -	280,000
„ Morris - -	93,700
Farmers' Bank, New Jersey - - -	100,000
New-Brunswick - -	90,000
Newark Banking and Insurance Co. -	350,000
Sussex - - -	27,500
Trenton Banking Co. -	214,740
Cumberland - -	52,025
Commercial - -	30,000
Farmers' and Mech's. Railway - - -	30,000
Orange Bank - -	50,000
People's ditto - -	75,000
Salem Banking Co. -	30,000
Salem and P. Man'g -	30,000
Washington Bank -	93,460
18 Banks	**2,017,009**

PENNSYLVANIA.

	Capital.
Pennsylvania - -	2,500,000
Philadelphia - -	1,800,000
North America - -	1,000,000
Farmers & Mechanics -	1,250,000
Chambersburgh - -	247,228
Chester County - -	90,000
Delaware County -	77,510
Gettysburgh - -	125,318
Pittsburgh - -	346,155
Carlisle - - -	171,466
Easton - - -	187,380
Farmers of Bucks Co. -	60,000
Farmers of Lancaster -	400,000
Farmers of Reading -	300,000
Harrisburgh - -	158,525
Lancaster - - -	134,235
Monongahela Bank of Brownsville - -	102,128
Northampton - -	112,500
Westmoreland - -	107,033
York - - -	168,720
Germantown - -	129,500
Montgomery County -	133,340
Northern Liberties -	200,000

	Capital.
Commercial - -	1,000,000
Mechanics of Philadel-	
phia - - -	529,330
Schuylkill - - -	500,000
Southwark - -	249,630
Kensington - -	124,990
Penn Township - -	149,980
Columbia Bridge -	395,000
Miners' Bank of Potts-	
ville - - -	40,000
Erie - - - -	20,000
Girard's - - -	1,800,000
33 Banks	14,609,963

DELAWARE.

Delaware Bank, Wil-	
mington - -	110,000
Farmer's Bank of Del.	500,000
Wilmington & Brandy-	
wine - - -	120,000
Bank of Smyrna -	100,000
Commercial Bank of Del.	Not known
Wilmington - -	ditto
4 Banks	830,000
2 not known	
6 Banks	

MARYLAND.

Bank of Baltimore -	1,197,550
Union - - -	1,500,000
Mechanics - -	384,000
Commercial & Farmers	318,400
Farmers and Merchants	414,045
Franklin - - -	406,500
Marine - - -	235,000
Hagerstown - -	250,000
Farmers of Maryland -	820,000
Susquehannah Bridge -	175,000
Westminster - -	175,000
Frederick County -	175,000
Bank of Maryland -	200,000
13 Banks	6,250,495

DISTRICT OF COLUMBIA.

Washington - -	479,120
Union, (George Town)	478,230
Alexandria - -	500,000

	Capital.
Potomac - - -	500,000
Mechanics of Alexandria	372,544
Farmers of ditto -	310,000
Metropolis - -	500,000
Farmers & Mechanics	
of Georgetown -	485,900
Patriotic - - -	250,000
9 Banks	3,875,794

VIRGINIA.

Bank of Virginia -	2,740,000
Farmers of ditto - -	2,000,000
Bank of the Valley -	654,000
North Western Bank of	
Virginia - -	117,100
4 Banks	5,571,100

NORTH CAROLINA.

Cape Fear - - -	795,000
Newbern - - -	800,000
State Bank - -	1,600,000
3 Banks	3,195,000

SOUTH CAROLINA.

Bank of State of South	
Carolina - -	1,156,000
Planters and Mechanics,	
Charleston - -	1,000,000
State Bank - -	800,000
South Carolina - -	675,000
Union - - -	1,000,000
5 Banks	4,631,000

GEORGIA.

Bank of State of Georgia	1,303,436
Planters Bank of ditto	566,000
Marine and Fire Ins.	Not given.
Augusta - - -	600,000
Darien - - -	484,276
Central - - -	922,317
Augusta Insurance -	110,000
Macon - - -	75,000
Merchants and Planters	142,000
9 Banks	4,203,029

LOUISIANA.	Capital.
Louisiana State Bank	1,248,720
Orleans - - -	424,700
Bank of Louisiana -	2,992,560
Branch of Bank of Louisiana - -	1,000,000
4 Banks	5,665,980

ALABAMA.	
Bank of State - -	495,503
„ of Mobile - -	148,000
2 Banks	643,503

MISSISSIPPI.	
Bank of State of Mississippi and Branches	950,600
1 Bank	

TENNESSEE.	
Bank of State of Tennessee - - -	737,817
1 Bank	

OHIO.	Capital.
Chilicothe - - -	500,000
Steubenville - -	100,000
Western Reserve Bank	82,386
Belmont Bank of St. Clairsville - -	100,000
Commercial of Scioto -	100,000
Farmers of Canton -	100,000
Farmers and Mechanics of Steubenville -	100,000
Franklin of Columbus -	100,000
Lancaster Ohio Bank -	100 000
Mount Pleasant -	100,000
Marietta - - -	72,000
11 Banks- -	1,454,386

MICHIGAN.	
Bank of Michigan -	100,000
1 Bank	

FLORIDA.	
Bank of Florida - -	75,000
1 Bank	

RECAPITULATION.

	No.	Capital.		No.	Capital.
Massachusetts -	66	20,420,000	Louisiana-	4	5,665,980
Maine - -	18	2,050,000	Alabama -	2	643,503
New-Hampshire	18	1,791,670	Mississippi	1	950,600
Vermont - -	10	432,625	Tennessee	1	737,817
Rhode Island -	47	6,118,397	Ohio -	11	1,454,386
Connecticut -	13	4,485,177	Michigan-	1	10,000
New-York -	37	20,083,353	Florida -	1	75,000
New-Jersey -	18	2,017,009		—	
Pennsylvania -	33	14,609,963		328	
Delaware - -	4	830,000	Delaware -	1	
Maryland - -	13	6,250,495		—	
Dist. of Columbia	9	3,875,794		329	
Virginia - -	4	5,571,100	Do. -	1	
North Carolina -	3	3,195,000			
South Carolina -	5	4,631,000		330	110,101,898
Georgia - -	9	4,203,029			

III. The following tables of the number and conditions of the banks in the respective states is taken from the American Almanack for 1837.

1. Number and Capital of all the Banks in the United States at different periods.—From the Letter of the Secretary of Treasury, Jan. 5, 1836.

* Returns of capital not complete.

States.	January 1, 1811. No. of Banks.	Capital.	January 1, 1815. No. of Banks.	Capital.	January 1, 1816. No. of Banks.	Capital.	January 1, 1820. No. of Banks.	Capital.	January 1, 1830. No. of Banks.	Capital.	January, 1835. No. of Banks.	No. of Branch.	Capital.
		Dollars.		Dollars.		Dollars.		Dollars.		Dollars.			Dollars.
Maine	6	1,250,000	8	1,380,000	14	1,860,000	15	1,654,900	18	2,050,000	36	…	3,549,850
N. Hampshire	8	815,250	10	941,152	10	998,121	10	1,005,276	18	1,791,670	26	…	2,655,008
Vermont	…	…	…	…	1	…	1	44,955	10	432,625	18	…	1,021,815
Massachusetts	15	6,292,144	21	11,050,000	26	11,650,000	28	10,485,700	66	20,420,000	105	…	30,409,450
Rhode Island	13	1,917,000	14	2,027,000	16	2,317,320	30	2,982,026	47	6,118,397	60	…	8,097,482
Connecticut	5	1,933,000	10	3,655,750	10	4,017,575	8	3,689,337	13	4,485,177	31	3	7,350,766
New York	8	7,522,760	26	18,946,318	27	18,766,756	33	18,988,774	37	20,083,253	87	3	31,881,460
New Jersey	3	739,740	11	2,121,932	11	2,072,115	14	2,130,949	18	2,017,009	24	2	2,707,135
Pennsylvania	4	6,153,050	42	15,068,818	43	15,384,597	36	14,681,780	33	14,610,333	44	…	17,958,444*
Delaware	…	…	5	966,990	5	974,500	6	974,900	5	830,000	4	4	830,000
Maryland	6	4,895,202	17	7,832,002	20	8,406,782	14	6,708,131	13	6,250,495	15	4	7,662,639
D. Columbia	4	2,341,395	10	4,071,097	10	4,294,013	13	5,525,319	9	3,875,794	7	…	2,613,985
Virginia	1	1,500,000	4	4,121,097	12	4,512,177	4	5,212,192	4	5,571,100	5	17	5,840,000
N. Carolina	3	1,576,600	3	1,576,600	3	2,776,600	3	2,964,887	3	3,195,000	4	7	2,464,925
S. Carolina	4	3,475,000	5	3,730,900	5	3,832,758	5	4,475,000	5	4,631,000	8	2	7,556,318
Georgia	1	210,000	2	623,580	3	1,502,600	4	3,401,510	9	4,203,029	13	10	6,783,308
Florida	…	…	…	…	…	…	…	…	1	75,000	3	…	114,320*
Alabama	…	…	…	…	…	…	3	469,112	2	643,503	2	4	6,107,623
Louisiana	1	754,000	3	1,432,360	3	1,422,300	4	2,597,420	4	5,665,980	11	31	27,172,145
Mississippi	…	…	1	100,000	1	100,000	1	900,000	1	950,600	5	10	5,890,162*
Tennessee	1	100,000	2	212,962	4	815,281	8	2,119,782	…	737,817	3	4	2,890,381
Kentucky	1	240,460	2	959,175	2	2,057,000	42	8,807,431	…	…	6	11	4,898,685
Missouri	…	…	…	…	…	…	1	250,000	…	…	1	1	278,739
Illinois	…	…	…	…	…	…	2	140,910	…	…	1	1	…
Indiana	…	…	…	…	…	…	2	202,857	…	…	1	9	800,000
Ohio	4	895,000	12	1,434,719	21	2,061,927	20	1,797,463	11	1,454,386	31	1	6,390,741*
Michigan	…	…	…	…	…	…	…	…	1	100,000	7	…	658,980
U. S. Banks	88	42,610,601	208	82,259,590	246	89,822,422	307	102,210,611	329	110,192,268	557	121	194,584,361
Estimated capital of seven banks from which no returns	1	10,000,000	…	…	…	…	1	35,000,000	1	35,000,000	1	25	35,000,000
													1,665,976
Total	89	52,610,601	208	82,259,590	246	89,822,422	308	137,210,611	330	145,192,268	558	146	229,584,361 — 231,250,337

Note.—Many of the above are from estimates made at different periods by different persons; but are believed to approximate accuracy as near as is now practicable.

TABLE II.

2. *Condition of all the Banks in the United States, as near Jan.* 1, 1835, *as returns could be obtained.*

	Whole No. of Banks	Whole No. of Branches.	No. from which returns Bank	No. from which returns Branches.	Specie Funds.	Specie.	Capital.	Circulation.
					Dollars.	Dollars.	Dollars.	Dollars.
Maine ...	36	...	35	...	28,196	171,923	3,499,850	7.709.320
N. H. ...	26	...	26	...	531,062	...	2,655,008	1.389.970
Vt.	18	...	17	...	286,116	50,958	921,815	1.463.713
Mass. ...	105	...	105	...	...	1,180,564	30,409,450	7.868.472
R. I. ...	60	...	60	...	...	473,641	8,097,482	1.290.785
Conn. ...	31	3	31	3	1,249,408	129,108	7,350,766	2.685.400
N. Y. ...	87	2	86	2	670,363	7,221,335	31,581,460	16.427.963
N. J. ...	24	...	1	...	8,736	...	50,000	30.247
Penn. ...	44	...	43	...	...	3,476,462	17,958,444	7.818.001
Del.......	4	4	3	3	...	173,183	730,000	622.397
Md.	15	4	14	4	...	972,090	7,542,639	1.923.055
D. of C.	7	...	7	...	...	474,199	2,613,985	692.536
Va.	5	17	5	17	...	1,160,401	5,840,000	5.593.198
N. C. ...	4	7	4	7	...	275,660	2,464,925	2.241.964
S. C. ...	8	2	2	2	...	754,219	2,156.318	2.288.030
Ga.	13	10	13	10	...	1,781,835	6.783.308	3.694.329
Fa.	3	...	2	...	41,305	14,312	114.320	133.531
Ala.......	2	4	2	3	...	916,135	5.607.623	3.472.413
La.	11	31	10	31	...	2,824,904	26.422.145	5.114.082
Miss.	5	11	2	8	...	359,302	5.890.162	2.418.475
Tenn. ...	3	4	2	4	...	290,472	2,890.381	3.189.220
Ky.	6	10	6	10	...	872,368	4.898.685	2.771.154
Mo.......	...	1	...	1	...	155,341	...	...
Illinois..	1	1	1	1	...	243,223	278.739	178.810
Ind.......	1	9	1	9	...	751,083	800.000	456.065
Ohio ...	31	...	29	...	...	1,906,715	6,390.741	5.654.048
Mich. ...	7	1	7	1	42,512	112,419	658.980	636.676
Estimate of Banks, returns are imperfect.	557	121	514	116	2,857,698	26,741,852	184.607.226	81.763.854
	...	...	43	5	204,121	1,487,404	11.643.111	4.588.844
			557	121	3,061,819	28,229,256	196.250.337	86,352,698
B. U. S.	...	...	1	25	...	15,708,369	35.000.000	17,339,797
Total	...	...	558	146	3,061,819	43,937,625	231.250.337	103,692,495

TABLE III.

3. *Condensed Statement of the Condition of all the Banks, at different intervals, in the United States.*

Date.	No. of Banks from which returns.	No. of Banks the affairs of which are estimated.	Total No. of Banks	Capital.	Deposits.	Circulation.	Specie.
				Dollars.	Dollars.	Dollars.	Dollars.
Jan. 1, 1811,	51	88	89	52,610.601	...	28,100,000	15,400,000
Jan. 1, 1815,	120	12	208	82,259,590	...	45,500,000	17,000,000
Jan. 1, 1816,	134	112	246	89,822,422	...	68,000,000	19,000,000
Jan. 1, 1820,	213	95	308	137,110,611	35,950,470	44,863,344	19,820,240
Jan. 1, 1830,	282	48	320	145,192,268	55,559,928	61.323,898	22,114,917
Jan. 1, 1835,	515	43	558	231,250,337	83,081,365	103,692,495	43,937,625

IV.—The following list of banks that have failed or
discontinued business is taken from Mr. Gallatin.

*A List of the Banks which have failed, or discontinued their business,
from 1st January, 1811, to 1st July, 1830.*

MASSACHUSETTS.
Capital.

Essex	300,000
New Bedford	150,000
Northampton	75,000
Farmers', (Belchertown)	100,000
Brighton	150,000
Sutton	75,000
6 Banks	**850,000**

MAINE.

Maine	300,000
Penobscot	150,000
Wiscasset	100,000
Hallowell	150,000
Kennebec	150,000
Passamaquoddy	50,000
Castine	100,000
Lincoln and Kennebec	200,000
8 Banks	**1,150,000**

RHODE ISLAND.

Farmers' & Mechanics', Pautuxet	200,000
Far. Exchange, Gloucester	
1 Bank	**200,000**

NEW HAMPSHIRE.

Coos	100,000
Concord	29,600
2 Banks	**129,600**

CONNECTICUT.

Eagle	500,000
Derby	100,000
2 Banks	**690,000**

NEW YORK.

J. Barker's Exchange	495,250
Utica Insurance Co.	100,000
Columbia	167,650
Hudson	110,000
Niagara	108,000
Plattsburgh	300,000
Washington and Warren	400,000
N. York Manuf. Co.	700,000
Franklin	510,000
Middle District	487,776
Catskill Aqued. Assoc.	
10 Banks	**3,378,676**

NEW JERSEY.

Jersey City Bank	200,000
Patterson	160,000
State Bank, Trenton	92,400
Protection and Lombard	200,050
Franklin	300,000
Monmouth	40,000
Manufacturing	150,005
Salem and Philadelphia.	
Hoboken	
7 Banks	**1,142,400**

PENNSYLVANIA.

Washington	92,070
Farmers' and Mechanics of Greencastle	74,485
Ditto ditto of Pittsburgh	65,337
Juniata	164,478
Marietta and Susquehannah Trading Co.	239,430
Pennsylvania Agril. and Man. Bank	110,102
Delaware Bridge	99,715
Allegheny	144,807
Beaver	78,985
Swatara	75,075
Centre	159,610
Huntingdon	123,122
Northumberland, Union and Columbia	116,980
North Western Bank	77,688
Union of Pennsylvania	124,792
Silver Lake	64,882
Fayette, New Salem	
Harmony	
Wilkesbarre Branch	
16 Banks	**1,811,558**

DELAWARE.	Capital.
Farmers'and Mechanics' of Delaware - -	45,000

MARYLAND.	
Elkton - - -	110,000
Conococheague - -	157,500
Cumberland - -	107,862
Somerset and W. -	90,000
Somerset - - -	195,850
Caroline - - -	103,045
Havre de Grace - -	132,075
City - - - -	838,540
Planters' P. George's Co.	86,290
9 Banks	1,821,162

DISTRICT OF COLUMBIA.	
Columbia - - -	901,200
Union of Alexandria -	340,000
Central - - -	252,995
Franklin - - -	163,265
4 Banks	1,657,460

VIRGINIA.	
Ohio Co. - - -	60,000
Charleston M. and C. Co.	32,580
Winchester - -	122,930
Monogalia - -	25,000
Farmers and Mechanics Harper's Ferry -	19,480
South Branch - -	25,000
Farmers, Merch., and Mech's. Jefferson Co.	26,425
Warrentown - -	60,000
Leesburg Union - -	20,000
Loudon Co. -	30,000
10 Banks	421,415

NORTH CAROLINA.	
Fayetteville	
Bertie	

SOUTH CAROLINA.	
Cheraw - - -	20,000
Hamburg	
1 Bank	20,000

GEORGIA.	Capital
Darien - - -	480,000
1 Bank	

LOUISIANA.	
Planters' Bank - -	200,000
Bank of Louisiana -	724,000
2 Banks	924,000

ALABAMA.	
Planters and Merchants	164,175
Tombeckbe - -	156,937
Steamboat - - -	16,000
2 Banks	337,112

TENNESSEE.	
Fayetteville Transfer -	110,000
Farmers' & Mechanics' of Nashville - -	180,200
Nashville & Branches	994,560
Tennessee Bank (old)	371,107
3 Branches of do. -	300,000
Nashville Branch of do.	206,775
Rogersville Branch do.	67,140
4 Banks and 5 Branches	2,229,782

KENTUCKY.	
Farmers' & Mechanics of Lexington, (stock & notes at par) -	489,700
Versailles - - -	111,180
Kentucky & Branches	2,756,220
Fleminsburgh - -	61,626
Limestone - -	135,825
Shepherdsville - -	55,880
Hinkston Exporting Co.	50,120
New Castle - -	40,520
Cynthiana - -	47,900
Centre Bank of Kentucky	120,000
Union of Elizabethtown	39,400
Farming & Com. Bank	37,219
Greenville - - -	46,640
Newport - - -	54,700
Southern Bank of Ky.	117,222
Farmers' of Harrodsburg	81,000
„ Somerset -	22,379
Lancaster Exporting Co.	39,900

	Capital.		Capital.
Insurance - -		Lebanon Miami Banking Co. - - -	86,491
Barboursville - -		Urbana Banking Co. -	49,685
Cumberland Bank of		Farmers' and Mechanics	
Burkville - -		Man. Chillicothe -	99,575
Burlington - -		Hamilton - - -	22,707
Bank of Colombia -		Zanesville Canal and	
Frankfort - - -		Manufacturing Co. -	79,125
Georgetown - -		West Union - -	100,000
Greensburg - -		Lake Erie - - -	100,000
Green River - -		Steubenville - -	100,000
Christian Bank - -		Muskingum of Zanes-	
Bank of Henderson -		ville - - -	100,000
„ of Washington -		Jefferson Co.	
Commercial Bank of		Bank of Xenia	
Louisville - -			
Mount Sterling - -		18 Banks	1,911,179
Morgantown - -			
Monticello - -		INDIANA.	
Farmers' Bank of Jes-		Farmers and Mechanics'	
samine - - -		Bank - - -	130,000
Owngsville - -		Bank of Vincennes -	127,624
Petersburg Steam Mill			
Farmers' Bank of Gallatin		2 Banks	257,624
Far. and Mech. of Logan			
Do. do. Shelbyville		ILLINOIS.	
Do. do. Springfield		Illinois - - -	105,720
Winchester Commercial		Edwardsville - -	57,190
Commonwealth Bank -	2,000,000		
	(nominal)	2 Banks	162,910
		MISSOURI.	
18 Banks	4,307,431	Bank of Missouri -	250,000
		„ „ St. Louis -	150,000
OHIO.			
Miami Exporting Co.,		2 Banks	400,000
Cincinnati - -	468,966		
Columbia, New Lisbon	50,000	MICHIGAN.	
Granville Alx'n Soc. -	12,002	Munroe - - -	10,000
Farmers' Bank of New		1 Bank	
Salem - - -	57,000	RECAPITULATION.	
German of Wooster -	25,000	129 Banks -	24,212,339
Muskingum - -	97,800	36 do. -	not known.
Farmers' and Mechanics			
of Cincinnati - -	184,776	165	
Cincinnati - - -	216,430		
Dayton Manufacturing-	61,622		

V. Those state banks, which have been selected by Congress to receive and transmit the revenue instead of the old bank of the United States, are called " deposit banks."

CONDITION OF THE DEPOSIT BANKS,

According to Returns made to the Treasury Department, Apr. 1, 1836.

Name.	Place.	Capital.	Specie.	Deposits. Treasurer United States.
		Dollais.	Dollars.	Dollars.
Maine	Portland	30,000 00	27,339 82	113,074 94
Commercial......	Portsmouth	102,000 00	11,065 56	128,338 33
Commonwealth.	Boston...	500,000 00	209,064 54	1,009,731 52
Merchants'	Do.	750,000 00	295,546 30	931,105 79
Burlington	Burlington	127,912 00	12,082 35	52,893 48
Far. & Mech. ...	Hartford	410,496 00	10,763 80	67,560 89
Mechanics'	New Haven.....	472,970 00	153,546 38	41,315 06
Arcade...........	Providence	300,000 00	52,231 26	115,132 40
Mech. & Farm	Albany............	442,000 00	114,032 33	217,430 22
Bank of America	New York	2,001,200 00	1,274,220 66	3,858,750 20
Manhattan Co...	Do.	2,050,000 00	1,028,946 33	3,462,800 38
Mechanics'	Do.	2,000,000 00	1,271.593 00	3,985,083 72
Girard	Philadelphia ...	1,500,000 00	461,374 86	2,516,858 76
Moyamensing ...	Do.	174,950 00	93,030 32	502,042 25
Union, Md......	Baltimore........	1,845,562 50	107,943 24	906,491 54
Franklin	Do.	508,970 00	124,197 74	347,388 74
Bank Metropolis	Washington......	500,000 00	217,219 39	200,394 40
Vir. & Branches	Richmond, &c...	3,240,000 00	633,700 07	358,230 56
North Carolina	Raleigh	1,206,100 00	292,018 15	38,471 07
Plant. & Mech.	Charleston	1,000,000 00	317,162 81	252,522 42
Planters' Geo....	Savannah.	535,400 00	178,472 45	111,862 48
Augusta	Augusta	897,000 00	313,750 03	129,770 95
Branch of Ala...	Mobile......	2,000,000 00	339,723 01	1,623,818 12
Commercial......	New Orleans ...	2,945,430 00	202,533 17	1,119,314 50
Un. Bank of La.	Do.	7,051,000 00	255,559 01	1,261,116 73
Merch. & Man.	Pittsburg	600,000 00	127,514 59	51,095 72
Franklin	Cincinnati	1,000,000 00	167,020 90	244,048 12
Commercial......	Do.	1,000,000 00	266,803 87	395,175 82
Clinton	Columbus	289,225 00	121,143 47	328,127 52
Savings Instit....	Louisville......	96,512 00	50,807 58	494,842 26
Union Bank Ten.	Nashville........	1,817,255 00	116,585 17	484,086 61
State	Indianapolis	1,279,857 78	964,758 34	1,379,949 98
Agency C. Bank Cincinnati ...	St. Louis		513,859 06	1,978,383 94
Planters'	Natchez	4,143,940 00	438,324 32	2,732,319 38
Michigan.........	Detroit............	448,200 00	62,139 34	1,070,820 03
Farm. & Mech.	Do.	150,000 00	59,923 70	703,675 25
Total ...		43,690,980 28	10,885,996 92	33,294,024 08

Recapitulation of Deposit Banks.

	Dollars.		Dollars.
Loans & Discounts......	68,850,287 67	Capital....................	43,690,980 28
Domestic Exchange ...	32,775,529 42	Treasurer of U. S.	33,294,024 08
Real Estate..............	1,929,056 68	Public Officers	3,477,252 42
Due from Banks.........	15,931,916 22	Due to Banks............	15,366,674 49
Notes of other Banks...	11,107,447 78	Contingent Fund	1,102,763 15
Specie	10,885,996 92	Profit and Loss, &c. ...	4,094,358 12
Foreign Exchange......	532,450 96	Circulation	28,796,186 68
Expenses.	184,901 22	Private Deposits.........	15,453,092 11
Other Investments.......	10,651,759 92	Other Liabilities	7,574,015 16
Total. .	152,849,346 79	Total ..	152,849,346 79

DISTRIBUTION OF THE SURPLUS REVENUE.

" A bill to regulate the deposits of the public money," which was passed by Congress in June, 1836, contains the following enactment relating to the surplus revenue :—' That the money which shall be in the treasury of the United States on the 1st day of January, 1837, reserving the sum of $5,000,000, shall be deposited with the several States, in proportion to their respective representation in the Senate and House of Representatives of the United States, which shall by law authorize their treasurer or other competent authorities, to receive the same on the terms hereinafter specified ; and the secretary of the treasury shall deliver the same to such treasurer, or other competent authorities, in such form as may be prescribed by the secretary aforesaid, which certificates shall express the usual and legal obligations of common depositories of the public money, for the safe keeping and repayment thereof, and shall pledge the faith of the State receiving the same to pay the said monies and every part thereof, from time to time, whenever the same shall be required by the secretary of the treasury, for the purpose of defraying any wants of the public treasury beyond the amount of the five millions aforesaid.

" Provided, that if any State declines to receive its proportion of the surplus aforesaid, on the terms before-named, the same may, at the discretion of the secretary of the treasury, be deposited with the other States agreeing to accept the same in deposit.

" And provided further, that when the said money, or any part thereof, shall be wanted by said secretary, to meet appropriations made by law, the same shall be called for in rateable proportions, within one year, as nearly as conveniently may be, from the different States with which the same is deposited, and shall not be called for in sums exceeding ten thousand dollars, from any one State in any one month, without previous notice of thirty days for every additional sum of twenty thousand dollars which may be required.

" The said deposits shall be made with the States, in the following proportions, and at the following times, viz.—one quarter part on the 1st day of January, 1837, or as soon after as may be ; one quarter part on the 1st day of April ; one quarter part on the 1st day of July ; and one quarter part on the 1st day of October, all in the same year."

VI.—The circulation of notes by the state banks.

A large portion of the profits of the banks is derived from the circulation of their notes. Thirteen of the States have, in consequence of the measures of the government with reference to deposit banks, abolished notes under five dollars. Several American writers have for some years past recommended this measure.

" In the United States," says Mr. Gallatin, " all the banks issue notes of five dollars. The States of Pennsylvania, Maryland, and Virginia, and perhaps some others, have forbidden the use of notes of a lower denomination, to the great convenience of the community, and without experiencing any of the evils which had been predicted. We have seen in Pennsylvania the chasm occasioned by that suppression instantaneously filled by silver, without the least diminution in the amount of currency. We cannot but earnestly wish that the other States may adopt a similar measure, and put an end to the circulation of the one, two, and three dollar notes, which are of no utility but to the banks. Those small notes are, as a currency, exclusively local and a public nuisance, and in case of the failure of any bank the loss arising from them falls more heavily on the poorest class of the community."

Another writer observes :—

" The natural and ordinary effect of the circulation of small notes is to cause the specie to leave the channels of circulation, and settle in the vaults of the banks, and for the most part in the banks of commercial towns. Consequently, when from the state of trade and currency it is in demand for exportation, being already collected it is silently and suddenly withdrawn ; and before the public at large can have any sufficient notice of its being gone, the banks are obliged to stop their issues, and the paper previously in circulation is withdrawn also, being returned to the banks by their debtors.

" It is owing to this effect of the universal issue of small notes— notes of one, two, three, and five dollars, that the banks in this city are ordinarily the depositories of nearly all the specie upon which depends the credit of the paper circulation of the whole State, and of the contiguous districts of several adjoining States. When, therefore, there is a demand for specie, the banks in the interior depend not upon their own vaults, but upon their credits in the city. When there is no such active demand, the city banks must hold and lose the interest on a quantity of specie far exceeding their proportion of the whole circulation of the state and adjacent districts, or hazard the occurrence of a demand beyond their means, and a necessity of instantly restraining their issues, ruining their debtors, and distressing the community.

" Were all notes under five or ten dollars suppressed, an amount of specie greater probably than the average quantity hitherto existing in the State, would constantly remain in the hands of the people ; in which condition, besides its effect in preventing an excess of circulation, it would, in the event of a demand for exportation, prevent a sudden and ruinous scarcity. It could not be silently and instantly withdrawn. It would be too much in the power of the people ; and a demand for it, would immediately enhance its exchangeable value. This, added to the progressive decline of prices and of confidence, and in short, all the circumstances which characterize such a period, the urgent wants of the circulation, and the disposition to hoard and conceal, would render the process of collecting and sending it out of the country extremely difficult, and to a great extent impracticable.

" It is a sufficient reason for the suppression of small notes, that they greatly multiply counterfeits, owing to the facility with which spurious imitations of them may be passed. Notes of ten dollars and upwards are comparatively but seldom counterfeited. Such notes are generally in the hands of persons capable of deciding on their genuineness. No one receives a note of that amount without attentive scrutiny; whereas the smaller denominations, especially those under five dollars, being in universal circulation among those who are without information or experience, unavoidably pass with little or no examination."—*Principles of Currency and Banking. By E. Lord. New York*, 1829.

VII.—The banks of the state of New York.

The following extracts respecting the banks of this state are taken from a work published a few years ago at New York, entitled "Report and Observations on the Bank and other Incorporated Institutions in the State of New York."

" The legislature aware that capital was essential to draw out the capabilities of the State, and that although individual capital was so employed, without its concentration the march of improvement would be slow over such an extent of country, met the wants of the community by acts of incorporation for every object calculated to draw forth the energies of the people, and by chartering companies for carrying on various public works, such as manufactories, working mines, and opening communications.

" In order to create a circulating medium for such establishments, the State granted charters for banks, authorizing them to create a capital threefold what they possessed. Thus, vesting in the directors of those banks a discretionary power to produce a circulating medium of about seventy millions of dollars, which being added to the capital authorized to be invested in other chartered institutions, shews an incorporated capital of one hundred millions of dollars, in all which any and every citizen or alien might invest such portions of their property as they thought proper without risking the remainder. It is evident, that without such acts of incorporation, reflecting and cautious men would not embark in new undertakings, however plausible; as the very questionable law of partnership, which is in force in this State as in England, would hazard the remaining property of the shareholders.

" It would betray great ignorance of the monied institutions of the State, were I to convey the idea that the authorized capital had all been paid in, or that the banks acted up to such their privileges of owing to three times the amount of their capital. However, I am safe in saying that the greater part of the capital of the banks has been paid in ; yet of the other monied institutions I am equally safe in stating, that save a few of those early established not one half the authorized

capital has been actually invested, but in lieu of cash the personal
security of the stockholder is accepted for a part of his subscription to
the stock standing in his name; which security is guaranteed by the
hypothecation of the stock so in part paid for, and sometimes secured
by a mortgage of his lands ; the balance so due is subject to interest
to the institution, and the stock so hypothecated is transferable, and
the purchaser assumes the debt; thus a fictitious capital is further
increased, thereby enabling persons of small available property to
become connected with these institutions. From all which facilities of
investment and accommodation afforded, every member of the community stands in some way or other interested in these institutions.

" In order to restrain the undue investment of property therein, as
well as to raise a revenue from them, the state legislature on the 23rd
April, 1823, passed an act by which all the incorporated associations
are to be taxed and assessed as in the case of individuals ; and requiring that the secretary, cashier, and treasurer of all such communities should pay the amount of the tax imposed upon the company.
Provided, however, that if the said companies, or either of them, should
elect or choose to pay directly to the treasurer of the county ten per
cent. upon all dividends, profits, or income made by the company, they
should be at liberty to do so, and the affidavits of the cashier, secretary,
&c. as to the amount of dividend, or profit, should be accepted.

" Thus has the State not only required from many of these institutions a bonus for granting their charters, from some loans, and from
others the privilege to subscribe for stock, thereby deriving an income
from their operations, as well as securing to various public institutions
the right to become shareholders ; but have subjected them to the
heavy tax of ten per cent., while the dividends payable to the
public institutions are exempt from such tax. At the same time, the
Bank of the United States has a branch at New York, which the
legislature has not the power of taxing, yet by this bank all the
customs and other revenue of the general government are managed,
and much of the money transactions of the public.

" While a created capital of such extent is thus operating upon the
community, it may be asserted there is not above one million and a half of
dollars in all the banks of the State in specie. In this opinion I am fully
borne out, by the opinion of many persons conversant with the subject,
as well as by those whose situation enables them to resort to the most
correct data. In 1824, when Mr. Manning, one of the house of Barclay
and Co. of London, the contractors for the loans, resorted to New
York from Mexico, to procure £73,000 sterling, to remit to Mexico,
although he had agents at Philadelphia and Boston, he could not procure it without so great delay, that he was obliged to send to London
and have it sent direct to Vera Cruz. Also in 1812 when but 240,000
dollars for the British Commissioners at Halifax was required, it was
necessary to send to Boston for 100,000 dollars, so that I am borne out
by facts, that an immediate demand for one million of dollars in specie
could not be met without resorting to the Bank of the United States, or
those of the neighbouring states. But at the same time, it should be
stated, that large demands are out of the ordinary transactions of the city,
and I feel the most assured conviction that the capital of many of these

banks is as well secured, and their issues being as much the representatives of real wealth, as those of any similar institutions in the world ; and were they liable for calls of larger sums in specie, their transactions would be regulated by such liability, but great curtailments in their issues would follow as well as general though temporary embarrassment.

" If bullion therefore is to be regarded as the only safe circulating medium, and if all securities not convertible into a metallic currency argues an unsound state of public credit—if according to the prevailing maxims of political economists, the existence of excessive fictitious capital is dangerous, then indeed are the people of this State and the United States in a truly awful condition ; but opposed to all these maxims stands the actual situation of the State of New York."

" The first act relating to banks passed by the legislature of the State of New York, bears date the 11th day of April, 1782. It was prohibitory ; namely, to prevent the establishment of any bank within the State, other than the Bank of North America, which had been chartered at Congress, and located at Philadelphia.

" The first act to incorporate a bank by the State legislature was passed in 1792, when the Bank of New York was chartered, by which the stockholders are allowed to issue notes to the amount of three times the capital paid in, as also to three times the amount of deposits. The amount authorized was one million dollars, and the charter was limited to May, 1811, but was afterwards extended to June, 1832 ; and as a bonus for such extension, the comptroller was to subscribe 15,000 dollars on the part of the commonwealth to the capital stock, the treasurer of Hamilton college 15,000 dollars, and of Columbia college 20,000 dollars. This bank has generally paid dividends of four and one half per cent. half yearly, and the stock has generally borne a premium of thirty per cent., but of late the dividends have been only equal to eight per cent. yearly.

" An act of incorporation passed in 1799, establishing an institution for supplying the city of New York with water, capital 2,000,000 dollars, surplus to be employed in money operations. Banking privileges are the chief objects of this company, which is called Manhattan Bank. Its stock has been very productive, and has generally sold from twelve to twenty per cent. above par, (the greater part of the stock is held by a gentleman in London.) Under the right to supply water this charter is deemed perpetual ; in granting it the State reserved the right to subscribe one thousand shares of fifty dollars each, which it still holds.

" The Mechanics Bank was incorporated in 1810, the State reserving the privilege of subscribing 200,000 dollars of the capital, (1,500,000 dollars) but afterwards accepted 32,500 dollars in lieu of the privilege of subscribing. This stock generally bears a premium of twelve per cent. advance.

" In 1812, an act was passed to incorporate the Bank of America, in the city of New York, with a capital of 6,000,000 dollars, for which a bonus was required of 400,000 dollars for the State, and two loans, 1,000,000 dollars at 5 per cent. and 1,000,000 at 6 per cent. These terms were subsequently reduced to a loan of 100,000 dollars, and a bonus of the like sum. This stock pays but five per cent. a year in dividends.

" In the same year, the city branch of New York was incorporated, with a capital of 2,000,000 dollars. For this act 120,000 dollars were paid as a bonus to the common school fund of the State, 50,000 dollars to the State itself, and 500,000 dollars were also lent to the State at 6 per cent. per annum.

From the year 1816 all acts of incorporation of banks required that their notes should be redeemed with specie under the penalty of being liable to pay at the rate of ten per cent. per annum interest, from the time of the demand in specie ; suits to be prosecuted in any court of law.

" In the several banks, the State has invested 606,800 dollars ; and several colleges in the State, hold 233,400 dollars, which stock was reserved as a privilege at the time of granting the charters."

" In the State of New York there is, by law, what is termed a " safety fund security." The idea of this fund has greatly increased the confidence of the community in the paper of that State. I have endeavoured to make myself acquainted with the system ; and if I understand it, there is little or no security in the fund. But many of the arrangements and restrictions connected with the system are bene- ficial. The fund can never consist of more than 500,000 dollars; and it is created by each of the banks paying annually half of 1 per cent. on their capital, until it amounts to the above sum. The contributions then cease, unless there is a defalcation in some bank. On such an event the contributions are continued, or re-commence, as the case may be, until the defalcation is made good, and the fund amounts to the specified sum. In this way, each bank is made liable, to a limited extent, for the paper of the others. It has been supposed, that by thus linking them together, a degree of watchfulness is created that otherwise would not exist.

" The salutary part of the system consists in requiring that the whole amount of the nominal capital of a bank shall be actually paid up before it commences operation ; that it shall report to the legislature annually, under the oath of its officers, the true situation of the institution ; that its books and vaults shall be open at all times to the inspection of bank commissioners, that are permanently appointed for the purpose of examining the state of these institutions ; that the Chancellor of the State, on the report of these commissioners, pur- porting that they are not satisfied, may suspend the business of a bank until a full and complete examination can be had ; and that they are all prohibited from making loans on their own stock.

" An objection has been urged against this plan with great warmth. It is said, that the commissioners are mere politicians, subservient to the views of the dominant party ; and that being so, they possess and exercise an undue influence on the directors of these banks ; and that, in point of fact, the whole plan is a piece of political machinery. This charge, on the other hand, is stoutly denied. The prevailing opinion

out of the State is, that the project is quite as much political as it is
financial."—*A Correspondent of the Times, who subscribes himself " a
Genevese Traveller."*

Mr. Gallatin says, that the safety fund appears
to be unjust—first, by making institutions properly
managed responsible for others at a great distance,
and over which they have no control; secondly,
because on account of the disproportion between the
aggregate of the circulation and deposits of the city
and country banks respectively, the former are made
to pay to the safety fund about twice as much in proportion as the country banks.

SECTION IV.

AN INQUIRY HOW FAR THE BANKING INSTITUTIONS OF AMERICA ARE ADAPTED TO THIS COUNTRY.

It will be seen from the preceding sections that the
banking institutions of America are different from
those of England. America has no national bank—
no private banks, and no joint stock banks upon our
system. Her banks are all chartered by the governments of the respective States in which they are
established. Whether the banking institutions of
America are upon the whole superior to those of this
country, is an interesting subject of investigation.
Those branches of the inquiry that have a reference
to a national bank or to the private banks, will not be
discussed in this section. I shall merely draw a comparison between our joint stock banks and the chartered banks of America, with a view to ascertain how
far the former may be improved by the adoption of
some of the regulations of the latter. As a guide to
the inquiry, I shall compare the act to regulate banks
and banking, passed by the State of Massachusetts in
1829, with the report of the secret committee of the
House of Commons upon joint stock banks delivered
in 1836. I must, however, premise that in the State
of Massachusetts American banking is exhibited in its

most prudent form. In consequence of their superior management, the banks of New England did not suspend payment in 1814, as did the banks in the other parts of America.

COMMONWEALTH OF MASSACHUSETTS.

An Act to regulate Banks and Banking.

" Sec. 1. Be it enacted by the Senate and House of Representatives, in general court assembled, and by the authority of the same, that from and after the passing of this act, every bank which shall receive a charter from or by authority of this commonwealth, and every bank whose capital shall be increased, or whose charter shall be extended, shall be governed by the following rules: and subject to all the duties, limitations, restrictions, liabilities, and provisions contained in this act."

This section implies that no bank shall be allowed to exist unless it have a charter, and that all the charters shall be drawn up according to the same general rules. In these respects, it stands opposed to the laws of this country. The following is the language of the parliamentary committee:—

" The law imposes on the joint stock banks no preliminary obligation, beyond the payment of a license duty, and the registration of the names of shareholders at the stamp office.

" The law does not require that the deed of settlement shall be considered or revised by any competent authority whatever, and no precaution is taken to enforce the insertion in such deeds, of clauses the most obvious and necessary."

An American bank has a charter, a joint stock bank has a deed of settlement. The general heads of this document are thus stated by the committee.

1. " The power of altering the regulations of the company."

2. " The mode of conducting the business of banking."

3. " The degree of publicity to be given to the proceedings."

4. " The terms on which the company is to be dissolved."

Although the law may not require that the deeds of settlement be revised by any competent authority, yet in fact, they always are, and precaution is taken by the directors of the company to insert clauses the

62 THE HISTORY OF

most obvious and necessary. After the deed has been
prepared by the solicitor, and approved by the directors, it is submitted to the inspection of an emi-
nent barrister. Still perhaps, it is desirable that
they be submitted to a barrister appointed by the
government, in the same manner as the rules of
savings' banks. This officer should not however have
a discretionary power; he might be allowed, 1st. to
strike out any clause which may be contrary to law.
2. He might object to any clause, which in his judgment would be injurious to the public or to the
shareholders, although not contrary to law. In this
case, the clause should not be inserted in the deed,
unless sanctioned at a meeting of the shareholders,
specially summoned for that purpose. 3.—In case he
stated that any provision was contrary to law, when
the directors did not believe it to be so, the clause
might be submitted to the Attorney or Solicitor-
General for the time being, whose opinion upon the
law should be final.

Although different deeds of settlement may require
some special clauses according to the circumstances of
different companies, yet in their general provisions
they must be very similar; and hence it would not
be difficult to draw up a list of clauses the most obvious and necessary. But it does not follow that
such clauses should be enforced by act of Parliament.
They who execute the deed, and who are to be bound
by its provisions, should be allowed to judge as to
what are the most necessary clauses.

Lord Althorp proposed the granting of charters to
all joint stock banks, on a plan somewhat similar to
that of America. The following is part of a speech
he delivered upon the renewal of the Bank of England
Charter, in 1833, as reported in the Times.

" He proposed that every banking company of more than six
partners, should be a joint stock company, such company to be
established by charter. These chartered banks would be subject to
certain regulations, but all advantageous to themselves and the country.
He would not propose that these banks should be banks of issue :
they were of two sorts ; some issued their own notes, and others the

notes of the Bank of England; but banks were prevented issuing notes payable in London for less than £50.

" In the plan he proposed, joint stock banks might exist within the sixty-five miles, if they used the paper of the Bank of England. The conditions on which he proposed government should grant charters to these joint stock banks were the following—first, that the partners in these banks should have half of their subscribed capital paid up, and deposited either in the government funds, or some equally good securities. He further proposed, that the partners should be liable to an unlimited responsibility—the corporation of the bank should not hold any shares in it ; and that the accounts of the bank should be yearly audited and published. Of course, it was plain there was a vast difference in those banks which possessed the power of issuing their own notes, and those which did not issue them. In their case, he proposed as the conditions on which charters should be granted, that one quarter of their subscribed capital, instead of one half, as required where they were banks of issue, should be paid up and deposited as before—that their shares should not be less than £100 each ;—and that the partners in such banks should be only liable to a responsibility to the amount of their shares. In a case where a charter was to be granted, it must be at the discretion of government to decide, whether the amount of capital subscribed was a sufficient amount for the locality in which the bank in question was situated. He hoped, however, that every proper facility would be given to the establishment of such banks."

If it were at all desirable to adopt Lord Althorp's plan, it is now too late. It would be unjust to compel the existing joint stock banks to take out charters, and to comply with burdensome conditions, of which they had no knowledge at the time of their formation. But, it may be worthy of inquiry how far charters may be granted without any material alteration of the laws respecting joint stock banks. Lord Althorp's plan appears objectionable—first, in requiring all joint stock banks to be chartered banks; and secondly, in giving the crown a discretionary power in granting the charters. Now might not Parliament prescribe the conditions on which charters might be obtained, and leave to the banks the power of complying with those conditions or not as they pleased ? And might not the mixture of banks of different sorts be attended with advantage to the country ? It is the opinion of Mr. Clay that the three chartered banks of Scotland " gave a tone to public opinion, and rendered it difficult for any bank commencing business to conduct

its affairs in a manner widely different." And Lord
Liverpool advocated the establishment of branches of
the Bank of England upon the ground that they
would operate as a check upon the country banks.
We know too that the extension of joint stock banks
in England has improved the private banks. Why
then, may not the establishment of a few chartered
banks tend to improve the joint stock banks?

" Sec. 2. And be it further enacted, that every bank incorporated
by the authority aforesaid, shall be a corporation by the name of the
president, directors, and company of the   bank (the blank
to be filled up as the case may require), capable in law to sue and
be sued to final judgment and execution, to have and use a common
seal, and the same at pleasure again to break, alter, and renew, and
also to establish and put in force such bye-laws and regulations as to
them shall appear necessary and convenient for the government of
said corporation."

The Americans have the sagacity to see that a bank
has occasion for the power of suing and being sued.
In this country joint stock banks above sixty-five miles
from London sue and are sued in the names of two
public officers, whose names are registered at the
stamp office. But joint stock banks situated within
sixty-five miles of London, although sanctioned by
law, have no prescribed mode of suing and being
sued. One would have imagined that in an act
which sanctioned the establishment of such banks,
this would have been considered one of the clauses
the most obvious and necessary.

The power to establish, alter, and renew by-laws and
regulations, seem very similar in both countries. In
England

" The active duties are generally delegated to a small body, called
the directors, while the main body of proprietors reserve to themselves
the power of re-electing the directors, and of altering from time to
time the rules by which the directors are to be governed."

" Sec. 3. Be it further enacted, that no bank, except such as are
now incorporated, shall go into operation, make discounts, loan money,
emit bills, or promissory notes, until fifty per centum, at least, of its
capital stock shall have been paid in gold and silver money, and existing
in its vaults, which shall have been examined by three commissioners
appointed by the governor, whose duty it shall be, at the expense of
the banks, to examine and count the money actually in the vaults, and

to ascertain by the oaths of a majority of the directors of said bank, that its capital hath been paid in by the stockholders of said bank, toward payment for their respective shares, and not for any other purpose ; and that it is intended to have it therein remain as part of said capital, and to return a certificate thereof to the governor, and no loan shall be made to any stockholder until the full amount of his shares shall have been paid into the bank ; and it shall not be lawful for any bank to have owing to it, on loan, on a pledge of its own stock, a greater amount than fifty per centum of its capital stock actually paid in ; and no part of the capital stock of any bank shall be sold or transferred until the whole amount thereof shall have been paid in."

England—

" The law does not impose any restrictions upon the amount of capital. This will be found to vary from £5,000,000 to £100,000 ; and in one instance an unlimited power is reserved of issuing shares to any extent.

" The law does not impose any obligation that the whole or any certain amount of shares shall be subscribed for before banking operations commence. In many instances banks have commenced their business before one half of the shares are subscribed for, and 10,000, 20,000, and 30,000 shares are reserved to be issued at the discretion of the directors.

" The law does not enforce any rule with respect to the nominal amount of shares. These will be found to vary from £1,000 to £5. The effects of this variation are strongly stated in the evidence.

" The law does not enforce any rule with respect to the amount of capital paid up before the commencement of business. This will be found to vary from £100 to £5."

The payment of a certain portion of the capital before the commencement of business, is a pledge that the project is not a mere bubble, and this is especially necessary when the proprietors have no farther liability. But even with unlimited liability a certain amount appears to be necessary. The employment of capital judiciously is sometimes a means of acquiring business ; and in case of loss there should always be a sufficient capital to fall back upon without recurring to the shareholders.

There is an evil in a bank having too small a capital. In this case, the bank will be but a small bank ; the number of proprietors will be few, and the number of persons eligible to be chosen directors will be few ; hence there will not be the same guarantee for good management. If a bank with a small capital have

F

also a very small business, it had much better cease as an independant establishment, and become the branch of a larger bank. If, on the other hand, it has a large business, with a large circulation, large deposits, and large loans or discounts, its losses will sometimes be large, and hence the whole capital may be swept away. It is true, that while it avoids losses the shareholders will receive large dividends, but these large profits had much better be left in the bank as an addition to its capital than shared among the proprietors in the form of dividends. There is danger too that the high premium on those shares may induce many shareholders to sell out and form other, and perhaps rival establishments.

On the other hand there is an evil in a bank having too large a capital. In this case, as the capital cannot be employed in the business, the directors are under the temptation of investing it in dead or hazardous securities for the sake of obtaining a higher rate of interest ; perhaps too they may speculate in the funds, and sustain loss. Hence it is much better that a bank should commence business with a small capital, and increase the amount as the business may require.

It is difficult to state in all cases what proportion a capital ought to bear to the liabilities of a bank. Perhaps the best criterion we can have, is the rate of dividend, provided that dividend be paid out of the business profits of the company. When we hear of a bank paying from fifteen to twenty per cent. dividend, we may be assured that the capital is too small for the business. The liabilities of the bank, either in notes or deposits, must far exceed the amount of its capital. As a general maxim, the greater the capital the less the dividend ; let the whole capital be employed at any given rate of interest, say four per cent., then the capital raised by notes or deposit, produce after paying all expenses, a certain sum as profit. Now, it is evident, that if this amount of profit be distributed over a large capital, it will yield a less rate per cent. than when distributed over a small capital. Sometimes however a large capital may have increased the rate of dividend, in consequence of having been the means of acquiring a large increase of business. It may have done this in consequence of inspiring the public with confidence in the bank, and thus inducing them to make lodgments or circulate its notes; or it may have enabled the bank to make large advances, and thus gained the support of wealthy and influential customers.

Although the proportion which the capital of a bank should bear to its liabilities may vary with different banks, perhaps we should not go far astray in saying it should never be less than one-third of its liabilities. I would exclude, however, from this comparison all liabilities except those arising from notes and deposits. If the notes and deposits together amount to more than three times the amount of the paid-up capital, the bank should call up more capital. It may be said, that the bank is liable also for its drafts upon its London agents, and for the payment of those bills which it has endorsed and re-issued: admitted; but in both these cases, the public have other securities besides that of the bank.

Presuming that banks are to commence with a moderate amount of capital, and to increase that amount as the business increases, the question is suggested, what is the best way of increasing the capital? The English banks have followed two ways of doing this; one, by a further issue of shares; and the other, by further calls upon the existing shareholders. The capital of all the joint stock banks in England is divided into certain portions, called shares; each proprietor holds a certain number of these shares, and pays a certain sum upon them. If he wishes to transfer a portion of his capital he cannot transfer a half share or a quarter share, but must transfer a whole share, or a certain number of shares. Thus, if the capital of a bank be £500,000, it may be divided into 5,000 shares of £100 each, or 50,000 shares of £10 each, and a certain proportion of the amount of each share will be paid up; and this proportion is called the real or the paid-up capital. Thus, if one-tenth of the above capital is paid up, then £50,000 will be the real or paid-up capital, and £500,000 will be called the nominal capital. In the chartered banks, on the other hand, there is usually no nominal capital, and the real capital is not divided into shares or portions, but any fractional sum may be transferred. The capital is then called stock. When there is no nominal capital, nor any way of increasing the amount of the real capital, this is the best way. But, in the other case, it is more convenient to have the capital divided into shares.

Some persons have objected altogether to a nominal capital; but their objections have been dircted more to the misrepresentations that may attend it, than to the thing itself. They say, " a bank announces that it has a capital of £500,000, whereas few shares are issued, and but a small sum is paid on each share; hence people are misled, and the bank acquires a confidence which it does not deserve." The objection here is against representing the nominal capital to be paid-up capital; it does not bear upon the principle of a nominal capital. In fact, we are misled by words. What is called nominal capital is nothing more than a farther sum, which the directors have the power of calling up. If this sum had not been called capital, it would not be objected to, as it could lead to no misapprehension. But the inquiry simply is, ought the directors to have the power of calling upon the shareholders for a farther amount of capital beyond that already paid up? Were they not to have the power, the bank would at its commencement probably have too large a capital, and after its business had advanced, would have too small a capital. And if the bank by any unforeseen occurrence became involved, and should have occasion for further sums to extricate itself from its difficulties, it could not make any further call upon its shareholders, although a very small advance might prevent its utter ruin. In case of a very large capital,

such as two or three millions, a nominal capital may
not be necessary, as so large a sum is likely to be in
all cases amply sufficient. But in banks of a second
class, it will always be best to give the directors the
power of making further calls upon the shareholders.

The second way of increasing the capital of a bank,
is, by the issue of new shares. The whole amount of
shares to be issued is fixed in the first instance, and
the bank commences as soon as a certain proportion
has been issued. If the bank was not allowed to
commence business until the whole of the shares were
taken, a small amount would be fixed upon, and the
bank would be proportionably weaker. But by
beginning with a small number of shares, you have
capital enough for your business, and you acquire
more as you proceed. Many persons will join a bank
after it is established who would not take shares at
the commencement. Some shares are therefore
reserved for persons of this description ; and as the
shares are more valuable when the success of the
undertaking is no longer doubtful, they are often
given out at a premium, and always a greater degree
of caution is exercised as to the persons to whom they
are distributed.

Some members of the committee appear to have an
objection to shares of a small amount; they apprehend that these shares are taken by an inferior class
of persons; and hence the body of proprietors are less
respectable. But it would appear from the returns, that
the general effect of small shares is, that each shareholder takes a greater number. Thus in the banks of
£100 shares each proprietor has taken upon an average
twenty-eight shares, on which he has paid the sum of
£444. In the banks of £20 shares, each proprietor
has taken forty-three shares, and paid £359. In the
banks of £10 shares, each proprietor has taken fifty-
two shares and paid £400. While in the only bank
of £5 shares, each proprietor has taken 117 shares, and
paid £585.* It appears to me that the chief objection

---

* See the last edition of my Practical Treatise on Banking.

to which small shares are liable is, that they do not
admit of a large amount of nominal capital. The
banks of £5 and £10 shares have usually the whole
capital paid up, and hence in case of necessity the
directors have no power to call for a further amount.
Could the Northern and Central Bank have made a
call upon their shareholders of £5 per share, this bank
might have been saved from destruction.

The latter part of this section notices a practice
which has very justly been condemned—the practice
of advancing loans to shareholders upon the security of their shares. Although in this country " the
law does not prohibit purchases, sales, and speculative traffic on the part of these companies in their
own stock, nor advances to be made on the credit of
their own shares," yet, I question if any joint stock
bank has carried this practice to any thing like the
extent which is here allowed in the very prudent
State of Massachusetts. I think it desirable that this
practice should be placed under restraint. No doubt,
sometimes it is convenient to advance a shareholder a
loan upon his own shares, and sometimes a customer
gets discounts more readily from the circumstance of
being a shareholder. But the conveniences do not
in general counterbalance its disadvantages. The
adoption of this principle in America has been one
great cause of the failure of their chartered banks.
In all our deeds of settlement there is a clause by
which every shareholder pledges his shares as security
for any debt he may owe the bank. Such a clause
is particularly useful, as the consciousness of having
this preference often induces the bank to give temporary loans and discounts to persons whose applica-
tions would otherwise be rejected.

In some cases, the circumstance of a bank making
advances upon its own shares arises from the heavy
stamp duties imposed upon the transfer of shares.
Could the shares in joint stock banks be transferred
like government stock without expense, a person who
wanted a temporary loan might obtain it in the money

market upon the transfer of his shares. But now if
he wished to borrow £1000 for a week upon shares on
which £1500 has been paid, the stamp duty on the transfer and re-transfer would be considerable. Under these
circumstances he very naturally applies to the bank to
make the advance, as the above-mentioned clause in
the deed of settlement supersedes the necessity for
an actual transfer. If the legislature wish to prevent
advances of this kind, the most effectual way of doing
so would be to abolish the stamp duties upon the
transfer of shares.

The committee state—

" In no instance is the company forbidden to become the purchaser
of its own shares ; but on the contrary, power is expressly given to
do so by means of the deeds, and that to any amount. The only
modifications of this power which your committee have found, are in
the case of one banking company, in which the directors are authorized to purchase shares in the case only of a refusal to admit as a
proprietor the person proposing to buy ; and in case of another bank,
in which the number of shares to be bought in by the directors is
restricted to forty."

In this, as in other cases, the committee have
fallen into the error of supposing that the directors
are in the habit of committing every fault which
is not prohibited by the deed of settlement. I have
never heard of a joint stock bank trafficking in its
own shares. It may sometimes be convenient for
them to buy a few shares in order to get rid of
an objectionable shareholder, but it can never be
worth their while to do so to a great extent. If a
bank issues new shares, it is quite proper that a premium should be charged proportionate to their increased value.

" *Sec.* 4. Be it further enacted, That the amount of bills issued by
any bank, shall not at any one time exceed twenty-five per centum
beyond the amount of the capital stock actually paid in, and no loan
or discount shall be made, nor shall any bill or note be issued by said
corporation, or by any person on their account, in any other place than
at the said bank.

" *Sec.* 5. Be it further enacted, That the total amount of debts which
any banking corporation shall at any time owe, whether by bond, bill,
note, or other contract, shall not exceed twice the amount of its capital

stock actually paid in, exclusive of sums due on account of deposits; nor shall there be due to said corporation at any one time, more than double the amount of its capital stock actually paid in. In case of excess of debts so due from said bank, the directors under whose administration it shall happen, shall be liable for the same in their private capacities, and an action of debt may in such case be brought against them, their, or any of their heirs, executors, or administrators, in any court proper to try the same, by any creditor or creditors of said corporation, and may be prosecuted to final judgment and execution, any condition, covenant, or agreement to the contrary notwithstanding: but this shall not be construed to exempt said corporation, or the lands, tenements, goods, or chattels of the same, from being also liable for, and chargeable with said excess. Such of said directors who may have been absent when said excess was contracted or created, or who may have dissented from the resolution, or act, whereby the same was contracted or created, may respectively exonerate themselves from being so liable by forthwith giving notice of the fact, and of their absence or dissent, to the governor and council, and to the stockholders at any general meeting, which they shall have power to call for that purpose."

These sections present to us two restrictions which are not noticed by the committee. We may therefore enlarge our catalogue of legal imperfections by two more startling articles, thus:—

" The law does not impose any restriction upon the amount of notes issued by these companies, however small may be their paid-up capital."

" The law does not limit the amount of loans advanced by these companies, however small may be their funds for granting them."

It is, however, worthy of inquiry, whether " these companies" should incur liabilities beyond a certain proportion to their paid-up capital? Is there no impropriety in a bank with £50,000 capital incurring liabilities to the extent of £500,000? If a bank by notes or deposits owes £500,000, it is liable to sudden calls for considerable amounts; and hence it should have a proportionable paid-up capital, to be better able to meet these sudden demands. And besides, this £500,000 must be employed, and losses may thereby be incurred to a large amount, and hence there should be a proportionable paid-up capital that the bank may be able to sustain these losses without making farther calls upon the shareholders.

As the circumstances of different banks vary very
much, it would be difficult to fix upon any proportion
that would not be liable to objections. The proportion
allowed in the State of Massachusetts is rather liberal
than otherwise : the notes may be $1\frac{1}{4}$ times the amount
of the capital ; and the total liabilities, exclusive of
the deposits, may be twice the capital. Mr. Gallatin
states that the average amount of notes issued by the
State Banks taken together did not exceed forty-four
per cent., nor the aggregate amount of their notes
and deposits eighty-one per cent. of their capital ;
and he believes that a positive restriction on the issue
of notes, so that they never should exceed two-thirds
of the capital, would be highly beneficial. The total
amount of notes issued by the joint stock banks are
supposed to be about one half the amount of their paid-
up capital.

The limitation of debts due to the bank appears to be
made with the view of limiting the issue of notes. The
most certain way would have been to limit the issues.
If the capital, and the notes, and the deposits are
limited, the loans made by the banks will necessarily
be limited by circumstances more forcible than any
law that could be passed on the subject ; that is, by
the ability of the bank to make them. But the plan
in America has been to limit the loans. Mr. Gallatin
says, " We think that no bank should be permitted to
extend its loans, including stocks of every description,
and every species of debt, in whatever manner
secured, beyond twice the amount of its capital.
We find provisions to that effect in the laws of
Massachusetts and Louisiana. The aggregate amount
of the loans made and of the stocks held by the
former bank of the United States never amounted to
seventy per cent., nor that of the existing bank to
fifty per cent. beyond the amount of their respective
capitals."

The act which incorporates the state bank of Massachusetts is in conformity with the above regulation,
but the charter of the North Bank in the same State

requires " that the amount of bills issued from said
bank at any one time shall not exceed fifty per centum
of the amount of the capital stock actually paid in."
A writer, I have already quoted, remarks, that " these
charters are founded upon that cautious policy which
marks the character of the people of Massachusetts;
a prudence, however, in the opinion of many, which
has neither promoted the interest of their monied
institutions, nor aided the enterprize of the community, and which happily for the prosperity of the State
of New York has not been hitherto followed here."

" *Sec. 6.* Be it further enacted, That no banking corporation within
and under the authority of this commonwealth, shall vest, use, or
improve any of its monies, goods, chattels, or effects, in trade or commerce, but any corporation aforesaid may sell all kinds of personal
pledges lodged with it by way of security, to an amount sufficient to
reimburse the sum loaned, with interest and expenses. Every banking
corporation as aforesaid, may hold real estate, lands, and tenements,
requisite for the convenient transaction of its business, not exceeding
twelve per centum on the amount of its capital stock, unless they have
been, or shall be thereto specially authorised, exclusive of what it may
hold on mortgage, receive on execution, or take as security for, or in
payment of, any debt to said corporation, and no more."

Although the law in England does not place any
limitation upon the amount of loans or advances
made by joint stock banks, yet restrictions upon some
descriptions of advance are imposed by most of our
deeds of settlement.   The committee state—

" Advancing money on real security is in no instance forbidden. The
deeds of three companies are silent on this subject, the rest expressly
allow it.
" The majority of the deeds are silent on the subject of the purchase of land.   The _____ Banking Company expressly allows it.
The _____ Banking Company and the Union Banking Company expressly forbid it.
" An advance of money on mining concerns is in no instance
expressly allowed, in many it is expressly forbidden, in the majority it
is passed over in silence.
" Advances of money upon any public foreign government stock or
the stock of any foreign chartered public " company" is directly sanctioned in the deeds of four banking companies.   Investment in foreign
government stock or funds is allowed by the deed of another bank.
Such advances are expressly forbidden by many of the deeds, and are
passed over in silence by many others."

In no case does it appear that any restriction is

placed upon loans granted upon individual security; that is, upon overdrawn accounts. In all our manufacturing towns it is the practice for the banks to make large permanent advances to the manufacturers. And as a remuneration they charge a commission of a quarter per cent. upon the account. Here the banks adopt the dangerous principle of running great risks for the sake of large profits. This practice has not been introduced by the joint stock banks. It has for many years been the practice of the private bankers, and has no doubt been exceedingly beneficial in stimulating our manufactures, and in giving worthy men of small means the opportunity of advancing themselves in the world. But now that our manufacturers are become wealthy, the same practice is not necessary. It is not the business of banks to supply their customers with capital to carry on their trade; it is a dangerous principle; because in the first place, there is a great risk upon individual security; and then, if the money is wanted, it cannot suddenly be called up. I think, therefore, that joint stock banks should limit their advances of this sort to a certain proportion of the amount of paid-up capital. And with regard to chartered banks, one condition of the charter should be that the bank admits of no overdrawn accounts.

" *Sec.* 7. Be it further enacted, That none but a member of the corporation for which he is chosen a director, being a citizen of, and resident in the commonwealth, shall be eligible to that office; and a majority of directors, in any bank, shall be residents within the county where the bank is located, and no person shall be a director in two banks at one and the same time ; no bank shall have less than five, or more than twelve directors, to be determined by their bye-laws. The directors shall choose one of their own number to act as president; and in case of the absence of the president, a chairman may be appointed for the time being. A majority of the directors shall always be necessary to constitute a quorum for doing business. The directors may make the president such compensation as shall appear to them reasonable.

" *Sec.* 8. Be it further enacted, That the directors shall be chosen by ballot annually, at a meeting held on the first Monday in October, by the stockholders, at such time and place, within the city or town where said bank is established, as the president and directors for the time being may designate, by giving public notice thereof fourteen days previous thereto, in some newspaper printed in the county; and if there be no newspaper printed in said county, then in some one in the city of Boston. The number of votes to which each stockholder shall be entitled, shall be according to the number of shares he shall hold, in the following proportion: That is to say—For one share, one vote; and every two shares above one shall give a right to one vote more, provided no one member shall have more than ten votes; and absent members may vote by proxy, such proxy being authorised in writing; vacancies occurring in the board of directors before the expiration of the term for which they were chosen, may be filled at any meeting of the stockholders called for that purpose, as hereinbefore provided. In like manner, the directors shall have power to call special meetings of the stockholders as often as they think the interest of the corporation may require it.

"*Sec.* 9. Be it further enacted, That the directors shall make half-yearly dividends of the profits of the bank. The directors shall have power to appoint a cashier, clerks, and such other officers, for carrying on the business of this bank, with such salaries as to them shall seem meet; and such cashier, clerks, and other officers, shall retain their places until removed therefrom, or others appointed in their place.

"*Sec.* 10. Be it further enacted, That the cashier, before he enters on the duties of his office, shall give bond, or bonds, with two or more sureties, to the satisfaction of the board of directors, conditioned for the faithful performance of the duties of his office: Provided, that in no case shall bonds be taken for a less sum than twenty thousand dollars, nor a greater than fifty thousand dollars. It shall be the duty of the cashier of any bank aforesaid, to call special meetings of the stockholders at any time hereafter, on the application, in writing, of the proprietors of twenty per centum of the capital stock thereof, by giving fourteen days public notice of such meeting, in the manner hereinbefore provided."

These sections are very similar to clauses that are inserted in our deeds of settlement. They refer to several matters of detail which can be arranged by the banks much better than by the legislature. It is worthy of inquiry, however, whether the legislature might not fix the qualifications of a director. The only tangible qualification is property. It seems essentially necessary that a bank director should be a man of property. Neither talent, nor rank, nor influence should be taken as a substitute for property. Most of our deeds of settlement require that a director should hold a certain number of shares. But the amount of property thus invested is usually inconsiderable. And it is not desirable, on several accounts, that a director should hold a large number of shares. It is understood that none of the directors of the Bank of England hold a greater amount of bank stock than their qualification. It appears that in the banks of Massachusetts all the directors go out every year, but may be re-elected by ballot. In the Bank of England eight directors go out every year, but are always re-elected. By the charter of the Bank of Ireland five new directors must be chosen every year. The deeds of settlement of the joint stock banks vary very much in this respect.

"*Sec.* 11. Be it further enacted, That in case the officers of any banking corporation aforesaid, in the usual banking hours, shall refuse or delay payment in gold or silver money, of any note or bill of said corporation, there presented for payment, the said corporation shall be liable to pay, as additional damages, at the rate of twenty-four per centum per annum, for the time during which such payment shall be delayed or refused."

This regulation is peculiar to America. In itself it may be very good, but the stoppage of payment ought also to be attended by the forfeiture of the charter. In this respect, the law of England in regard to joint stock banks is very defective. If the banks stop payment it does not appear that the creditors have any power to interfere, or to obtain possession of the funds of the bank. Each creditor may sue the public officer, and having obtained judgment may issue execution against the funds of the bank, and the private property of the shareholders. It is proposed as a subject of inquiry, whether in case of stoppage, the affairs of a bank ought not to be placed immediately in the hands of government commissioners, for the purpose of winding it up, and an extent in aid issued against the property of all the directors, that in case it should be necessary to come upon the property of the proprietors to make good the deficiency; that of the directors should be first taken.

"*Sec.* 12. Be it further enacted, That in case of any loss or deficiency of the capital stock in any bank aforesaid, which shall arise from the official mismanagement of the directors, the persons who are stockholders at the time of such mismanagement, shall in their private and individual capacities, be respectively liable to pay the same : Provided, however, that in no case shall any one stockholder be liable to pay a sum exceeding the amount of the stock actually then held by him.

" *Sec.* 13. Be it further enacted, That the holders of stock in any banking corporation aforesaid, in this commonwealth, when its charter shall expire, shall be chargeable in their private and individual capacities, and shall be holden for the payment and redemption of all bills which may have been issued by said corporation, remaining unpaid, in proportion to the stock they may respectively hold.

" *Sec.* 14. Be it further enacted, That any stockholder of any bank who shall have been obliged to pay any debt or demand against said bank out of his individual property, shall have a bill in equity, originally to be tried in the supreme judicial court, to recover the proportional parts of such sums of money as he may have so paid, from the other stockholders, who may be equally liable for the same, and such damages and costs as the court may decree, and said bill in equity may be inserted in a writ of attachment, or original summons."

In America, the banks are chartered banks, and the shareholders, in most cases, have no liability beyond the amount of their respective shares. In England, every shareholder is liable to the full extent of his property for all the debts of the bank.

Unlimited liability gives greater security to the public. It will hardly be denied that all the property of five hundred partners gives greater security for the debts of the bank than any small portion of that property that may be advanced in the form of paid-up capital. It is not necessary to prove that the paid-up capital and the remaining property of the partners form a larger fund than the paid-up capital alone. The unlimited liability of the partners constitutes therefore a higher guarantee for the ultimate payment of the debts of the bank, whether those debts arise from notes or deposits.

Unlimited liability, is to a certain extent, a guarantee for prudent management. As the directors are liable to the full extent of their property, they will take care not to incur such risks as will place that property in jeopardy. And the shareholders will take care to choose directors, whose wealth and

character render them worthy of confidence; and
they will also attend to the annual report of the
directors, and will be alive to any event that may
endanger the prosperity of the bank. It is no
objection, to say that private bankers run risks,
although their whole property is liable, and hence
the directors of joint stock banks would run risks in
the same way. First. Private bankers, for the most
part, have not run risks as bankers, but as manufacturers and merchants, and the failure of their commercial enterprizes has brought down their banks.
Secondly. The private bankers had greater inducements to run risks, because all the profit of the risk
went to themselves; but bank directors have no such
inducement, because the profit that comes to themselves is very small, being only in proportion to the
shares that they hold, while the failure might endanger their whole property, as the directors [would
be the first that would have judgment issued against
them. Nor is it any objection to say, that the shareholders will not pay any regard to the administration
of the bank, so long as they receive good dividends.
It may be very true, that when the shareholders have
provided for the good management of the bank, by
choosing efficient directors, that they will then attend
no farther to its administration beyond receiving the
half-yearly or annual reports. But let it be once
even rumoured that the directors are acting unfaith-
fully towards the shareholders, or let it be suspected
that the dividends are not paid out of the profits, and
then see if the shareholders will not meet, and show
by their conduct, that they are alive to the sense of
unlimited liability.

The unlimited liability of the shareholders attracts
the public confidence. It is not enough that a bank
is ultimately safe, the public should believe that it is
safe. A want of confidence in our banking establishments has been the cause of much misery. The panic
of 1825 would have been far less calamitous had there
existed no suspicion of the banks; but in consequence

of the general suspicion, many stopped payment, who
were afterwards proved not only to be solvent, but
wealthy. It will not be denied, that the public will
place greater confidence in a bank, where, in addition
to the paid-up capital they have a claim upon the property of all the partners, than where they have to depend upon the paid-up capital alone. It is remarkable
that this tendency of unlimited liability to inspire
public confidence should be advanced as an objection
against it. It has been said, that the public confidence
may be abused, and that banks presuming on the confidence they know they have acquired, may engage in
speculations to which they would not otherwise resort.
We grant that the public confidence may be abused;
but is there no way of guarding against these abuses,
but by rendering the banks less deserving of confidence? If a commander presuming on the goodness
of his ship were to attempt a dangerous voyage, in
which he should peril the ship and cargo, that might
be a very good reason for displacing the commander,
or for prohibiting him making the same voyage a
second time; but would that be a sufficient reason for
damaging the ship, so as to render her less sea-worthy?
They who assert that unlimited liability acquires an
excessive degree of public confidence, admit that the
public opinion is in opposition to their own. They
think that unlimited liability renders a bank less
worthy of confidence; the public think the reverse,
and they act accordingly.

But it is said, that if the liability were limited,
a more respectable class of persons would become
shareholders in joint stock banks. Perhaps this is
the case with a few of the landed gentry, but certainly
not with any large portion of them. They are the
principal declaimers against joint stock banks. But
why is it so desirable that they should become partners? Is it on account of their habits of business,
or their superior knowledge of banking? No; it
is because their large properties would give weight
and respectability to the bank. But of what value

would their property be to the bank, if their liability was limited to the amount of the paid-up capital? Besides, it is not necessary that every man of property in the country should be a shareholder in a joint stock bank; and if we have a sufficient number of wealthy men to make the banks safe and respectable, why need we alter the law to meet the scruples of others whose assistance is not required?

But it is said that unlimited liability has been tried and failed. The private banks in England were all founded on unlimited liability, and yet large numbers of them have failed. Is it believed that if these private banks had been founded on limited liability, the failures would have been less numerous? Besides, is it fair to infer that because the unlimited liability of six partners fails to produce a good bank, that therefore the unlimited liability of six hundred partners would be equally ineffectual? And if in some cases even this has been found to fail, are there no failures on the other side? Has not limited liability been also tried and failed? Are the one hundred and sixty-five chartered banks that have failed in America to go for nothing? And what are all the returns, the oaths of the directors, the examinations and countings of the money by government commissioners, but so many acknowledgments that limited liability is not to be trusted?

If limited liability is to be tried at all, it should be under heavy restrictions—restrictions more severe than those imposed upon the banks of America. It is perhaps possible to frame charters with such provisions as might justify the limitation of the liability to three or four times the amount of the paid-up capital. I may have occasion to notice some of these provisions at the end of this section.

"Sec. 15. Be it further enacted, that every bank shall be kept in the city or town in which it is, or shall be originally established, and in such part of such city or town as is prescribed by its charter."

The Americans have adopted the district system.

The banks of every state confine themselves to that state, and do not extend their branches into the neighbouring states. Analogous to this is the district system of banking adopted by the joint stock banks in England. Had the law of 1826 permitted joint stock banks to be established in London, we should probably by this time have had ten or a dozen banks having their head quarters in London, and extending their branches throughout the country. But as the law prohibited these banks being established within sixty-five miles of London, it necessarily gave rise to banks occupying particular districts in the country. The advantages which are alleged to belong to the district system are the following—that the bank will be better adapted to the wants and habits of the people—that a local feeling will be excited in its favour, hence the inhabitants of the district will take shares, and the occurrence of runs upon the bank will be less probable—that a better system of management may be expected, as it can more easily be governed, and will be more under controul—that a panic in the district will not affect the other parts of the country, and hence supplies may be more easily obtained — that banks will be of a moderate size, and hence will be attended with the advantages arising from numerous banks acting as checks upon each other, instead of a few large banks who may combine for objects injurious to the nation ; and that as each bank will have an agent in London, the bills they draw will thus have two parties as securities, and the public will have a pledge that there is no excessive issue in the form of kites or accommodation bills. On the other hand, it may be contended, that in Scotland the large metropolitan banks which have branches extended throughout the country, have generally been more successful than the provincial or district banks—that there is a greater security to the public for the notes or deposits—that advances are not so likely to be made to speculative parties merely on account of their local influence—that the capital raised in one part of the country can be employed in another—that the transmission of money from one part of the country to another is more rapid and direct—that the establishment of the bank being on a larger scale, you have a superior class of directors, and can demand the services of higher talents in those who are employed as officers.

It does not appear that these two systems are necessarily at variance with each other. County or districts banks have no doubt many advantages, but they do not seem to supersede banks on a larger scale.

Both the district and the extended system of banking are attended with a system of branches. The Bank of the United States had a branch in every state, and several of the state banks have also branches. It will be seen at page 48 that the 558 banks have 146 branches.

When the law existed in England that no bank should have more than six partners, the branch system scarcely existed. In some cases, a bank had a branch or two a few miles distant, but no instance occurred of a bank extending itself throughout a county or a district. But with joint stock banking arose the branch system—the head office was placed in the county town, and branches were opened in the principal towns and villages around. The credit of the bank being firmly established, its notes circulated freely throughout the whole district. The chief advantages of this system are the following:—

There is greater security to the public. The security of the whole bank is attached to the transactions of every branch; hence there is greater safety to the public than could be afforded by a number of separate private banks, or even so many independent joint stock banks. These banks could have but a small number of partners—the paid-up capital and the private property of the partners must be comparatively small; hence the holder of a note issued by one of the independent joint stock banks could have a claim only on that bank : but if that bank, instead of being independent, were a branch of a large establishment, the holder of a note would have the security of that large establishment; hence the branch system unites together a greater number of persons, and affords a more ample guarantee.

The branch system provides greater facilities for the transmission of money. The sending of money from one town to another is greatly facilitated, if a branch of the same bank be established in each of those towns, for all the branches grant letters of credit upon each other. Otherwise you have to ask the banker in the town from which the money is sent to give you a bill upon London, which is transmitted by post, or you request him to advise his London agent to pay the money to the London agent of the banker, who resides in the town to which the money is remitted. This takes up more time, and is attended with more expense. A facility of transmitting money between two places usually facilitates the trade between those places.

The branch system extends the benefits of banking to small places where independent banks could not be supported. An independent bank must have an independent board of directors who in most cases will be better paid—the manager must have a higher salary because he has a heavier responsibility, and a large amount of cash must be kept unemployed in the till, because there is no neighbouring resource in case of a run. There must be a paid-up capital, upon which good dividends are expected; a large proportion of the funds must be invested in exchequer bills, or other government securities, at a low interest, in order that the bank may be prepared to meet sudden calls; and the charge for agencies will also be more. On the other hand, a branch has seldom need of a board of directors, one or two being quite sufficient—the manager is not so well paid : there is no necessity for a large sum in the till, because in case of necessity the branch has recourse to the head office, or to the neighbouring branches; nor is a large portion of its fund invested in government securities that yield but little interest, as the head office takes charge of this, and can manage it at a less proportional expense. Besides at some branches the manager attends only on market days, or once or twice a week. The business done on those days would not bear the expense of an independent establishment.

The branch system provides the means of a due distribution of capital. Some banks raise more capital than they can employ, that is, their notes and deposits amount to more than their loans and discounts. Others employ more capital than they raise, that is, their loans and discounts amount to more than their notes and deposits. Banks that have a surplus capital usually send it to London to be employed by the bill brokers. The banks that want capital must either restrict their business, or send their bills to London to be rediscounted. Now if two banks, one having too much, and the other too little capital, be situated in the same county, they will have no direct intercourse, and will consequently be of no assistance to each other : but if a district bank be established, and these two banks become branches, then the surplus capital of one branch will be sent to be employed at the other—thus the whole wealth of the district is employed within the district, and the practice of rediscounting bills in London will be proportionably diminished.

The branch system secures a better system of management. The only way to secure good management is to prevent the formation of small banks. When banks are large the directors are men of more wealth and respectability—they can give large salaries to their officers, and hence can command first-rate talent — there will be a more numerous proprietary ; and in a large number there will be always some active spirits who will be watchful of the conduct of the directors and the manager ; besides, in a numerous proprietary there is a greater number of persons eligible to be directors, and consequently there is a wider choice. In populous cities such as London or Manchester, a large bank may be formed without branches—but in smaller places there is no way of forming a large bank but by giving it branches throughout the district. A branch bank in a small town will probably be better managed than an independent bank in the same place. The directors and manager of the branch will be appointed by the directors at the head office, assisted by the general manager, who are very competent to judge what qualifications are necessary for these offices, and who would not be biassed by local partialities. But the directors of the independent bank would most likely be self-appointed or chosen by the proprietors, because no others could be obtained, and these directors would appoint some friend of their own to be manager. The manager of the branch, besides the superintendence of the directors, which he has in common with the manager of the independent bank, will be subject to visits from the general manager or the inspector; and he must send weekly statements of his accounts to the head office. The consciousness of responsibility will thus secure a more anxious attention to his duties; and besides, he will probably be looking forward for promotion to a higher branch as a reward for his successful management. These circumstances seem to ensure a higher degree of good management to the branch.

At the same time it must be admitted that banks with numerous branches require a proportionate paid-up capital, and that the capital be kept in a disposeable form; it also requires vigilant and constant inspection, and a rigid system of discipline.

A proportionate paid-up capital is necessary, because in case of a run there are a greater number of points of attack; hence the funds must be divided to meet all these possible attacks, for if one branch be overpowered, the whole bank is immediately exposed to suspicion.

Another danger arises from the incompetency or negligence of the managers of branches. Among a number of men it is not likely that all are clever, and all prudent; and one case of neglect on the part of one manager, may in times of alarm throw discredit on the whole establishment. Besides, there is sometimes danger even from the zeal of the branch managers. Each manager is naturally anxious to increase the business of his own branch ; and he will perhaps find that the most easy way of doing this is to extend his loans and discounts. Hence each manager tries to employ as much capital as he can ; and the urgent remonstrances he receives from head quarters, requiring him to restrict his discounts, are either evaded or delayed. Thus the bank proceeds until some heavy demand for money arises at head quarters, and it is then found that all the capital of the bank has been absorbed by the branches. These advances cannot be suddenly recalled, and thus the bank is ruined.

What number of branches a bank ought to have, and what distance they ought to be from the head office, have been the subject of much discussion. No general rules can be given. The subject may very safely be left to the discretion of the banks themselves. Several of the banks in Scotland have from thirty to forty branches. The Provincial bank of Ireland, whose head office is in London, have branches spread all over Ireland. I am not aware that in these cases any danger or inconvenience has been experienced. When branches are found troublesome or unprofitable, they will very soon be discontinued. In some instances, even in Scotland, the branches of the larger banks have been withdrawn in consequence of being unable to sustain a competition with the local banks of the district.

" Sec. 16. Be it further enacted, that, upon any requisition of the legislature, each banking corporation shall loan to the common wealth, a sum not exceeding five per centum on its capital stock at any one time, reimbursable by five annual instalments, or at any shorter period, at the election of the commonwealth, with the annual payment of interest, at a rate not exceeding five per centum per annum: provided, that the commonwealth shall never at any one time stand indebted to any corporation, without its consent, for a larger sum than ten per centum of its capital. It shall be the duty of the treasurer of this commonwealth, whenever he shall have occasion to borrow any sum of money of any incorporated bank, under and by virtue of any authority for that purpose given by an act or resolve of this commonwealth, to give notice in writing to the president or cashier of any incorporated bank of the amount which he has occasion to borrow, and demanding of said bank a loan of the same, conformably to the provisions of this act, and the commonwealth will hold itself responsible for any money borrowed of any bank by the treasurer; and if any incorporated bank aforesaid, shall neglect or refuse for the space of thirty days after notice given as aforesaid, to loan to the said treasurer the sum so demanded, said bank shall forfeit and pay into the treasury of this commonwealth, the sum of two per centum per month upon the amount of any sum so demanded, and so after that rate for a shorter or longer time, so long as said neglect or refusal to comply with such demand of said treasurer shall continue: provided, that the notice demanding such loan shall be accompanied by an attested copy of such act or resolve, and shall be approved by the governor in writing ; and it shall be the duty of the treasurer, at the expiration of one month after said demand shall have been made, to institute an action, in the name of and for the use of this commonwealth, in any court of competent jurisdiction, against the bank so neglecting or refusing for the recovery of the said penalty, and so from month to month, to institute similar suits for the recovery of the penalty aforesaid, so long as such neglect or refusal shall continue ; and it shall also be the duty of said treasurer, upon obtaining judgment and execution on any such action or actions, to cause the amount thereof to be forthwith levied upon the goods, chattels, or lands of the bank, against which the same shall have been obtained. It shall be the duty of the treasurer, in making the demand aforesaid of any bank or banks, to equalize, as far as is conveniently practicable, the amount of such demand among the several banks within the commonwealth, having reference to the amount of the obligation of each bank to loan to the commonwealth, and to the amount previously borrowed of each bank, under the authority thereof."

This arrangement is bad—the government will require these loans only in seasons of distress, and in these seasons the banks are least able to spare it. To raise this money for the state they must restrict their loans to individuals, and hence the distress will be increased. It would be much better for the commonwealth to borrow ten per cent. of the capital at the time the charter was granted.

Several American writers have recommended as an

improvement on their system of banking, that the whole of the capital should be lent to the state.

" The business of all those banks consists in receiving money on deposit, in issuing bank notes and in discounting notes of hand or bills of exchange. A portion of the capital is sometimes invested in public stocks, but this is not obligatory, and in this they differ essentially from the Bank of England. The capital of this institution being loaned to government, and not depending on the solidity of the paper discounted, affords a staple guarantee to the holders of notes and to the depositors. The bank can loan to individuals or advance to government (beyond its capital as above-mentioned) nothing but the difference between the aggregate of its notes in circulation, and of the credits in account current on its books, and the amount of specie in its vaults. But the American banks lend to individuals, not only that difference, but also the whole amount of their capital, with the exception only of such portion as they may find it convenient, but are not obliged to vest in public stocks. It follows, that the security of the holders of notes, and of the depositors generally, rests exclusively on the solidity of the paper they have discounted. It might seem, on the other hand, that as the Bank of England cannot apply its original capital to any immediate use, whilst the American banks may, by curtailing their discounts, call in their capital on any emergency, they might, without risk, put in circulation a greater proportionate amount of notes. But such curtailments can never be made to any considerable extent without causing much distress ; and in point of fact, a large portion of their loans consists of what the merchant considers as permanent accommodation, and in the country often rests on real security. This departure from what has been deemed the true banking principle, must, it is believed, be ascribed to the original disposition of the capital."—*Gallatin, page* 40.

" The modifications of the banking system to be proposed and recommended for adoption, may be briefly described, as requiring the capitals of banks to be invested in permanent securities, and their credits founded alone on the known amount, and condition of their capitals to be employed in the operations of discount, to an extent not exceeding in any instance the amount of capital invested.

" By the investment of the capital the security of the public and of individual creditors may be considered as increased to that amount. For under this system, while the capital will be exempt from the risks of commercial paper, the issues made will be at least as well secured by the notes and bills discounted, as is possible in the case of banks employing both capital and credit. If, therefore, such events should occur, as to render the discounted paper unavailable, the capital existing in another form, and not being liable to the same casualties, would supply the defect ; whereas, under the present system, there is no such fund in reserve.

" Should a bank on this plan issue a quantity of paper equal to the whole of its capital, it is obvious that the whole of the commercial notes and bills discounted must be proved bad, and be bad before the

holders of the bank paper could be injured ; and in the extreme case
of such an entire loss, the capital reserved from hazard would still
protect the utmost possible amount of outstanding issues.

" But the safety of this system would result chiefly from its effect
in preventing over-issues of paper, and consequently, drains of specie,
and contractions of the circulation ; and thereby preventing those
reductions and fluctuations of prices, which bring about suspensions
and failures, and render the present system so unsafe, both to individuals and banks.

" On the proposed system a far greater degree of confidence would
exist, and be maintained even in the periods of adversity and depression
in the solvency and stability of the banks, than is possible on the
existing plan, and consequently, unless in very extraordinary cases,
agitation and panic would be depressed or wholly prevented."—*Lord's
Principles of Currency and Banking, page* 72, 84. *New York,* 1829.

It has often been suggested in this country, that the
private bankers should make deposits with government
as a security for their notes, but the plan has never
been carried into effect. To compel either a private
or a joint stock bank to deposit that which could not be
withdrawn in case of emergency, would be to cause a
lock-up of capital liable to all the objections advanced
against lending money upon dead security ; and even
should those funds be available, it would be unjust
unless the same amount of money that was invested
should be returned. It is no doubt advisable that
every bank should invest some portion of its capital in
government security. The objection to buying stock
is, that the stock is sure to be low when the money is
wanted ; and were a law to be made requiring banks
to invest their funds in a security, that in case of
emergency could not be realized without loss, it would
be little better than an act of confiscation. It may
therefore be worthy of inquiry, how far government
might issue to joint stock and private banks a kind of
bank debentures similar to exchequer bills. These
debentures to bear interest, say at four per cent.
receivable every year, and to be granted only to
bankers ; the banks not to be at liberty to sell their
debentures, but might borrow money upon them from
the Bank of England, or from other parties as they
think proper.

" *Sec.* 17. Be it further enacted, that any committee especially appointed by the legislature for the purpose, shall have a right to examine into the doings of any banking corporation chartered under the authority of this commonwealth, and shall have free access to all their books and vaults ; and if, upon such examination, it shall be found, and after a full hearing of said corporation thereon, be determined by the legislature, that said corporation have exceeded the powers granted them, or failed to comply with any of the rules, restrictions, and conditions provided in the laws relating to them, their charter thereupon may be declared forfeit and void ; and if an officer of any bank, or other person having charge of the books and property of any bank, shall refuse or neglect to exhibit said books and property, or shall in any way obstruct said examination by a committee as aforesaid, he or they so offending shall be guilty of a misdemeanor, and on conviction thereof, shall be punished by a fine not exceeding ten thousand dollars, or imprisonment not exceeding three years, at the discretion of the court.

" *Sec.* 18. Be it further enacted, that in addition to the capital stock to which any bank may be entitled by its act of incorporation, the commonwealth shall have a right to subscribe thereto an amount not exceeding fifty per centum of its authorised capital, whenever provision shall be made thereto by law : and the commonwealth, from the time of making any such payment towards the capital stock of any such bank, shall be entitled to their proportionate share of the profits and dividends arising from the amount thereof.

" *Sec.* 19. Be it further enacted, that, in addition to the directors authorized by law to be chosen by the stock-holders in the several banks, the legislature shall have a right from time to time to appoint a number of directors in any bank, in such proportion as the sums paid from the treasury of the commonwealth towards the stock of said bank shall bear to the whole amount of stock actually paid into the said bank, if at any time hereafter they shall see fit to exercise that right.

I presume the object of this provision is to secure the good management of the banks. If the government have reason to believe that a bank is not well managed, they can appoint directors of their own, through whose influence a better system of management may be introduced. But if the securing of good management be the sole object, where is the necessity of the commonwealth making an addition to the capital, and receiving a proportion of the dividends ? If a bank be prosperous, why should the government step in and share its profits ? If a bank be not prosperous, why should the property of the state be invested in a losing concern ?

The directors of the Bank of the United States were twenty-six, of whom six were appointed by the president and senate. There does seem a propriety in some of the directors of a national bank being appointed by the government. First, it seems to connect the bank more closely with the government, and thus to render the government to a certain extent responsible for the conduct of the bank. Secondly, it may prevent the occurrence of disputes between the government and the bank, that might be injurious to the public. Thirdly, it might secure a more enlightened system of management, by introducing directors of a different class in society from those chosen by the proprietors; the union of merchants and statesmen is always desirable in the formation of a board of directors. Fourthly, the bank would be less likely to incur the charge of conducting their affairs upon principles of hostility towards other banks; directors appointed by the state would not be disposed to enter into all the petty jealousies of commercial bodies, and hence would not be suspected of wishing to employ the privileges of the company as a means of crushing rival establishments.

"*Sec.* 20. Be it further enacted, that every bank shall be liable to pay to any *bona fide* holder the original amount of any note of said bank altered in the course of its circulation to a larger amount, notwithstanding such alteration.

"*Sec.* 21. Be it further enacted, that every bank shall, within ten days after the first Mondays in October and April, annually pay to the treasurers of this commonwealth, for the use of the same, a tax of one-half of one per centum on the amount of such part of their original stock as shall have been actually paid in by the stockholders in the respective banks : provided, that if any portion of the capital stock shall not have been paid in six months previous to said days, then the tax on such portion shall be paid in proportion to the time that has elapsed since it was actually paid in. It shall be the duty of every bank which shall be incorporated after the first Monday in October, in the year of our Lord one thousand eight hundred and thirty-one, or which, on that day, shall not have completed the payment of their several instalments, to furnish the treasurer of the commonwealth, on or before the first Mondays in October and April, with an abstract of the amount of stock actually paid by the stockholders into their respective banks, together with the time when the several instalments were paid. And if any bank shall neglect to pay the aforesaid tax for the space of thirty days after the same shall become due, it shall be the duty of the treasurer to issue a warrant of distress, directed to the sheriff of the county in which such bank is situate, or his deputy, commanding them to levy and collect the sum due from the estate and effects of such bank, which warrant shall be in the same form, *mutatis mutandis*, as warrants of distress against delinquent sheriffs are by law directed to be issued."

The Americans tax the capital of their banks—the English tax their notes, their bills, their bonds, and their transfers ; the latter plan seems preferable, as the banks are taxed in proportion to their business.

The composition of the stamp duty upon notes is a great improvement. The banks pay only upon the amount in circulation. When the notes were actually stamped, the banker paid a duty upon those also in his possession.

Bills drawn upon London at not more than twenty-one days date, are included in the composition. This arrangement should be extended to all bills drawn upon London. It is much better than stamping the bills, as the duty would vary, not only with the amount of the bill, but with the time it has to run. It is quite fair that a bill which is drawn two months after date should pay twice the duty which is paid by a bill drawn only one month ; and it would do so under the composition, but on the existing plan it pays precisely the same. The composition upon duties should not only be extended to all bills, but the returns ought to be made separately. At present the amount is unknown, as the twenty-one day bills and the notes payable on demand are included in one sum.

Banks also contribute to the state by the stamp duties paid on cash credit bonds, surety bonds, and other legal instruments ; they also greatly increase the sums derived from the stamp duties on bills of exchange, and the post-office revenue.

There is also a heavy duty upon the transfer of shares in joint stock banks. It seems hardly fair that a transfer of shares in a joint stock bank should pay

the same tax as a transfer of a landed estate of equal
value : the estate will probably not be sold again for a
life-time ; the shares in the bank may change hands
several times in a year.   If the tax were lightened the
transfers would be more numerous, and possibly the
revenue more productive.

" *Sec.* 27. Be it further enacted, that the cashier of every bank,
shall, in every year, make a return of the state of such bank, as it
existed at two o'clock, afternoon, of the first Saturday in such preceding month as the governor may direct, and shall transmit the same
as soon as may be, not exceeding fifteen days, to the secretary of this
commonwealth, which return shall specify the amount due from the
bank, designating in distinct columns the several particulars included
therein, and shall also specify the resources of the bank, designating
in distinct columns the particulars included therein. Which return shall
be signed by the cashier of each bank respectively, who shall make
oath or affirmation before some magistrate qualified to administer oaths,
to the truth of said return, according to his best knowledge and belief,
and a majority of the directors of each bank shall certify and make
oath, or affirmation, before the same magistrate, as their respective
cashiers, that the books of such bank indicate the state of facts so
returned by their cashier, and that they have full confidence in the
truth of the return so by him made, and no further or other return
shall be required from said banks.
  " *Sec.* 28. Be it further enacted, that the secretary of this commonwealth be, and he hereby is authorized and directed to procure, at the
expense of the commonwealth, printed copies of the form of the
return required by this act, and to furnish four such copies of the
same, to the cashier of every bank, in the months of March, or April,
annually.
  " *Sec.* 29. Be it further enacted, that it shall be the duty of the
secretary of this commonwealth, after he shall have received the returns
from the several banks, as aforesaid, to cause to be prepared, and
printed, a true abstract from those returns, each column to be footed
up as soon as practicable after they shall have been received, and the
secretary shall transmit, by mail, one copy thereof to the cashier of
each bank incorporated by authority of this commonwealth."

Perhaps these are some of the most useful of the
American regulations.   Returns are required from
each bank, and from the whole is prepared an abstract
exhibiting the actual condition of the currency, and
the state of banking in the country.   Every man
who has paid much attention to the question of
the currency in England must be conscious that he
has not sufficient facts to enable him to form con-

clusions upon many important questions. The paucity of facts is one cause why we have so many theories. The received opinions upon this subject are for the most part, rather the result of abstract reasoning than deductions from facts. Had we more ample information there would be less room for speculation, and we should arrive at certain knowledge instead of being wafted about by fluctuating theories. But the science of statistics has received till lately but little attention in this country, and perhaps, the statistics of banking have received less attention than any other portion of that science. It is only since 1833 that we have periodical publications of the circulation of the Bank of England, and of the country banks, and even these are imperfect.

First, then, we ought to have more minute accounts of the circulation of the Bank of England.

We ought to have, not merely the quarterly averages of the circulation, but the actual weekly amounts, in order that the fluctuations caused by particular events may be clearly perceived.

The circulation of the London office should be given separately from that of the branches. At present they are all included in the same amount.

The amount of notes payable on demand should be given separately from the bank post bills drawn at seven days sight, and from the drafts drawn by the branches upon the head office.

It is quite clear that returns made as at present can be of very little use as a means of forming any correct principles upon the subject of the currency. Let it be supposed, for instance, that the last return shows a considerable reduction in the quarterly average of notes in circulation, and I wish to trace the effects of this reduction upon the money market of London. How can I do this? I know not whether the reduction took place at the beginning or at the end of the quarter, whether in the issues of the London office, or in those of the branches, whether in the notes payable on demand, or in the bank post bills, or in the branch drafts on London. If then, I found my reasonings upon the supposition that the reduction took place at the end of the quarter, and in the notes payable on demand, issued by the London office, I may be led to very erroneous conclusions.

There is another piece of information which it is desirable to possess relative to the circulation of the Bank of England, and it is one which the bank cannot supply. It is desirable to know the difference in the amount of the active circulation and the dead circulation, so as to be able to trace their respective fluctuations. That portion of the notes of the Bank of England which is passing from hand to hand, may be called the active circulation. That portion which is hoarded, or kept in reserve to meet possible demands, may be called the dead circulation. Now it is quite certain that the dead circulation, while it remains in that state, has no effect upon the prices of commodities, the spirit of speculation, or the foreign exchanges. These are effected only by the active circulation. In seasons of pressure the dead circulation is increased at the expense of the active circulation, because people hoard their money to meet contingencies. Hence we find the pressure is often more severe than the reduction of ' the bank circulation would seem to warrant. But the fact is, that the pressure is in proportion to the reduction of the active circulation, and not in proportion to the reduction of the whole circulation. On the other hand, in seasons of abundance, the dead circulation is diminished, the active circulation proportionably increased; and hence, the stimulus given to trade and speculation is much greater than the returns of the Bank of England would warrant us to expect. Now what means do we possess of getting at the amount of the dead circulation? The Bank of England can give us no information on the subject. But it seems probable that almost all the dead circulation is in the hands of the different banks: very few private individuals keep any hoard of bank notes. If then, all he bankers and banks be required to produce returns of the amount of Bank of England notes in their possession, this might enable us to form a judgment as to the amount of the dead circulation.

It is well known that bills of exchange serve the purpose of promissory notes. It is therefore of importance, in all discussions upon the currency, to ascertain the amount of the bill circulation. It may be justly supposed, that a large proportion of the bills in existence are in the hands of the banks. In their periodical returns, the banks, therefore, should state the amount of bills of exchange in their possession ; and the country banks should state the amount of outstanding bills they have drawn upon their London agents.

Banks of deposit serve the same purpose as banks of circulation. Payments are made by cheques as well as by notes. The amount of the deposits should therefore be known.

· If then it be not desirable to require a balance-sheet, every bank in England, whether private or joint stock, should at least once in three months render to government the following returns :—

LIABILITIES.
An account of all the notes in circulation.
The amount of their deposits.
The amount of undue bills they may have drawn.

ASSETS.
The amount of the Bank of England notes in their possession.
The amount of gold and silver.
The amount of undue bills discounted.
The amount of government securities they held.
Also, the amount of bills lodged by customers to be placed to their credit when due.

These returns might be consolidated, and published in the following form—

Notes payable on demand.

Bank of England notes issued at the London office.
Ditto issued at the branches.
Notes issued by the private bankers.
Notes issued by the joint stock banks.

Total amount of notes upon demand in circulation.

Bank Post Bills and Bills drawn upon London by Joint Stock and Private Bankers.

Bank of England post bills issued at the London office.
Drafts drawn by Bank of England branches upon ditto.
Drafts on London by private bankers.
Ditto ditto by joint stock banks.

Total amount of post bills and drafts upon London.

Deposits.

Deposits in the joint stock banks that issue notes.
Ditto in ditto that do not issue notes.
Ditto in private banks that issue notes.
Ditto in ditto that do not issue notes.
Private deposits in the Bank of England.

Total amount of private deposits.
Public deposits in the Bank of England.

Total deposits.

Bills of Exchange.

Discounted.   Deposited.

Bills of exchange in joint stock banks that issue notes.
Ditto in ditto that do not ditto.
Ditto in private banks that do.
Ditto in ditto that do not ditto.
Ditto in Bank of England.

Total amount of bills of Exchange.

An account of Bank of England notes, gold, government stock, &c. might also be stated in the same manner, distinguishing the different classes of banks.

Had we returns such as these for a series of years, we should probably be able to confirm or to correct some of the received opinions respecting the currency. We might also be able to judge how far the accusations advanced against some of our banking establishments are well or ill-founded, and we might discover some practical measures for preventing those evils that now result from the alternate expansions and contractions of the circulating medium. To the statesman this information would be useful in other respects, as it would furnish a criterion of the wealth and commerce of the country. Lord Althorp wished to adopt some measure of this sort in 1833. In his speech upon the renewal of the bank charter, he stated—

"It appeared to him very desirable, that a better mode should be established for regulating the estimation of the circulation of the country banks. It was essential that the amount of their notes in circulation should be accurately known. It was for that purpose he proposed, that those country banks, instead of having the option as now enjoyed by the Bank of England of making a composition for the stamp duty payable on the gross amount of their notes issued, should be compelled to pay 7s. per cent. stamp duty upon the notes which they issued; thus government would know at all times the exact amount of country bankers' notes in circulation. No evil could happen in the case of any country banker from such an arrangement. He did not wish to expose the affairs of individual bankers; for though he thought it desirable to make the affairs of joint stock banks known to the public, he did not think it expedient to extend it to private bankers. He proposed that every individual bank should send up a statement to London, as a strictly confidential paper, which was not to be published in a separate form, but the accounts being added together, the total result would be given to the public periodically. These were the grounds of the pro-positions which he felt it his duty to submit to the committee on this important subject. He should observe, that the country banker could state the whole of his available assets.—(Sir Robert Peel asked whether the statement would include landed property.) As to that point, landed estates, although not immediately convertible, tended certainly to an increase of security for the ultimate solvency of the banker, and on that ground it might be matter of consideration, whether the descrip-tion of property referred to should not be included in the account. These were the propositions which he would submit to the committee."

From this quotation, it appears that Lord Althorp did not contemplate the publication of the affairs of any individual bank. The committee of 1836 state, "The law does not provide for any publication of the liabilities and assets of those banks, nor does it enforce the communication of any balance-sheet to the pro-prietors at large." It may be a subject of inquiry how far such a measure would be beneficial. The publica-tion of a balance-sheet by individual banks seems liable to the following objections.

1. That it is not a fair criterion by which you can form any judgment of the real condition of the bank. You might see that the bank had a certain amount of securities, or had advanced a certain sum upon loans;

but whether those securities were available, or whether those loans could suddenly be called up, are points upon which the balance-sheet could give no information. The Agricultural and Commercial Bank of Ireland published a very satisfactory balance-sheet a few weeks only before they stopped payment.

2. It would lay the bank open to attacks from its rivals or opponents. The balance-sheet will shew in what way the funds of the bank are employed, but it will not state the reasons why they are so employed. The opponents of the bank may attack every item of the balance-sheet, and the directors may not be able to repel those attacks without a breach of confidence that would be injurious to the establishment. Suppose, for instance, the balance-sheet should shew that the bank had advanced a few thousand pounds upon mortgage. This might be justly considered as a departure from the sound principles of banking; yet it might in this case be justified by some peculiar circumstances, which nevertheless the directors could not publish without serious injury to the parties concerned. The production of a balance-sheet is advocated upon the ground that it would enable the shareholders to judge of the ability and prudence of the directors. But how can they do this without knowing the reasons by which the directors are influenced in their decisions ?

3. It would cause a great deal of speculation in the shares. The shareholders and the public would form their opinions of the bank from the statements in the balance-sheet; and according to these opinions the price of the shares would fluctuate in the market. Suppose it were seen that the bank had invested a large portion of its funds in government securities, and it was known that during the year the price of those securities had experienced a considerable fall, would not the bank shares immediately fall too ? Again, suppose at the end of a year like 1836, it should appear that the bank held a considerable amount of overdue bills, the apprehension of loss would cause the

bank shares to fall; soon afterwards these bills might be paid and then the shares would rise again.—Thus, the publication of balance-sheets would keep the prices of shares in perpetual fluctuation, and furnish a most fruitful source of speculation and gambling.

4. It would be perfectly inefficient as a protection against fraud. The balance-sheet it seems is to be a check upon the directors, and yet the directors themselves are to prepare the balance-sheet. They must be stupid knaves indeed, if they produce such a balance-sheet as shall expose their own knavery. Besides, the balance-sheet merely shews the state of the bank on one day in the year. Would it not be easy to put the bank on that day in such a condition as would give satisfaction to the shareholders? An American writer will give us a lesson upon this subject.

" If we had all these accounts collected and arranged to our hand, a question might arise as to the sense in which they should be understood. There is an ambiguity in many bank statements, which renders them useless. The word " cash" under the pens of some bank officers, contracts and expands its meaning with as much facility as bank medium contracts and expands its amount. Sometimes it includes " mint certificates," because cash can be got for them in the market. Sometimes, in the case of a country bank, it includes city bank notes, because they are to the country bank "as good as cash;" sometimes cash and " bills of exchange" are given together.

" If all ambiguity were removed from bank statements, another question might arise, and that is, how far they are to be depended upon. We have seen a committee of the legislature of Connecticut accusing one of the banks of that state of rendering a false account of the amount of notes in circulation.

" No doubt, the accounts of many banks are fairly rendered, but it is impossible, in a general view of the subject, to say how many bank returns are faithful, and how many are not. There may be a literal exactness in the returns, and yet some fact may be suppressed, which, if generally known, might entirely change the impression the public receives from a bank statement. " I could," says a writer in a Portsmouth, New Hampshire paper, "name more than one bank in this state, where a considerable portion of the debts mentioned in the return, were worth nothing ; and much of the specie was borrowed from individuals or banks, laid in the vaults those two days, and then returned to the owners with the seals unbroken." The author of a pamphlet, published at New York in 1828, entitled " a Peep into the Banks," objected to a new law of that state, requiring the banks to make semi-annual returns of the amount of specie in their vaults for the following reasons. " It is well known, that institutions which heretofore have been required to make these exhibitions, have prepared, previous to the period of making them, to present as favourable statements as possible. If all the banks in the state are to do so, it will produce a semi-annual pressure for money. Paper, payable a short time previous to these periods, will be discounted freely, when a general curtailment will be made. The notes and bills payable out of the state, will obtain a preference, that thereby funds of specie, in Philadelphia, Boston, &c., may be made for a few days the property of banks in this state. In this and other contrivances, the officers will be employed to make a display of that which has no permanent existence."*

Most of the English deeds of settlement guard against any degree of publicity being given to the accounts of individuals. Their provisions in this respect form the best answer to those who assert that the transactions of individuals with joint stock banks are universally known.

" No principle seems to be more attended to or prominently put forward, than that of preserving secrecy as to the state of accounts of the customers of the banks. To this principle there does not appear to be an exception.

" The directors are in general required to sign a declaration, pledging themselves to observe secrecy as to the transactions of the bank with their customers, and the state of accounts of the individuals. In some of the companies this declaration is also to be signed by all the clerks and officers. One banking company goes so far as to require an oath to this effect. If the proprietors are dissatisfied with the statement of accounts made by the directors, a power is generally reserved to appoint auditors or inspectors for the examination of the books; but these auditors or inspectors are required to sign a similar declaration of secrecy.

" No proprietor, not being a director, is entitled to inspect any of the books of the company.

" The directors are in general bound to exhibit to the general meeting of the shareholders a summary or balance-sheet of their affairs, and to make such further statement or report as the directors may deem expedient and conducive to the interests of the company. In the case of one of these banks, even this is not obligatory by terms of the deed, which leave it to the discretion of the directors whether they do or do not exhibit a balance-sheet. In a very extensive bank, the proprietors annually appoint auditors to examine the affairs of the company, and to report thereon.

" In some of the companies the principle of secrecy is carried still further; two of the directors, selected from the rest, are the exclusive

---

* Gouge's Short History of Paper Money and Banking in the United States.

depositors of the power of inspecting the private accounts of customers. These persons are sometimes called 'confidential directors.' This provision is stated to be made, 'in order that the credit and private transactions of individuals may be preserved inviolate.' Sometimes they are called 'managing directors,' sometimes 'special directors.' In other companies, though all the directors have the power of inspection of the accounts of customers, two of the directors are selected to inspect bills and notes, 'in order to prevent the exposure of such bills of exchange and promissory notes as may pass through the bank.' These two directors are called 'the bill committee.' In two of the companies, a single person, called 'the manager,' has the exclusive power of inspecting the notes."

"Sec. 30. Be it further enacted, that the president, directors, and company of any bank established by authority of this commonwealth, on application, within one year from the passage of this act, shall be authorized, with the assent of the legislature for the time being, to continue its operations as a banking company for the further period of twenty years from and after the first Monday in October, in the year of our Lord one thousand eight hundred and thirty-one, with all the powers and privileges, and subject to all the duties and requirements, of this act."

In our deeds of settlement the duration of a company is not usually limited to any number of years; its existence depends upon contingencies.

" The deeds of all these companies contain some provision for dissolution in certain contingencies. It is in general provided that a dissolution of the company shall take place by reason either of a certain amount of loss, or of a voluntary agreement. Dissolution by reason of loss in the great majority of the deeds is provided for in the following manner :—

" It is necessary to premise that the directors of each of these companies are bound to set aside a certain portion of the profits to form a fund to meet extraordinary demands, which fund is sometimes called the ' surplus fund,' sometimes the ' reserve fund,' but more usually the ' guarantee fund.' The ordinary provision for dissolution is to this effect :—That if the losses sustained shall at any time have absorbed the whole of this guarantee fund, and also one-fourth of the capital paid up, then any one shareholder may require the dissolution of the company, which shall take place accordingly, unless two-thirds in number and value of the shareholders shall be desirous of continuing the company, and shall purchase the shares of those proprietors who wish to withdraw. In one bank the dissolution of the company takes place upon a loss of one-fifth instead of one-fourth of the capital. In two other banks no mention is made of the guarantee fund.

" The provision of the great majority of deeds, as above stated, is, that in the event of a given amount of loss, any one shareholder may propose the dissolution. In some, three shareholders are required. In the Banking Company A. the requisition for dissolution must be made by ten shareholders holding 200 shares ; in the Bank B. by one-fourth of the company; but if the loss amount to one half of the capital, then by any single shareholder.

" By the general provisions of the great majority of deeds, the dissolution of the company, though duly proposed, may be averted by two-thirds of the proprietors; but in some there exists no such restriction; and on the occurrence of a given amount of loss, the dissolution, if proposed, is to take place immediately, even though no partner should propose it.

" The Banking Company C. has provisions for dissolution peculiar to itself, and among others it is set forth, that the partnership shall determine on the 1st of January, 2001.

" The Bank of D., besides the usual provision for dissolution in case of a loss, has a provision for dissolution if the company shall not repay a contribution to a shareholder who shall have been compelled to pay a debt of the company.

" A dissolution, by voluntary agreement, may in general be directed by a majority of two-thirds of the shareholders in the number and value, but with the concurrence of a certain number of the directors.

" In some companies a voluntary dissolution may be effected by three-fourths of the shareholders; in others by a majority; in a few others there is no provision for a voluntary dissolution.

" *Sec.* 31. Be it further enacted, that if, during the continuance of any bank charter, granted or renewed under the provision of this Act, any new or greater privileges shall be granted to any other bank now in operation, or which may hereafter be created, each and every bank in operation may be entitled to the same.

" *Sec.* 32. Be it further enacted, that no bill or note, of the denomination of one hundred dollars or less, shall be issued by any bank aforesaid, unless the same shall be impressed from Perkins' stereotype plate: provided, that no greater sum than one cent shall be charged for each bill impressed from the class of plates on which is the fine writing, nor more than two cents for bills of either of the other classes; but the legislature may, at any time hereafter, authorise and require the use of any other plates.

" *Sec.* 33. Be it further enacted, that all Acts and parts of Acts heretofore passed in relation to banks, inconsistent with the provisions of this Act, be, and the same are hereby repealed, so far as the same might apply to all banks whose charter may be extended under the provisions of this Act."

The committee conclude their analysis of the deeds of settlement thus—

" The House will see from this analysis that these deeds of partnership, on which depend the whole transactions of the banks and their responsibility to the public, so far from being framed according to one common and uniform principle, differ materially from each other in many most important particulars; and, in some instances, the deeds contain provisions open to very serious objections, as entailing possible consequences highly injurious to the interests of the public, and of the banking establishments themselves."

It may be questioned whether any deed of settlement can be framed which shall not contain provisions that may by possibility become injurious. Hence arises the propriety of inserting a clause, giving the proprietors the power of altering the deed, as circumstances may require. The committee state, that with one single exception, " the main body of the proprietors reserve to themselves the power of selecting the directors, and of altering from time to time the rules by which the directors are to be governed." " The deeds of all the other companies expressly give a power to the shareholders to make new laws and regulations."

Whether we view the history or the principles of the respective institutions, I think it is abundantly evident, that as a whole the system of chartered banks acted upon in America, is inferior to the system of joint stock banks as acted upon in Scotland : nor does it appear that there are many of the American regulations that could be advantageously introduced into our joint stock system. The restrictions on the amount of notes, deposits, and loans, are merely nominal ; and were they reduced to so low a proportion as to be real restrictions, they would most probably be pernicious. Under the American system of limited liability, these regulations may be proper enough, for it is quite proper to limit the debts of a bank, if you limit the fund from which those debts are to be discharged. The most important of the American regulations, are those that refer to the paid-up capital, and that require the periodical returns to be made to the government ; and these I think may very usefully be engrafted upon our system.

While, however, separately considered, the American system seems inferior to the joint stock system, I see no objection to their existing together, provided that neither be forced upon the public by the power of the legislature, but that they are left to depend entirely on public support. We have the means of trying the system of chartered banks, either in connection with the system of joint stock banking, or in a state of separation from that system. According to the existing law, no joint stock bank of issue can be established within sixty-five miles of London. If chartered banks were established beyond that distance, they would have to contend against joint stock banks, and hence their comparative merits might be easily observed. But if chartered banks of issue were also allowed at a greater distance than ten miles from London, the space between ten and sixty-five miles, a space greater than the fourth of all England and Wales, might have an extensive system of chartered banks, and here we should perceive their operation in a state of separation from the system of joint stock banks.

It may therefore be worthy of inquiry, whether the legislature might not improve our banking institutions by the adoption of regulations somewhat similar to the following—

I. With regard to joint stock banks.

1. All deeds of settlement to be submitted to a public officer who should have power to strike out those provisions that are contrary to law, and to object to those he might consider injurious to the public or to the shareholders.

2. That a list of the shareholders and the amount of the paid-up capital shall be inserted once a year in the London Gazette, and a printed copy given to all the shareholders and customers of the bank.

3. No bank to commence business until a capital of £20,000 was paid up; to have £50,000 paid up by the end of the first year, and £100,000 by the end of the second year, or else to cease. Banks in London and Manchester to commence with a capital of £100,000.

4. The bank to make to government the periodical returns I have described; and to lay a balance-sheet before the shareholders *when requested by them to do so, but not otherwise.*

5. In case of a stoppage of payment, the affairs of the bank to be placed immediately in the hands of government commissioners, for the purpose of being wound up, and an extent in aid to be issued against

the property of the directors, that in case it should be necessary to come upon the property of the shareholders to make up a deficiency, that of the directors may be first taken.

II. That those joint stock banks that require it may have charters upon the following conditions.

1. That the paid-up capital shall be at least £250,000, and the nominal capital £1,000,000.

2. The shareholders shall not be liable beyond the amount of the nominal capital.

3. The bank shall make periodical returns to government in the manner described, and shall lay before its shareholders an annual balance-sheet, certified by two auditors who are not directors.

4. The bank shall not permit any overdrawn accounts, nor advance any money upon mortgage, railways, &c. &c., nor in any other way except by discounting bills or investments in government securities.

5. The bank shall not issue notes beyond the amount of its paid-up capital, nor incur liabilities beyond three times the amount of its paid-up capital.

6. The bank shall not discount or rediscount any bills it may have discounted, nor reissue any bills having more than three months to run.

7. The bank shall not draw bills upon London at more than two months after date.

8. The bank shall not have any branches.

9. The charter shall be limited to ten years, and the bank shall be established beyond ten miles from London.

10. In case the bank should stop payment, its affairs shall immediately be placed in the hands of the government commissioners, for the purpose of being wound up. In case of a deficiency, all the shareholders shall be answerable to make it good, but only in proportion to their respective shares; and an extent in aid, or some other process equally summary, shall enforce these claims.

It will be seen that I have not suggested any

method of limiting the value of the shares, the amount of the nominal capital, or the number or distance of the branches. I am inclined to think that these are matters which the legislature had better let alone.

We must always bear in mind that it is not the business of the legislature to lay down rules for the management of banks; but merely to establish such laws as shall have the effect of placing the banks under the guidance of persons who know how to manage them. Upon this subject I need only quote the speech delivered from the throne at the opening of the present session of parliament.

"The best security against mismanagement of banking affairs must ever be found in the capacity and integrity of those who are entrusted with the administration of them, and in the caution and prudence of the public; but no legislative regulation should be omitted which can increase and ensure the stability of establishments upon which commercial credit so much depends."

This may be regarded as a truism, but it is a truism that is often forgotten, and hence it very properly found a place in the royal speech. It is useful to legislators to be reminded of the limits of legislation.

SECTION V.

A COMPARISON BETWEEN THE ENGLISH AND THE AMERICAN SYSTEMS OF BANKING, WITH REFERENCE TO THE CURRENCY AND TO THE FOREIGN EXCHANGES.

In 1810 two bank directors stated to the bullion committee, that in regulating the general amount of their loans and discounts, they did not "advert to the circumstance of the exchanges, it appearing upon a reference to the amount of the notes in circulation, and the course of the exchange, that they frequently have no connection."

Since that period the opinion of the directors of the Bank of England have undergone a change; and it is now admitted, that the amount of notes in circulation has a considerable effect upon the foreign exchanges. The mode in which this effect is produced is thus described in the History and Principles of Banking.

" The effect which the amount of notes in circulation has upon the foreign exchanges has been the subject of much discussion. One party contended, that as the amount of notes increases, the exchange must become unfavourable. Another party maintained, that the exchanges were not at all affected by the issue of notes, but by the state of foreign trade. The authors of the report of the bullion committee expressed the former opinion, some of the bank directors maintained the latter.

" It is obvious that the exchanges are regulated by the amount of gold that is required to be sent abroad, either to pay the balance of trade, or to pay our armies, or to subsidize foreign powers, or as rents to absentees, or for some other purpose. Now it is clear that an increased or diminished issue of notes will in no way diminish the amount of gold that is to be sent abroad, and therefore have no direct effect upon the exchanges ; if we owe gold, we must pay it. We may diminish our issue of notes, but that will not pay our debts. If, then, the issue of notes have any effect upon the exchanges, it must be in an *indirect* way.

" I have already stated that an increased issue of notes can have no effect upon the prices of commodities at home, but by influencing either the supply or the demand. If the increased quantity of money raises the demand for commodities beyond a certain point, it will advance the price ; and if it increases the supply, it will lower the price ; but in no way can the quantity of money in circulation affect the prices of commodities but through the channels of supply and command. Just so with the foreign exchanges ; an unfavourable course of exchange arises generally from our owing a sum of money which we have to pay, in consequence of our imports having exceeded our exports. An increased quantity of money, therefore, to affect the exchanges, must diminish the amount of our foreign debt, and it can do this only by either increasing our exports or diminishing our imports. When money is abundant, our merchants can import more than formerly ; this increases our debt. The importers are disposed to lay in stocks of goods, and the competition between the importers raises the prices they give to the foreigner ; hence there are heavy sums to be sent abroad. It is true, that when money is abundant our manufacturers and exporters can also export more goods, but the competition among exporters diminishes the price to the foreigner, and hence we have a less proportionate sum to receive. The exporter, too, having abundance of money, gives the foreigner long credit, and hence the money is not received in England for a considerable time after the goods have been shipped ; in the mean time the exchanges become unfavourable, and gold must be sent abroad. Now suppose in this state of things the bank contract their issues; money becomes scarce, bills cannot be discounted, and trade is dull. Now, then, the importer having already a heavy stock of goods, will buy no more, he is anxious to sell, for he has not now sufficient capital to keep so large a stock—a general desire of selling will cause a fall of price. Fewer commodities will now be imported, and these obtained at a less price; hence there is less money due to the foreigner. The exporters on the other hand, deprived also of their usual accommodation, cannot carry on business to the same extent; the supply will be reduced, the competition is less, and prices rise to the foreigner. The exporters, too, cannot now give such long credit as formerly; they will call in the sums due to them, and hence more money must come in from abroad. As, then, we have to pay other nations a less amount of money for our imports, and they have to pay us a greater amount for our exports, the exchange will become favourable. It is obvious that this operation will cause great embarrassment to trade; in fact it is only by producing embarrassment that a contraction of the currency can affect the exchanges.

" The amount of notes in circulation affects the foreign exchanges in another way. When an increased issue takes place, money becomes more abundant; the lenders are more numerous, and the supply of capital is increased; hence the price given for the loan of money, that is the rate of interest, falls. Persons who have money to employ will find they cannot obtain the same interest as formerly, hence they will be disposed to invest it in the foreign funds, where it can be employed to greater advantage. In order to remit this money, they will purchase foreign bills; this demand for foreign bills will advance their price, and the exchanges will consequently be unfavourable. On the other hand, when the circulation is considerably reduced, money becomes scarce, a higher price will be given for the use of it, the rate of interest rises; persons who have property abroad will be disposed to bring it home, where it can be more profitably invested; they will draw bills against it, and sell them in the market. This new supply of bills will lower the price, and make the exchanges favourable.

" It should always be recollected that the transmission of money as subsidies, loans, or for investment in the foreign funds, will have the same effect upon the exchanges as though it were transmitted in payment of commodities imported. Whenever, therefore, the issue of notes shall, directly or indirectly, cause a transmission of money from one country to another, the exchanges will be affected; but when this shall not be the case, the expansion or contraction of the currency will have no effect upon the foreign exchange."

It is also an admitted principle in America, that paper issued to excess will have the effect of raising prices, stimulating speculation, and rendering the exchanges unfavorable. The operation of the currency upon the exchange in America was thus described a few years ago by Mr. Biddle, the President of the Bank of the United States.

"The currency of the United States consists of coin, and of bank notes promising to pay coin. As long as the bank can always pay the coin they promise, they are useful; because, in a country where the monied capital is disproportioned to the means of employing capital, the substitution of credits for coins enables the nation to make its exchanges with less coin, and of course saves the expense of that coin. But this advantage has by its side a great danger. Banks are often directed by needy persons, who borrow too much, or by sang uine persons, anxious only to increase the profits, without much pecuniary interest or personal responsibility in the administration. The constant tendency of banks is, therefore, to lend too much, and to put too many notes in circulation. Now the addition of many notes, even while they are as good as coin, by being always exchangeable for coin, may be injurious, because the increase of the mixed mass of money generally, occasions a rise in the price of all commodities. The consequence is, that the high price of foreign productions, tempts foreigners to send a large amount of their commodities; while the high price of domestic productions, prevents these foreigners from taking in exchange a large amount of our commodities. When, therefore, you buy from foreigners more than they buy from you, as they cannot take the paper part of your currency, they must take the coin part. If this is done to a considerable extent, the danger is, that the banks will be obliged to pay so much of their coin for their notes, as not to leave them a sufficient quantity to answer the demand for it, in which case the banks fail, and the community is defrauded. To prevent this, a prudent bank, the moment it perceives an unusual demand for its notes, and has reason to fear a drain on its vaults, should immediately diminish the amount of its notes, and call in part of its debts. So on a large scale, when the banks of a country perceive such a demand for coin for exportation, as diminishes too much the stock of coin necessary for their banking purposes, they should stop the exportation. This they can always do, if their affairs have been well managed: and here lies the test of bank management.

"The law of a mixed currency of coin and paper is, that when, from superabundance of the mixed mass, too much of the coin part leaves the country, the remainder must be preserved by diminishing the paper part, so as to make the mixed mass valuable in proportion; it is this capacity of diminishing the paper which protects it. Its value consists in its elasticity, its power of alternate expansion and contraction, to suit the state of the community; and when it looses its flexibility it no longer contains within itself the means of its defence, and is full of hazard: in truth the merit of a bank is nearly in proportion to the degree of this flexibility of its means.

If a bank lends its money on mortgages, on stocks, for long terms, and to persons careless of protests, it incurs this great risk, that, on the one hand its notes are payable on demand, while, on the other its debts cannot be called in without great delay, a delay fatal to its credit and character. This is the general error of banks who do not always discriminate between two things essentially distinct in banking, a debt ultimately secure, and a debt certainly payable. But a well-managed bank has its funds mainly in short loans to persons in business; the result of business transactions payable on a day named, which the parties are able to pay, and will pay at any sacrifice in order to escape mercantile dishonour. Such a bank has its funds, therefore, constantly repaid into it, and is able to say whether it will or will not lend them out again. A bank so managed, if it finds too much demand for its coin to go abroad, begins by not lending more than it receives every day, and then goes farther, by not lending as much as its income, declining to renew the notes of its debtors, and obliging them to pay a part or the whole; making it a rule to keep its discounts within its income. The operation proceeds thus: by issuing no new notes, but requiring something from your debtors, you oblige them to return to you the bank notes you lent them, or their equivalents. This makes the bank notes more scarcer — this makes them more valuable— the debtor in his anxiety to get your notes, being willing to sell his goods at a sacrifice—this brings down the prices of goods, and makes every thing cheaper. Then the remedy begins. The foreigner finding that his goods must be sold so low, sends no more. The American importer, finding that he cannot make money by importing them, im- ports no more. The remainder of the coin, of course, is not sent out after new importations, but stays at home where it finds better employ- ment in purchasing these cheap articles; and when the foreigner hears of this state of things he sends back the coin he took away. He took away merely because your own domestic productions were so high that he could not make any profit in his country by taking them. But when the news reaches him that his productions are very cheap in our country, he will also learn that our productions are cheap too, and he sends back the coin to buy these cheap productions of ours. We therefore get back our coin by diminishing our paper, and it will stay until drawn away by another superabundance of paper. Such is the circle which a mixed currency is always describing. Like the power of steam, it is eminently useful in prudent hands, but of tremendous hazard when not controlled; and the practical wisdom in managing it lies in siezing the proper moment to expand and contract it, taking care, in working with such explosive materials, whenever there is doubt, to incline to the side of safety.

" These simple elements explain the present situation of the country. Its disorder is over-trading brought on by over-banking. The remedy is, to bank less and to trade less.

" During the last year, money was very abundant, that is, the de- mand for coin being small in proportion, the banks distributed freely their discounts and notes. This plenty concurred with other causes, especially the expectation of a new tariff, to induce an increased im- portation of foreign goods, and at the same time furnish great facility for procuring them on credit. For instance, in the difficulty of pro- curing profitable investments, there were found capitalists who exported the coin of the country, and sold their bills for it on credit; thus obtaining a small profit on the shipment, and a greater on the discount of the notes taken for their bills.

" This fraction of a per centage on the shipment of coin, seems to be a trifling gain for the great inconvenience to which it often subjects the community; but the profit though small, is lawful, and no odium should

be attached to the agents, for the operation is often a wholesome correc-
tive of excessive issues of paper.   The effect was, that by the month of
February, the exportations of specie to France and England had become unusually large, amounting probably, in the preceding twelve
months, to between four and five million dollars ; and great importations were constantly arriving, and which when sold would require
remittances to Europe.   Hitherto at this season, the demand for
exchange had been supplied by the bills drawn on the produce of the
South, when shipped to Europe ; but this year the crop, and with it
the bills produced by it, has come tardily into the market, so that the
demands of exchange for the proceeds of the arriving shipments were
directed immediately to the exhausted vaults of the bank.   Such an
effect was to be averted without loss of time.   The directors of the
Bank of the United States, as was their natural duty, were the first to
perceive the danger, and the bank was immediately placed in a
situation of great strength and repose.   The State Banks followed its
example.   They began by restraining their loans within their income,
and gradually and quietly decreasing the amount of them, and more
especially directing their retrenchments on those whose operations were
particularly connected with the exportations they desired to prevent.
The course of business has been this : a merchant borrows from the
banks and sends abroad £100,000 in coin, or he buys bills from one
who has shipped the coin.   With these he imports a cargo of goods,
obtaining a long credit for the duties, sends them to auction, where
they are sold, and the auctioneer's notes given for them.   These notes
are discounted by the bank, and the merchant is then put in possession
of another £100,000, which he again ships, and thus he proceeds in an
endless circle, as long as the banks, by discounting his notes, enable him
to send the coin, and tempt him so to do, by keeping up prices here by
their excessive issues.   The banks, therefore, begin by diminishing or
withdrawing these artificial facilities, leaving the persons directly concerned in this trade to act as they please with their own funds, but not
with the funds of the banks.   The immediate consequence is, that the
auctioneers can no longer advance the money for entire cargoes, that
they no longer sell for credit but for cash, that the price of goods fall,
that instead of being sold in large masses they are sold slowly and in
small parcels, so that the importer is not able to remit the proceeds in
large amounts.   This diminishes the demand for the bills and for specie
to send abroad.   In the meantime, the importer finding the prices of his
goods fall, imports no more, and the shipper of coin finding less demand
for exchange, and that he can make more of his money by using it at
home than by exporting it, abstains from sending it abroad.   Time is
thus gained till the arrival of the Southern exchange, which will supply
the demand without the aid of coin, and then every thing resumes its
accustomed course.

" This is the point to which the present measures of the banks are
tending.   The purpose must be accomplished, in a longer or shorter
time, with a greater or less degree of pressure, but the effect must or
will be produced."

While however the admitted principles of the cur-

I

rency are the same, there is a considerable difference
in the mode of its administration.   In America there is
no national bank: even the late Bank of the United
States had no monopoly; its only privileges consisted
in being the banker of the government, and in being
able to establish branches in the respectives states,
without being subject to local taxation.   All the banks
issue notes, even for so low an amount as five dollars,
and in many of the States for even one dollar.   If there
is an evil in unlimited competition in the issue of
notes, that evil must be experienced in America.   It
is therefore worthy of inquiry, whether derangements
have occurred in the American currency more frequently than in this country; and if so, whether they
have arisen from a spirit of competition between the
issuing banks, or from the circumstance of their issuing very small notes ?

With regard to England, the case is this :—In London, and for ten miles round, we have exclusively the
circulation of Bank of England notes.   From ten to
sixty-five miles round London, we have exclusively the
notes of private bankers.   Beyond sixty-five miles from
London, we have the notes of private bankers, the notes
of joint stock banks, and the notes of branches of the
Bank of England.

First, we shall consider the circulation of London.

The bank charter committee of 1832 proposed to
themselves the following inquiries :

1. "Whether the paper circulation of the metropolis
should be confined as at present to the issue of one
bank, and that a commercial company; or whether a
competition of different banks of issue, each consisting
of an unlimited number of partners, should be permitted?

2. "If it should be deemed expedient that the
paper circulation of the metropolis should be confined
as at present to the issues of one bank, how far the
whole of the exclusive privileges possessed by the Bank
of England are necessary to effect this object ?"

Upon these points, the committee declared they

could not give a decided opinion.   Lord Althorp thus referred to them in the speech I have already quoted.

A GOVERNMENT BANK.

" The advantages of having the bank altogether in the hands of Government, instead of a private company, would be greater responsibility, and in that respect greater security to the public, and the whole of the profit ; but these were more than counterbalanced by the political evils to which it would give rise.   Government would have a constant temptation to abuse this additional power: besides, in times of distress, Government could not give the accustomed accommodation which would be desirable from a banking company.   But supposing they could give this assistance, the power which they would acquire, might be destructive to the constitution of the country.   Now, if the bank were tied down by fixed rules, to prevent their making advances, he thought that from one evil, they would fly to another, and it would be impossible to provide for all the cases, in which the aid of a bank to the public might be required."

A SINGLE BANK.

" The first question then was whether it would be more desirable that the circulating medium should be conducted by a single body, as bankers of issue, or by a competition of different banks or bankers?   There were advantages in both systems.   It must be to the interest of banks competing with each other, to issue each as much paper circulation as they could.   They would be a check upon each other.   It was therefore clear that no one of these banks could issue more than its due proportion of the circulation wanted.   Suppose there should be a great demand for accommodation, though it might be in the power of each to increase the amount of the circulation, it would not be in the power of any of them, to have more than his due proportion of the amount of that increase; and when again, in consequence of a depreciation of the currency, a failure of credit takes place, in consequence of the turn of the exchange against us, each bank must contract its issues, and thus produce a sudden contraction to the currency of the country.   Hence you would from such a competition cause greater fluctuation than from a single bank.   There was another point on which a single bank having the control of a larger part of the circulation of the country might be of advantage ; and that was, the assurance that in times of distress it could assist the commerce of the country.   In times of panic the exchanges turn in favour of this country : there was no objection to the banks increasing its accommodation ; but if there should be many banks, no one would dare to come forward, from fear of the competition of its rivals."

The great objection to freedom of banking in London, arises from the apprehension, that if there were numerous banks of issue, the rivalry between them would put into circulation an excessive amount of notes; the prices of commodities would thus be advanced, speculation would be encouraged, the foreign exchanges would become unfavourable; and there would be a consequent demand upon the banks for gold to be exported, and this demand the banks might be unprepared to supply. To this it has been replied—granting all these effects would result from numerous banks of issue, should we be worse off than at present? Are not all these evils experienced when we have only one bank of issue?

But it may be contended, that rival banks of issue tend to diminish these evils. If the Bank of England put into circulation an excessive amount of notes, these notes are not returned for payment until the foreign exchanges become unfavourable; but were there numerous banks of issue, the notes issued by one bank would soon find their way into the others, and be returned for payment in the daily exchanges. All the witnesses from Scotland, who were examined before the parliamentary committees in 1826, concurred in saying, that the exchanges between the banks was an effectual check to an excessive issue of notes. Why should not a check, which is found·so effectual in Scotland, be equally effectual in London?

But even admitting that one bank of issue were preferable to an unlimited number, another subject of inquiry would present itself, that is, whether four or five chartered banks, each having a large capital, and founded on principles of unquestionable stability, would not be preferable to one bank. Here the ·checks, arising from frequent exchange of notes, would exist without the evils arising from unlimited competition; and as neither one of these banks could calculate upon being able by its individual exertion to turn the foreign exchanges, they would be careful to be always in a position to meet their engagements.

Besides, it is worthy of inquiry, whether there might not be a proper division of labour in banking, and different banks be chartered for different purposes. The Bank of England is a bank of circulation, a bank of deposit, and a bank of discount. It is the bank of the government—a bank having eleven branches—a bank whose notes are a legal tender all over the country, and which has to watch and regulate the foreign exchanges. Is it not worthy of inquiry, whether these various functions could not be performed better by separate establishments?

Secondly. From about ten to sixty-five miles from London, the circulation consists exclusively of notes of the private bankers.

The distance of sixty-five miles happened to be fixed upon, because in an act passed a short time before, a bank having more than six partners was prohibited within fifty Irish miles from Dublin; and fifty Irish miles are equal to about sixty-five English miles. But as Dublin is situated on the sea-coast, the bank of Ireland has a monopoly of only a semicircle, whose radius is fifty Irish miles. But London being situated inland, the Bank of England has a monopoly of a whole circle of one hundred and thirty miles in diameter. She has not, however, shown any disposition to avail herself of this monopoly:—she has not established a single branch within this circle, but leaves it to the uninterrupted possession of the private bankers. This circle, after deducting the space equal to ten miles round London for the bank of England circulation, will leave above thirteen thousand square miles: and as the whole of England and Wales contains about forty-nine thousand square miles, it follows, that a space equal to one-fourth of England and Wales, and taken from the heart of the country, is in the exclusive possession of the private bankers.

It would be very desirable to have returns of the circulation of the private bankers within this circle, from December, 1833, to December, 1836, in order to ascertain whether those private bankers who were free from competition with joint stock banks, did or did not increase their circulation during that period. We know that the total private circulation decreased, and the joint stock circulation advanced; but upon investigation, it would probably be found that the private circulation within the sixty-five miles had from the increase of trade and speculation advanced, and that more than the whole diminution had taken place in the circulation of those private banks, that are situated beyond the sixty-five miles.

Thirdly. The circulation beyond sixty-five miles consists of the notes of private banks, the notes of joint stock banks, and the notes of branches of the bank of England.

From the circumstance that the circle of sixty-five miles radius, contains about one-fourth of England and Wales, we may perhaps hazard a conjecture that the circulation bears about the same proportion. This will give about four millions; and it will lead us to suppose that the circulation beyond the sixty-five miles, is pretty equally divided between the private bankers, the joint stock banks, and the branches of the bank of England. I again quote from the report of the Parliamentary Committee.

" The most important facts which have come under the consideration of your committee are connected with the operation of the joint stock banks on credit and circulation. It appears that a great extension has been given to both; and that if the operations of all banks, whether private, or formed on joint stock principles, are not conducted with prudence and with caution, measures adopted by the Bank of England with a view to the state of the foreign exchanges, and of the consequent demand for bullion, may be contracted by the advances and increased issues of country banks. The following table will exhibit the progress of the circulation for some time past; and it is to be inferred, from the increased issues of joint stock banks at periods when the Bank of England was endeavouring to limit the amount of paper in circulation, that a due attention was not given by them to the returns published in the Gazette under the Act of the 3rd and 4th Will. IV. c. 98.

An Account of the aggregate number of notes circulated in England and Wales by private banks and joint stock banks and their branches, distinguishing private from joint stock banks.—(From returns directed by 3 and 4 Will. IV. c. 83.)

—	Private Banks.	Joint Stock Banks.	Total.
Quarter ending			
28 December, 1833	8,836,803	1,315,301	10,152,104
29 March, 1834	8,733,400	1,458,427	10,191,827
28 June, —	8,875,795	1,642,887	10,518,682
27 September, —	8,370,423	1,783,689	10,154,112
28 December, —	5,537,655	2,122,173	10,659,828
28 March, 1835	8,231,206	2,188,954	10,420,160
27 June, —	8,455,114	2,484,687	10,939,801
26 September, —	7,912,587	2,508,036	10,420,623
26 December, —	8,334,863	2,799,551	11,134,414
26 March, 1836	8,353,894	3,094,025	11,447,919
25 June, —	8,614,132	3,588,064	12,202,196

BANK OF ENGLAND.

—	Circulation.	Deposits.	Bullion.	Securities.
28 December, 1833	17,469,000	15,160,000	12,200,000	24,576,000
29 March, 1834	18,544,000	13,750,000	8,753,000	25,787,000
28 June, —	18,689,000	15,373,000	8 885,000	27,471,000
27 September, —	18,437,000	12,790,000	6,917,000	26,915,000
28 December, —	17,070,000	13,019,000	6,978,000	25,551,000
28 March, 1835	18,152,000	9,972,000	6,295,000	24,530, 00
27 June, —	17,637,000	11,753,000	6,613,000	25,221,000
26 September, —	17,320,000	13,866,000	6,284,000	27, 24,000
26 December, —	16,564,000	20,370,000	7,718,000	31,764,000
26 March, 1836	17,669,000	12,875,000	8,014,000	25,521,000
25 June, —	17,184 000	15,730,000	6,868,000	28,847,000

" Your committee cannot too strongly recommend to all parties engaged in banking the utmost caution and prudence in these respects, both at the present and in their future operations."

The former part of this quotation probably refers to the practice of rediscounting bills in London by joint stock banks in the country.

Banks situated in agricultural districts have usually more money than they can employ. Independently of the paid-up capital of the bank, the sums raised by circula ion and deposits are usually more than the amount of their loans and discounts. Banks, on the other hand, that are situated in manufacturing districts, can usually employ more money than they can raise; hence the bank that has a superabundance of money sends it to London to be employed by the bill brokers, usually receiving in return bills of exchange. The bank that wants money sends its bills of exchange to London to be rediscounted. These banks thus supply each other's wants through the medium of the London bill brokers. Other funds besides those remitted by the country banks are employed in the same manner. Many merchants and others lodge money at the bill brokers, either as loans or in rediscount of bills. Thus the superfluous capital of London is directed into channels where it is employed in rewarding labour, encouraging manufactures, and increasing the wealth of the community.

But this system is not confined to the production of positive good; it prevents an immensity of evil. In a wealthy and commercial country there must always be a large amount of floating capital, and at the same time a spirit of enterprize. When there is no immediate employment for this floating capital, it bursts out in some wild speculation, such as foreign loans; and hence the rediscounting of bills in London has a tendency to prevent speculation, by drawing off the surplus cash from London into the country. Had the joint stock banks been in as active operation in 1835 as they were in 1836, the speculation in Spanish bonds would probably never have occurred: even in 1836 the speculative undertakings in London were far less numerous than in Manchester and Liverpool.

If this system considerably increased in the years 1835 and 1836, it was because money was then very cheap in London, and the joint stock banks had therefore an inducement to do as much business as they could. Had the Bank of England contracted its London circulation, and raised the rate of interest during that period, money would have become dearer, and the amount of bills discounted for the country banks would have been considerably diminished.

As far as regards the effect upon the foreign exchanges, it is evident that this rediscounting must have an effect precisely the reverse of rendering them unfavourable. By drawing off the surplus capital of London, its employment in foreign loans, and its consequent transmission to other countries is prevented. This capital too being now employed chiefly in manufactures, of which a larger portion is exported, the exchanges are to this extent rendered favourable.

In reply to the charge, that the joint stock banks and the country bankers do not regulate their issues by the foreign exchanges, and by counteracting the efforts of the Bank of England, are often the means of causing the gold to be withdrawn from the country —we may observe

1. That it is not the business of the joint stock banks to regulate the foreign exchanges.

The legislature has made Bank of England notes a legal tender. It is therefore the duty of the joint stock banks to be prepared to give Bank of England notes in exchange for their own; but it is not also their duty to provide gold for those Bank of England notes. It is the duty of the Bank of England to provide gold for their own notes; and if they are not prepared to do this, upon whom but themselves is the blame to fall? The claim that is made upon them to supply gold for exportation, arises from their being the sole bank of issue in London, and from their notes being made a legal tender. If they take to themselves all the advantages of their monopoly, they should put up without murmuring to all its inconveniences. Nobody can demand gold from the Bank of England except as payment of their own notes; and as to pay their notes in gold upon demand, is what they profess to do, it ought not to be regarded as a grievance. The following question was proposed by the committee to the director of a joint stock bank.

" If you saw upon a series of returns from the Bank of England, that the amount of bullion had been gradually lessening, and that there was a drain upon the resources of the Bank of England, do you

conceive that that would be a matter to which would
be your duty to give attention as a practical banker
in the country."

Answer. "We have not the charge of providing
bullion to pay our notes; the charge rests with the
Bank of England to provide bullion."

2. It may be stated, that in many cases the business
of a country banker does not admit of being regulated by the foreign exchanges.

It is desirable that the business of a country bank
should be carried on in a steady and uniform manner.
But this can never be the case if the banker regulates
his advances to his customers by the state of the
foreign exchanges: these are in a state of perpetual
fluctuation. The production and manufacture of commodities intended for domestic consumption, must
proceed. And even the manufacture of those intended
for foreign consumption cannot be *suddenly* arrested
without throwing thousands of persons out of employment. How then can a country bank regulate its advances by the foreign exchanges? What would a
tradesman in a country town say on presenting a
£100 bill for discount to his banker, if he were told—
"Really, I cannot do it. I perceive the foreign exchanges
are unfavorable. I have noticed the price of gold at
Paris and at Hamburgh, I have made my calcula-
tions, and find there is a profit upon the exportation
of gold ; and as the Bank of England has only four
millions in its coffers, I should not like to press
hard upon them. Call upon me again this day week,
and if in the mean time the exchanges become
favorable, I will then discount your bill." The customer might reply, " I do not understand what you
mean about the foreign exchanges; I am a tanner,
and have drawn this bill upon a shoemaker, to whom
I have sold leather. I shall pay the money to a
butcher of whom I have bought hides : he will pay the
notes for rent to his landlord, who will lodge them with
you on his account. If you will not discount my bills
as you have done hitherto, I must restrict my business.

But I cannot see why the quantity of leather in my pits should be regulated by the quantity of gold in the Bank of England."

A banker will notice the foreign exchanges with a view to the profitable employment of his surplus capital. If the exchanges are likely to become unfavorable, he will presume that the rate of interest will advance, and that the price of the public securities will fall, and he will act accordingly. But these operations are performed in London and not in the country. The director of a country joint stock bank stated to the committee, in answer to the inquiry —" Does not the state of the exchanges and the amount of gold in the hands of the Bank of England, affect the country banks of this country?" " I do not think it does in general—I think it only operates with a very few banking companies."

3. It may be replied, that supposing it had been the duty of the joint stock bank to regulate their issues by the state of the exchanges, the returns published in the Gazette are not sufficient for this purpose.

The average amount of the bullion in the Bank of England for the preceding three months is published monthly in the Gazette. From these returns it can easily be seen whether there be a less amount of gold in the bank than there was three months ago, but it cannot be perceived whether the amount is increasing or diminishing at the time of publication. Now it is not the past but the present state of the exchanges that ought to be known, and that is studiously concealed. Besides, it is stated in the bank evidence, that the quantity of gold in the Bank may be diminished by other causes than an unfavorable course of exchange.

The following question was proposed to Mr. Horsley Palmer.

" No. 131.—Does it not occasionally happen, that whilst the par of exchange according to the general estimate of it with another country, France for instance, is considerably in favor of this country, and would therefore indicate a power of importing gold, there is at the same time a demand for gold upon the bank, and an export actually taking place arising from particular circumstances abroad? Certainly."

Another bank director, Mr. William Ward, gave the following evidence.

" 1935.—Does it not often happen, that merchants having large remittances to make abroad, where it is important for them to make them rapidly, and when it is important for them not to shew the nature of their business to all the world by being large takers on the exchange—frequently make their remittances by bullion or by coin of this country, when you could not trace by the rates of exchange that it would precisely answer to do it in that manner?—It is so.

" 1941.—Supposing you had a large sum to remit to Paris, and wanted it there within a short period—supposing you wanted to remit half a million, and you found by the quotation of the exchanges that bills would pay an eighth to a quarter per cent. better than bullion, might it not still be more to your interest to send the bullion in preference to the bills, considering the rapidity with which you can execute your business, considering you run no risk in taking bad bills, and considering that you might before you had executed your operation upon the exchanges by taking bills, have moved the course of exchange more than the difference at which it then stood?—Certainly.

" 1942.—Has not that mode of remittance by coin and by bullion, very much grown into a practice in this country, since the law permitting the free exportation of coin, and since the perfection in the manufacture of the coin?—There is no doubt, that facility of communication has materially increased that description of business; it was a description of business not frequently had recourse to in former periods."

It appears, then, that the diminution of the amount of gold in the bank is no evidence of an unfavourable course of exchange, and consequently, no reason for a contraction of their circulation by the country banks. The committee infer that the joint stock banks have not paid a due attention to these returns; but, in fact, the object of these returns was not to instruct joint stock banks, but to restrain the circulation of the Bank of England. The following is the language of Lord Althorp on the subject.

" Now it was well known that the exchanges were against us, from August, 1830, to February, 1832; during this period, there was a corresponding contraction of the circulation, which at one time fell below its usual amount by £7,000,000. This might have been productive of great pressure, and some distress; but no convulsion similar to that which had been experienced in former times. Now, the publicity to which he alluded, would be a check how the bank acted on this principle; he was aware the directors were not responsible to the public for adopting any course they thought proper in the management of their affairs, but they would still be under the control of public opinion. He would therefore propose, there should be a single bank as at present, but subject to such control as the publicity of their accounts would produce. He proposed that the bank should make a weekly return to the treasury, of the amount of bills and notes in circulation, and also of deposits, and that the average of such issues and deposits, should be published quarterly. Such a publication would be sufficient to shew whether the bank acted on sound principles, and could not be productive of evil consequences."

4. It may also be stated, that the country banks have many checks against over-issue, which do not apply to the Bank of England.

" The amount of notes issued by a bank must be limited by the demand of its customers. No banker is so anxious to put his notes into circulation, that he gives them away. He advances them either by way of loan or discount; and he always believes that the security on which he makes his advances is sufficiently ample. He expects that the money will be repaid with interest. It is true, that like other commercial men, he is sometimes deceived in his customers; and by placing too much confidence in them, he sustains losses. But this is a misfortune against which he is always anxious to guard. The issues of bankers are limited, therefore; on the one hand by the wants of the public, and on the other by the bankers' desire to protect their own interests.

" A further check upon the issues of banks is, that all their notes are payable on demand. Although a banker has the power of issuing his notes to excess, either by advancing them as dead loans or on slender security, yet he has not the power of keeping them out: their remaining in circulation depends not on him, but on the public; and the uncertainty, as to the time of their return for payment, compels him to keep at all times a sufficient stock of money, to meet the most extensive demand that is likely in the ordinary course of business to occur.

" Another check upon an extensive issue of notes, is the system of exchanges that is carried on between the banks. Every banker that issues notes, has an interest in withdrawing from circulation the notes of every other banker, in order to make more room for his own. When a banker receives the notes of another banker, he never reissues them. If the two bankers live in the same place, they meet once or twice a week, as they may find convenient, and exchange their notes. The balance between them, if any, is paid by a draft on London, payable on demand; or, which amounts to the same thing, the London agent of the one party, is directed to pay the amount to the London agent of the other party. If the country banker lives at a distance from the banker whose notes he has received, he sends them to his London agent to present for payment. Hence it is that country notes seldom travel far

from the place of issue ; they are sure to be intercepted by some of
the rival banks ; and in a country where banks are so numerous as in
England, it is obvious that the notes of any individual bank must move
in a very limited circle. If a banker attempts to force out a higher
amount of notes than the wants of this circle require, he will soon find
that the notes will be returned to him by the neighbouring banker, or
else they will speedily find their way for payment to his London agent.

" Another check upon an over issue on the part of the banks is
their practice of allowing interest upon money lodged in their hands.
No man will keep money lying idle in his hands, if he can obtain interest
for it, and have it returned to him upon demand. If a banker attempts
to force out a large number of notes, they will get into the hands of
somebody. And those who do not employ them at their trade will
take them back to the bank and lodge them to their credit, for the purpose of receiving the interest. Thus, if the notes of a banker are put
in motion by the operations of commerce, they are soon intercepted by
rival bankers ; and if they attain a state of rest, they are brought back
and lodged upon interest : so that in either case they are withdrawn
from circulation.

" It cannot be denied that if any bank have the privilege of issuing
notes not convertible into gold, that is, not payable in gold on demand,
the notes may be issued to such an amount as to cause considerable
advance in prices. It is now generally believed that the issues of the
Bank of England during the operation of the Restriction Act, did produce
this effect.

" It may also be admitted, that in a country where there is one chief
bank, possessing an immense capital and unbounded confidence, the
notes of such a bank, even if payable in gold, may be issued to such an
extent as to cause an advance of prices, until an unfavorable course of
the exchange shall cause payment of the notes to be demanded in gold.
For gold will not be demanded until the course of the exchange is so
unfavorable as to cause the exportation of gold to be attended with
profit. Hence the issues of the Bank of England being at present
under no other restraint than liability to pay in gold on demand, may
for a time cause an advance in prices."*

5. The issues of the joint stock banks have not so
great an influence in rendering the exchanges unfavorable as those of the Bank of England.

If a joint stock bank makes an advance of money
to an importer, a large quantity of commodities may
be imported, and this will tend to render the exchanges unfavorable ; but the advance cannot be
made in notes. The importer cannot pay for his
imports in country bank notes ; he will want a bill,
or a credit upon a London banker, in favour of

---

* History and Principles of Banking—Section, Banks of Circulation.

the foreigner of whom he buys his goods.   In either case, the money is paid in London, and no circulation is given to country notes.   If a joint stock bank makes an advance to an exporter, it encourages exportation, and this tends to render the exchanges favorable. Here the advance may be made in notes.   The exporter takes these notes, and purchases of the producer, or the manufacturer the commodities he exports.   Thus it appears that the issues of notes by country banks have a tendency to render the exchanges favorable, and that those advances that tend to render the exchanges unfavorable, cannot be made by notes, but must be made, if made at all, out of real capital.   On this subject I shall quote part of a memorial presented in 1833, by the country bankers to Earl Grey and Lord Althorp.

" Your memorialists are prepared to prove that the issues of country bankers have less tendency to promote fluctuations in the country than those of the Bank of England, and that their efforts in throwing the exchanges against the country is comparatively insignificant.   It is indisputable that adverse exchanges that endanger the bank always succeed great importations of foreign produce, and that they never can be effected by large exportations of domestic productions.   Now it is notorious that the circulation of country bankers acts almost exclusively in promoting these productions; and that when it is in an extended state, the direct and proper influence even of an alleged excess of that circulation would be to provide the means of paying for the exportations of foreign produce, without causing so great an export of gold as to derange and endanger the monetary system of the country.   All experience shews that great fluctuations have originated in the speculations of influential merchants, and never originated in the channels to which the issues of the country bankers are confined: their source is in great mercantile cities, and they are promoted by the issues of the bank of England."

These observations are equally applicable to the issues of joint stock banks, most of which are situated either in agricultural districts or in manufacturing towns.   None of them issue notes either in London or Liverpool.

6. In many cases the joint stock banks cannot avoid putting into circulation an increased amount of their notes.

When the trade of the country requires an increased

amount of currency, notes will be withdrawn from the banks in repayment of deposits. On this subject I quote from the evidence delivered by the late T. Kinnear, Esq. before the committee of the House of Lords, in 1826.

" An increased trade which regards an increased circulation to carry it on, will cause a demand for an addition to the circulating medium of any country, and if the country possess the means of answering, it will be answered. If a reverse of circumstances discredit the trade, and a smaller medium be in consequence sufficient, the public will then return that part of the medium which is not required to the sources from which it had been derived. The bank cannot prevent the public from taking their share in the regulation of this part of its issues. To illustrate this by what happened last year—a restless and speculative spirit induced many persons who had not been accustomed to trade in any shape to employ themselves by engaging in the purchase and sale of stocks and property of various descriptions. This led to increased demand, not so much for the loan of capital, or for discounts, as for an increased circulating medium which the banks were made sensible of by increased drafts upon them by their creditors, and by the circumstance that the notes which they issued did not return upon them as usual ; in short, by the increased demand for bank notes, and the increase of their circulation. When time and experience had shewn, as they soon did to those traders and speculators, the unprofitable and injudicious conduct into which they had plunged, they gradually withdrew from those pursuits ; part of the circulating medium became in consequence useless, and immediately began ·to be returned by the public to the banks. Their circulation has probably now returned to what is necessary for the fair and legitimate industry and trade of the country. In this fluctuation the banks were passive ; they paid, as a matter of course, the demands upon them by their creditors, and their notes, contrary to the usual routine, did not return for payment for a great many months, during which time the banks continued ready to restore them. Against this sort of over circulation the exchanges offer no remedy, although they palliate the evil, nor could any human device afford a remedy, for the cause of it was a moral one, and operated in the minds of the public. Their ignorance, perhaps folly, induced them to enter upon transactions, to carry on which they found it necessary to withdraw part of their capital from the banks and add it to the circulating medium'; and had that circulating medium been increased by them to a much greater extent than it was, the banks could do no more than refrain from encouraging the evil, they could not arrest it.''

Confirmatory of the above sentiments are the following statements:

The average circulation of all the banks in Scotland in 1823, 1824, and 1825, was as follows:—

1823—£3,087,624   1824—£3,428,851   1825—£4,058,655

The average circulation of the Bank of Ireland:—

1823—£5,117,389   1824—£5,622,845   1825—£6,411,348

The average circulation of all the banks in Ireland :—

1823—£6,023,847   1824—£6,543,123   1825—£7,604,234

" All speculation by increasing the number and amount of commercial transactions, puts into motion a greater quantity of money. This money is supplied by the bankers either in the way of repayment of deposits, or of discounting of bills or of loans. Now as increased issues on the part of the banks are almost simultaneous with a spirit of speculation, it has been inferred that the issues of the notes have excited the spirit of speculation, whereas it has been the spirit of speculation that has called out the notes. In the years 1824 and 1825, as the speculations increased the issues of notes increased ; and when the speculations were over the notes returned. This was the case not merely in England, but also in Scotland, though none of the Scotch banks sustained the least diminution of public confidence."*

7. It may also be stated that the joint stock banks cannot so suddenly reduce their circulation as the Bank of England.

Those banks that issue notes are also like the Bank of England, banks of deposit, and banks of discount.

As far as regards the operation on their deposit accounts, the joint stock banks have no control over the circulation. The amount of notes that are issued will depend upon the amount of checks that are presented for payment; and when the notes are put into circulation, the banks have no means of withdrawing them. When they will come back, depends not upon the banks but upon the public.

As banks of discount they may cease to issue, but they cannot recall the notes they have issued. When the bills they have discounted become due, they may not be paid in the notes of the bank that discounted them. Hence the decline of the amount of notes on circulation must be gradual, and depends always upon the will of the public.

As a bank of deposit the Bank of England has no more control over the amount of its notes in circula-

---

* History and Principles of Banking—Section on Banks of Circulation.

K

tion than a joint stock bank. As a bank of discount it may cease to issue, but all the bills when due will be paid in Bank of England notes, by which the amount in circulation will be reduced.

But the Bank of England has other means by which it can reduce its circulation more rapidly. It can sell government stock or exchequer bills. It will be paid for these in its own notes, which will thus be withdrawn from circulation. If a joint stock bank should sell stock or exchequer bills, it would not be paid in its own notes, but in those of the Bank of England. Hence no reduction would take place in its own circulation. It is not therefore quite fair to blame the joint stock banks for not reducing their circulation as rapidly as the Bank of England, when they have not the power so to do.

8. But even could it be proved that the joint stock banks had issued an excessive amount of their notes, it might then become a matter of inquiry whether that excess could counteract any measures adopted by the Bank of England with a view to the state of the foreign exchanges.

The bank can control the foreign exchanges only through the means of its own circulation. Let us suppose that the circulation of the country is in excess, and that under these circumstances the Bank of England contracts her issues. The immediate effect in London will be, that the interest of money will advance, money will become scarce, traders will be less disposed to purchase, and more disposed to sell, and consequently the price of commodities will fall. Now this will produce an effect upon the country circulation in two ways; first, through the means of trade; and secondly, through the direct monetary transactions.

With regard to trade we shall simplify the illustration by taking an individual case. A wholesale grocer, who has travellers in every part of the kingdom collecting money and receiving orders, will write them to avoid taking bills as heretofore, at two or three months date, and to allow a liberal discount for cash. Now, money being abundant, the country shop-keepers will be glad to take the discount and pay cash. Instead of bills the travellers will get country notes, which they will take to the banks for payment, or transmit to London for presenting to the London agents. Here the country circulation is reduced by the withdrawal of notes in circulation.

This is the case of a house that sells to the country. Now let us take the case of a house that buys from the country. A wholesale ironmonger has been in the habit of receiving weekly a quantity of goods from Sheffield, against which he had accepted a bill : the Sheffield manufacturer had taken this bill to the bank to be discounted, and had put into circulation the notes of the Sheffield bank to that amount; but in consequence of the contraction of the notes of the Bank of En-gland, the wholesale ironmonger discontinues his orders, believing that money will become scarce, and that prices will fall. The Sheffield manufacturer having no orders, sends no goods, and draws no bills, and consequently puts no notes into circulation. Here the country circulation is diminished by a diminution of the issues; hence we perceive that the operations of both the export and import trade of London with the country have a necessary effect of reducing the cur-rency in the country to a level with that of London.

But this effect will be still more rapidly produced by direct monetary transactions.

The country banks that rediscounted their bills in London, finding that their bills are rediscounted with difficulty, and only at an advanced rate of interest, will also reduce their discounts in the country, and hence their issues will be diminished. They will also call up any loans they may have advanced, and these will be paid to them in their own notes, or in the notes of the neighbouring banks, and hence the country circulation will be reduced by a withdrawal of those in circulation. Parties too that have money will send it to London for employment, as the high rate of interest, and probable fall in the public securities, will offer profitable means of investment, and this will draw off a further portion of the country circulation. These are some of the ways in which a contraction of the London currency will rapidly and necessarily contract the country circulation.

If indeed it be admitted that a variation in the dearness or cheapness of money will cause it to pass from London to all parts of the world, it seems hardly necessary to prove that the same variation will cause it to pass from the country parts of England to London. If then, the Bank of England has the power of reducing the country circulation, how can the country banks render the exchanges unfavourable, in opposition to the exertions of the Bank of England?

But it may be still further a matter of inquiry, whether the Bank of England ought to place herself in a situation that shall render necessary the adoption of any measures, with a view to the regulation of the foreign exchanges; whether a national bank ought not, like other banks, to keep funds sufficiently ample to meet her engagements; and whether the foreign exchanges ought not to be regulated by the legitimate operations of commerce, and not by operations on the currency. A bank that has the control of the foreign exchanges has an interest opposed to the interest of the community. It is the interest of the community that the national bank should always hold an amount of treasure adequate to meet all the demands that may come upon it. It is the interest of the bank to hold as little treasure as possible, to employ its funds in securities, upon which she gains interest; and then if the demands should exceed her means, to avoid stopping payment by a sudden operation on the currency that may involve the nation in distress. The notion of regulating the currency is peculiar to England. Who regulates the currency of Scotland or America? A short time ago we had institutions for regulating the price of bread, the wages of labour, and the import and export of a variety of commodities. Now it is found that these things can regulate themselves. Such probably will be the case with the currency. After a few more years have elapsed, after some thousands of fortunes have been destroyed, and some millions of families ruined, we shall then possibly discover that the amount of the currency, the prices of commodities, and the course of the foreign exchanges would have gone on better without our interference.

With regard to the tables given by the committee, we may observe,

1. That the table referring to the country circuculation, states the quarterly averages, but the table referring to the Bank of England merely states the circulation, &c. on those days that are there mentioned. To form a proper comparison, the two tables should refer to the same periods. The following table is formed entirely upon the quarterly averages.

A table of the London and branch circulation of the Bank of England, and the circulation of the private and joint stock banks:—

Date.	London Circulation.	Branch Circulation	Total Bank of E. circulation.	Private Banks.	Joint Stock Banks.	Total Country Circulation.
Dec. 1833...	15,000,000	3,200,000	18,200,000	8,836,803	1,315,301	10,152,104
April, 1834 .	15,800,000	3,200,000	19,000,000	8,733,400	1,458,427	10,191,827
July	15,700,000	3,200,000	18,900,000	8,875,795	1,642,887	10,518,682
Sept.	15,800,000	3,300,000	19,100,000	8,370,423	1,783,689	10,154,112
Dec.	14,800,000	3,300,000	18,100,000	8,537,655	2,122,173	10,659,828
March, 1835	15,200,000	3,300,000	18,500,000	8,231,206	2,188,954	10,420,160
June	15,000,000	3,300,000	13,300,000	8,455,114	2,484,687	10,939,801
Sept.	14,900,000	3,300,000	18,200,000	7,912,587	2,508,036	10,420,623
Dec.	13,800,000	3,400,000	17,200,000	8,334,863	2,799,551	11,134,414
March, 1836	14,400,000	3,600,000	18,000,000	8,353,894	3,094,025	11,447,919
June	14,200,000	3,700,000	17,900,000	8,614,132	3,568,064	12,202,196
Sept.	14,500,000	3,600,000	18,100,000	7,764,824	3,969,121	11,733,945
Dec.	13,500,000	3,800,000	17,300,000	7,753,500	4,258,197	12,011,697

2. The daily amounts of the circulation present no certain means of forming a comparison. Thus, if we wish to prove that the Bank of England had diminished its circulation, we might compare March 1834, with June, 1836, and say, that the circulation had considerably decreased. On the other hand, if we wished to shew that the circulation had increased, we might take the two points of comparison three months farther back, and shew that between December 1833, and March 1836, the circulation had considerably advanced.

3. In noticing the London circulation of the Bank

of England, we shall find that the first and third
quarters in the year are usually higher than the other
quarters. The dividends payable in January and
July are to a larger amount than those paid in April
and October. Hence the quarters that take in January and July have a higher circulation of notes.
If therefore we wish to mark the increase or decrease
of notes in circulation, we must not compare the
highest quarter in one year with the lowest quarter in
a subsequent year, but compare the correspondent
quarters. Thus we find the difference between December 1835 and December 1836, there is a diminution of £300,000.

4. It will be seen that the branch circulation of the
Bank of England does not fluctuate so much quarterly
as the circulation of London. There seems to have
been a steady increase. The increase between December 1835 and December 1836, is £400,000. From
the evenness in the amount of the branch circulation,
I should infer that the branches have very little business in the way of current accounts.

5. It will be perceived that the circulation of the
joint stock banks has considerably increased, while
that of the private banks has diminished. This
arises, in the first place, from a number of private
banks having merged in joint stock banks;* and
secondly, from a transfer of accounts from private
banks to joint stock banks. Had we returns of the
circulation of those private banks which are not
exposed to the competition of joint stock banks, those
for instance within sixty-five miles of London, we
should probably find that these banks had increased
their circulation, and that the total diminution had
fallen upon those private banks that are beyond the
sixty-five miles.

In judging of the effects produced upon the foreign
exchanges, we must take the whole amount of the
country circulation; for the circulation of the joint
stock banks could not have produced any effects, if
it merely filled up the void occasioned by the with-

* See a list of these in the Appendix.

drawal of the private circulation. Nor is it fair to consider the increase in the whole amount of the circulation, as produced solely by the increased issue of the joint stock banks. The circulation of the joint stock banks is about one-third of the whole circulation, and consequently they are chargeable only with one-third of the excess.

7. Every variation in the amount of notes in circulation of the Bank of England, must be produced either by the action of the public, or the action of the bank. The public act upon the circulation through the deposits and the bullion. If I take £10,000 in bank notes, and lodge them as a deposit in the bank, I diminish the circulation £10,000, and increase the deposit by the same amount. And if I withdraw £10,000 from the deposit, I diminish the deposits and increase the circulation. So if I demand gold for notes to the extent of £10,000, I diminish the stock of gold in the bank, and diminish the circulation. If I take gold to the bank, I increase both the stock of gold and the circulation. The action of the bank is indicated by the change in the amount of securities. But did we not know the amount of the securities, we might ascertain the action of the bank by calculating the results of the action of the public.

The circulation of the Bank of England

28th December, 1833, was	£17,469,000
25th June, 1836	17,184,000
Showing a diminution of	£285,000

Now we may easily ascertain whether the diminution was produced by the action of the public, or that of the bank. Thus—

Circulation, 28th December, 1833	£17,469,000
Diminished by an increase of deposits.........	570,000
	16,899,000
Diminished by a diminution of bullion...	3,332,000
Amount by the action of the public	13,567,000
Increase by the action of the bank	3,617,000
	£17,184,000

8. The increase of the circulation by the action of the bank is denoted by the increase of the securities. The only way the bank can affect the circulation, is by increasing or diminishing the securities. If the bank buy exchequer bills, or discount bills of exchange, she increases the circulation and also the securities. If she sells exchequer bills, she diminishes the circulation, and also the securities. It will be seen that from December 1833, to June 1836, the securities of the bank were increased £4,271,000. Now it may be observed, that the increase of the country circulation from £10,152,104 to £12,202,196, may not have been by any voluntary action on the part of the banks; it may have been by the withdrawal of deposits. But the increase of the Bank of England circulation must have been occasioned by a voluntary action. These tables therefore, do not seem to present us with sufficient ground for holding up the Bank of England as a model to the country banks, for making exertions to limit the amount of paper in circulation.

THE BRANCHES OF THE BANK OF ENGLAND.

The Bank of England first established branches in 1826. The object was to improve the country circulation by operating as a check upon the private banks. The circulation of all the branches in 1831 was £2,372,000. It has since increased, as will be perceived by the table to £3,800,000. In 1832, Mr. Horsley Palmer was asked—

" Have the bank taken any measures, and what measures, for extending the circulation of bank notes through their branch banks?

" The measures they have taken have been permitting individuals of supposed credit to open discount accounts with the branch banks; they have also afforded every facility to the transmission of money from London to the country, through the branch banks; and to those bankers who have proposed (for the bank have made no proposition themselves to the bankers) to withdraw their circulation, the bank have given the same amount of circulation in coin and bank notes, that they previously stated to possess in their own notes, at three per cent. per annum upon approved bills of exchange; those are the three sources."

Mr. Horsley Palmer has stated in his recent publication, that the late increase in the branch circulation has arisen from new contracts of this kind. It is no doubt an advantage to a country bank to be able to re-discount its bills at three per cent. instead of five— to re-discount at home, instead of sending to London— and to re-discount without depending on the fluctuating supplies of the London money market. On the other hand, as the country bank must give up its circulation, the arrangement is not convenient for those banks that have many branches, or which are situated at a distance from a branch of the Bank of England.

Upon public grounds the arrangements made between the branches of the Bank of England and the joint stock banks, appear liable to the following objections:—

First, that they tend to promote a spirit of speculation, by increasing the amount of the currency. The amount of re-discounts granted to several of these banks, is much larger than any amount of notes they could maintain in circulation. And even supposing the amount of discount were limited to the amount of the circulation, yet as the country bank is relieved from the necessity of keeping a reserve of cash to meet the notes daily presented for payment, the currency will be increased to the amount of that reserve. The issues of the Bank too being made in Bank of England notes, they are not withdrawn from circulation by the exchanges between the local banks. Secondly; they promote speculation by reducing the rate of interest. The bank that can obtain money at three per cent. can discount for its customers at a less rate than those that have to pay four or five per cent. This will attract the customers of the other banks; and these banks, unwilling to lose their

customers, will be compelled to extend their accommodation, and at a lower rate of interest. Thirdly ;
this reduction of the rate of interest is not confined
to the country districts; but also affects the market
rate of discount in London, in consequence of the
demand for money being proportionably reduced.
Fourthly; the evil effects of this system appear to
be shown by the fact, that in the beginning of the
year 1836, the chief speculations did not originate in
London, but in Manchester and Liverpool, the places
where the Bank of England made the largest advances
at the lowest rate of interest. The subject was noticed
by two witnesses examined by the Parliamentary Committee last year.

MR. VINCENT STUCKEY.

" Have you understood that the Bank of England has advanced to
joint stock banks money at three per cent. to a considerable extent ?—
I have.

" Do you consider that, in reference to the monetary transactions of
the country, a prudent transaction ?—I take the liberty of saying, I do
not think it is ; and as a proprietor of the bank stock, I have so stated
to some of the directors.

" Is not that a measure very stimulating to imprudent speculation ?—I
think so, but I wish to give my opinion on this point with considerable
doubt, as the directors of the Bank of England have much better
opportunities of judging than I can have.

" If the money be advanced at three per cent. to render it a profitable transaction, some interest must be made of this money in their
hands, which could be created only by cash speculation ?—We have
had nothing of this kind in the West of England; but it was stated in
a public discussion by a gentleman from the North, that if there was
any mischief likely to result from the joint stock banks, it might arise
from those banks which had borrowed from the Bank of England, and
having their cash at less than the market rate of interest, they had
been induced to lend it again improperly in Lancashire.

" In your opinion is as much danger to be apprehended from such
advances at three per cent. on the part of the Bank of England as from
over-issues of joint stock banks ?—Yes, perhaps some banks do issue
bank paper improvidentially, but they are kept in check by being liable
to pay their cash notes on demand in gold."

MR. W. G. CASSELLES.

" What, in your opinion, is the effect of that accommodation afforded
by the Bank of England ? what effect has it upon the operations of
the banks to which it is granted ?—It facilitates their operations, and
enables them to discount more paper than they otherwise would be
enabled to do.

" Does it give them a confidence in affording accommodation to their customers, which in your opinion they would not with their own circulation of notes?—Undoubtedly it does; I should think, if a larger quantity of paper were presented to that bank which has a constant discount account with the Bank of England, they would be encouraged to discount a larger amount, because they know that by going to the Bank of England, and giving in those bills again, under their agreement with them, they will be pretty certain of their being discounted by the Bank of England; the other banks, which have not an account with the Bank of England, must make their discounts in proportion to their means.

" Is it, as far as your experience goes, a facility which has tended considerably to increase the amount of accommodation given in the town of Manchester?—I understand it has increased very much the business of the Manchester and Liverpool district bank, which is the only one I know of at present. Of the banks established two or three months ago, I do not know any thing ; but of the four banks established previously to the commencement of this year, I think it has increased the business of that particular bank, that they have continued their intercourse with the Bank of England.

" By enabling them to discount freely, does it force upon other banks, not having the same engagement with the Bank of England, the necessity of more freely supplying their customers ?—I think it does in this way, that where customers are liberally supplied at one bank, those in the same line of business with them, and possessing equal means, and whose business could be done with equal safety, say, " Why, cannot we have our business done in the same way ? it is very strange that you should pinch us." And I think it is their interest to increase as far as they safely can ; therefore it has an effect upon the whole.

" Therefore that must tend to foster speculation to the extent to which such accommodation is increased ?—I should be sorry to say it fostered speculation. I consider a circulation, founded on the trade of that part of the country, to be a circulation perfectly safe, and I do not think they have gone further than prudence justified.

" In whatever degree the accommodation may tend to extend the disposition to trade to that extent, the accommodation afforded by the Bank of England has had its effect ?—It has rendered it more easy.

" In your opinion, has it any effect on the London market for interest?—I think it has a little effect upon it.

" In what way has it that effect?—If all the four banks of Manchester, for instance, had no account whatever with the Bank of England, for any thing that they rediscount, they must depend upon the floating capital of the country, which generally centres in London ; any thing done in the country bears a small proportion to that done in London. I think there is generally a large amount of floating capital required to be vested for a temporary purpose, or for a certain period. Banks in the country send their bills to their broker and agent in London to rediscount; if four of them were bringing all their bills to bear upon the floating capital, that would make a very great demand upon it ; if that was confined to three-fourths of that demand, the floating capital will not be affected to so great an extent as it otherwise would be. In that way, perhaps, if a fourth part of the whole demand for rediscount be transacted by the Bank of England, that takes away from the demand upon the floating capital, and I think those other three banks will obtain their discounts at a cheaper rate than if all four were competitors for it.

"Do you know the extent to which the Manchester and Liverpool district bank has the power of discounting with the Bank of England?— I have heard it is to the extent of £400,000 or £500,000, constantly running; I do not give that as a matter of fact I am acquainted with, but I have no reason to believe it is incorrectly given.

"Supposing it be, for illustration, £500,000, the effect is, it gives greater accommodation to the business of the bank having that accommodation?—Certainly.

"It has a tendency to compel other banks also more freely to accommodate their customers? They would not do it except they complain of it, but it is an inducement.

"It also, by the assistance it affords to the bank having that account with the Bank of England, has a tendency to lower the general rate of interest?—I think so; that must follow.

"Do you mean that it lowers the market rate of interest in London or Manchester?—In London.

"Do you mean that many bills being sent from Manchester to London for discount, will lower the rate of interest in London?—Bills being sent from Manchester to London for discount, will increase the rate of interest; but the Bank of England giving a greater facility, and preventing one-fourth part of the bills coming to London, prevents the interest on money being so high in London."

If it be desirable to increase the efficiency of the "measures adopted by the Bank of England, with a view to the state of foreign exchanges, and of the consequent demand for bullion," the bank should, first, discontinue their branches; and secondly, cease to act as a bank of private deposit in London. If the branches were replaced by independent chartered banks, their circulation would be controlled by the daily exchanges with the neighbouring banks. The Bank of England would be more watchful of the country circulation, and be better able to judge when it was excessive; whereas now she feels no alarm at the extent to which the country circulation is increased, provided that increase consists of her own notes: and if the bank ceased to act as a bank of private deposit in London, she would have a more effective command of the exchanges. At present, if she makes money scarce, merchants and others who have accounts at the bank draw out their deposits; some to employ them in their business, others to lend them at interest; thus more notes are put into circulation, and the bank must make a farther contraction to counteract this operation. If the bank did not act as a bank of private deposit, a demand for gold would necessarily contract her circulation to the extent of the gold withdrawn. If these deposits were in the hands of the London bankers, they would be more effectively employed in assisting trade and commerce in seasons of pressure. It may be said that the bank employs these deposits—so she may, but it is not in small advances to individual traders, but in large masses on the money market. As to their influence in fertilizing commerce there is as much difference between these two ways of employing money, as there is between a shower of rain and a water-spout.

SECTION VI.

AN INQUIRY INTO THE CAUSES OF THE RECENT PRESSURE ON THE MONEY MARKET.

As the recent pressure for money has extended to America, an inquiry into the causes to which it may be ascribed, is not unsuitable to an essay on American Banking.

In the beginning of last year there was no appearance of distress; but on the contrary, every symptom of prosperity, attended by its usual concomitant—a readiness to engage in speculative undertakings.

The following description of this period is taken from the speech of Mr. Clay, on introducing his motion respecting Joint Stock Banks, May 12, 1836.

" To what extent the operations of the joint stock banks may have contributed to create the present state of excitement in the commercial world, must, of course, be mere matter of conjecture. That they have

142 THE HISTORY OF

had some considerable influence is probable, from the fact that the excitement and rage for speculation is greatest in those parts of the kingdom, where the operations of those establishments have been most active. London has been comparatively unmoved, but Liverpool and Manchester have witnessed a mushroom growth of schemes not exceeded by the memorable year 1825. I hold in my hand a list of seventy contemplated companies for every species of undertaking, which have appeared in the Liverpool and Manchester papers within the last three months. This list was made a fortnight or three weeks since, and might probably now be considerably extended. It is impossible also, I think, not to suspect that the facility of credit and consequent encouragement to speculation to which I have alluded, cannot have been without its effect in producing the great increase of price in almost all the chief articles of consumption and raw materials of our manufactures. That increase has been enormous—not less than from twenty to fifty, and even one hundred per cent., in many of the chief articles of produce, of consumption, and materials of our manufactures. I am quite aware that there is every indication of this advance of price being sound; that it has arisen from consumption outrunning supply; and that our manufacturers are working on orders rather than speculation. But I cannot forget that the excitement of 1825 commenced legitimately—that the rise of prices will infallibly check consumption, whilst it stimulates supply ; and when we look at the amount of our paper currency resting at this moment on the somewhat narrow metallic basis of the bullion and specie in the vaults of the Bank of England, it is impossible not to feel apprehension, or at least the propriety of caution and forethought.

" The circulation of the Bank of England, as appeared by the last average in *The Gazette*, is—

Circulation of the bank	£18,063,000
Deposits with ditto	14,751,000
	32,814,100
Private and joint stock banks	11,447,919
	44,261,919
Probable amount of Scotch and Irish currency .	10,000,000
	54,261,919

Specie and bullion at the bank. . . £7,801,000 ―――――――

" It is right that I should say, I cannot approve of the course taken by the Bank of England in this matter. The directors of that establishment—acting, I doubt not, with the most conscientious desire to protect the interests of the community,—have not taken, in my opinion, the wisest course to effect that object. With a desire to discourage the circulation of the notes of joint stock banks, they afford facilities, as I have said, to such as issue Bank of England notes. I cannot think that this mode of forcing issues is a legitimate proceeding on the part of that corporation, combining, as it evidently does combine, an increase of the currency which may not be required, with a temptation to the joint stock banks thus supplied with its notes, to afford indiscreet accommodation.

These appearances continued with little alteration until the month of July, when the Bank of England raised the rate of discount to four and a half per cent. It then became known that there had been a demand upon the bank for gold from the preceding April, and this measure was adopted by the bank as a means of rendering the foreign exchanges more favourable. This being found ineffectual, the bank in September raised the rate of discount to five per cent. Besides raising the rate of interest, the bank adopted other measures of increasing the value of money. A large amount of American bills upon first-rate houses had been offered for discount and rejected. A high degree of alarm was immediately spread throughout the community. The dread of a panic similar to that of 1825 almost universally prevailed. Those who had money were unwilling to part with it—trade became suddenly stagnant—the prices of all commodities fell considerably, and numbers of commercial houses, chiefly of the second class, suspended payment. Many railway and other projects now fell into oblivion.

The alarm that existed was kept up by the monthly accounts of the bullion in the Bank of England. The public returns shewed a gradual decline from April, 1836, to February, 1837. It was therefore supposed, that the Bank of England would be under the necessity, for her own safety, of still further contracting her issues, and thus increasing the existing pressure. This apprehension caused all persons who had money, to retain it in their possession, and bankers and others withheld accommodation they would otherwise have been disposed to grant.

This state of alarm was considerably augmented by the publication of the Report of the Secret Committee of the House of Commons upon Joint Stock Banks. This committee had been appointed, on the motion of Mr. Clay, the Member for the Tower

Hamlets, whose speech on the occasion might be termed a bill of indictment. The joint stock banks had rapidly increased; they had issued small shares; they had large nominal capitals; they had circulated an excessive amount of notes; they had promoted speculation. These were the charges brought against them; and they had greater weight from being advanced by a member who was known to be friendly to joint stock banking. The report of the committee appeared to sustain all Mr. Clay's accusations. This report was highly creditable to the talents and industry of the committee, but marked by a decided hostility of tone. While it enumerated all the actual or possible imperfections of the joint stock banks, it ascribed to them scarcely a single excellence. At the same time, the committee deferred to the succeeding session, the proposal of any measures for their improvement; thus the public were led to suppose, that in the following session some astringent measures would be adopted with reference to joint stock banks, but what they would be none could conjecture.

Had the report appeared at any other period it might possibly have done good; but as its appearance was contemporaneous with a pressure on the money market, and a high state of alarm, it unquestionably tended to weaken public confidence, at a time when it required to be strengthened. Persons who were unfriendly to joint stock banks, seized the opportunity of dispraising them, and believed or pretended to believe that the banks were unsound, and would certainly stop payment. Others, who were friendly, were apprehensive that the banks being still in their infancy, would be found too weak to withstand the storm now raised against them. But though this alarm began with respect to joint stock banks, it did not end there. It was soon foreseen that if a few joint stock banks were to stop payment, the private banks in their neighbourhood would be put to a severe trial; and if the banks should even be compelled to withhold their usual advances to their customers, the credit of individuals must suffer. Hence the private bankers and the merchants, as well as the joint stock banks, made preparations to meet any event that might occur, and by thus increasing the pressure on the London money market, occasioned still farther apprehensions.

The alarm was augmented by the stoppage of the Agricultural and Commercial Bank of Ireland, in the month of November, and the demand for gold which that stoppage occasioned in Ireland. The joint stock banks of England now became subject to increased suspicion; the accommodation they had been accustomed to obtain by the re-discount of their bills in the London market was considerably restricted; and in the beginning of December, the Northern and Central Bank at Manchester, a bank having a paid-up capital of £800,000, with above 1,200 partners, and forty branches, applied for assistance to the Bank of England. This was afforded upon condition, in the first instance, that they should wind up all their branches except that at Liverpool; and afterwards further assistance was granted, upon condition they should discontinue business after February, 1837. Their life was saved, on condition they should commit suicide. At the commencement of the present year the old and respectable London banking-house of Messrs. Esdaile and Co. received assistance upon similar terms.

The pressure which existed in England rapidly extended to America. A large amount of American securities, consisting chiefly of bonds of the respective States, had been remitted to the agency houses in England. This circumstance, in connection with the exportation of gold to America, attracted the notice of the Bank of England. The following letter, written by a respectable London house, was published in the American newspapers:

" LONDON, AUGUST 20, 1836.
" DEAR SIR,
" We were informed to-day, by an active intelligent director of the Bank of England, that more British capital has been ab-

sorbed by American and Continental houses than can be spared, without injury to the commercial and manufacturing interests of this country ; that the directors of the bank have decided, that they will take measures to check the sale of such securities, by refusing to discount bills of exchange drawn in those countries on houses here, however high may be their standing or credit.

"This decision places all houses in jeopardy that do business with American dealers in British merchandise, because remittances are usually made in payment for such merchandise in bills of exchange on such houses; and if the decision referred to is rigidly enforced, such remittances will be unavailable till due. Under these circumstances, we deem it prudent to state, that we do not feel bound to continue our usual facilities to dealers in British merchandise, and that we reserve to ourselves the right of regulating them according to existing circumstances. We hope this decision will not be rigidly enforced ; and, if not, that we shall be able to act with more liberality than we now think probable. It is desirable that our correspondents should be made acquainted with this state of things, that they might be governed by it in making out orders for merchandise the ensuing season, which we hope will be unusually small."

The Bank of England did carry into effect the measure intimated in the above letter. A large amount of bills drawn from America upon first-rate London houses was rejected. In America the pressure became severe—money was wanted to remit to England to meet the drafts that had been drawn upon England, either upon credit or against securities that could not now be sold. The rate of discount at New York rose to two, and even to three per cent. per month.

From the pressure upon the money market, and from the great fall in the price of American produce, the cotton and other commodities sent from America to meet drafts upon the English agents, could not be sold except at a ruinous loss. And other remittances not having arrived, several houses in the American trade, who were said to have given extensive credits to parties in America, applied for assistance to the Bank of England.

It is unquestionably a most important inquiry—to what cause we ought to attribute this severe pressure— a pressure by which thousands have been ruined, and trade and commerce and manufactures greatly depressed. Several publications upon the subject have appeared, written chiefly by practical men of high standing in the monied and commercial circles, and whose opinions, on account of the station and talents of the writers, are worthy of every consideration. The principal are the following :—

1. A Letter to the Right Honourable Lord Viscount Melbourne, on the Causes of the recent Derangement in the Money Market, and on Bank Reform. By R. Torrens, Esq. F.R.S.

2. A Defence of the Joint Stock Banks, an Examination of the Causes of the present Monetary difficulties, and Hints for the future management of the Circulation. By David Salomons, Esq.

3. The Causes and Consequences of the Pressure upon the Money Market, with a Statement of the Action of the Bank of England, from 1st October, 1833, to the 27th Dec. 1836. By J. Horsley Palmer, Esq.

4. Reflections suggested by a perusal of Mr. J. Horsley Palmer's Pamphlet, on the Causes and Consequences of the Pressure on the Money Market. By Samuel Jones Loyd.

5. Observations on the recent Pamphlet of J. Horsley Palmer, Esq. on the Causes and Consequences of the Pressure on the Money Market, &c. By Samson Ricardo, Esq.

6. The Cause of the present Money Crisis explained, in answer to the Pamphlet of Mr. J. Horsley Palmer, and a remedy pointed out. By W. Bennison.

7. Reply to the Reflections, &c. &c. of Mr. Samuel Jones Loyd, on the Pamphlet, entitled, " Causes and Consequences of the Pressure upon the Money Market." By J. Horsley Palmer.

The recent pressure upon the money market has been assigned by the above writers to some one or more of the following causes.

First. It has been ascribed to the excessive issue of notes by the joint stock banks. This opinion is stated by Mr. Horsley Palmer.

" Immediately subsequent to the panic of 1825, which affected almost every banking establishment in London as well as the country, the Government of that day was unfortunately induced to call upon the Bank of England to relinquish, beyond sixty-five miles from London, its exclusive privilege as to the number of partners authorized by law to be associated for the formation of banks, in order to enable ministers to frame regulations authorizing the establishment of joint stock banks throughout all parts of the country beyond the limit above specified, thereby virtually declaring that the existing private banks were unworthy of credit. The term " unfortunate" is used ; for perhaps there never was a measure more uncalled for by the wants of the community. The existing system was intimately connected with the prosperity of the country, and was good in all its parts, excepting the power of issuing paper-money ad libitum. The change in question laid the foundation of a new system to be brought into the field by competition in the issue of paper-money, the most prejudicial means that could be devised.   A reluctant concession was obtained from the bank ; and in order to place the whole subject before the public, the correspondence which then took place between the government and the bank is annexed to the present statement.   Very little progress was made in the formation of those projected institutions prior to the year 1830, when a further application was made by government to the bank for concessions intended to have formed part of the conditions at that time for the renewal of the charter.   The opinion of the bank remained unchanged as to the danger to be apprehended from the extension of the system of joint stock banks, and this opinion was pressed upon the government at that period.   The ministry under the Duke of Wellington having soon after been dissolved, no further discussion of the subject took place until the negotiation under the government of Earl Grey, which terminated in the renewal of the charter of the bank in 1833. Pending the discussions which then took place the strongest representations were verbally made to Earl Spencer (then Chancellor of the Exchequer), of the necessity of placing joint stock banks of issue under some regulations to be proposed by his majesty's government, which might tend to a prevention of excess in their issues of paper-money.   It is well known that that noble lord was desirous of submitting such regulations for the consideration of parliament ; but these he was prevented from carrying into effect.   The system of joint stock banking was further facilitated by permitting the formation of direct agencies in London ; and a declaratory clause was inserted in the Bank Charter Act authorizing the establishment of those bodies in the metropolis.   It is conceived that the bank had the more reason to complain of the ministers' proceeding upon that occasion, it having been distinctly understood during the negotiation, that the law affecting the formation of banks within sixty-five miles of London should remain untouched, and upon the faith of that understanding Earl Spencer undertook to bring the bill into the House of Commons for the renewal of the charter of the bank.

   " Having thus briefly stated the proceedings which have occurred in the establishment of joint stock banks prior to the renewal of the charter of the Bank of England, it may, perhaps, be proper to state the periods of the increase of those of issue from the year 1826; they are as follow, taken from returns furnished by the stamp office.

IN ENGLAND AND WALES.

1826,	were	established -	-	-	-	- 3
1827,	,,	-	-	-	-	- 4
1828,	,,	-	-	-	-	- nil
1829,	,,	-	-	-	-	- 7
1830,	,,	-	-	-	-	- 1
1831,	,,	-	-	-	-	- 8
1832,	,,	-	-	-	-	- 7
1833,	,,	-	-	-	-	- 10
1834,	,,	-	-	-	-	- 11
1835,	,,	-	•	-	-	- 9
1836, from 1st January to 26th November -						- 42

Total   -   -   - 102

IN IRELAND.

There were formed prior to 1834 -   -   -   - 3
In 1835   -   -   -   -   -   -   -   - 2
     1836   -   -   -   -   -   -   -   - 8

Total   -   -   -   13

" Until the year 1833 the action of the banks, as already stated, appears to have been perfectly regular. From that period the increase in the number of joint stock banks, in England and Wales, to the 26th of November last, has been seventy-two, and in Ireland ten, making an aggregate of eighty-two, exclusive of their innumerable branches formed in almost every town in the two kingdoms, which are, in fact, equivalent to so many additional banks."

" Having thus endeavoured to explain the causes which have operated to reduce the bullion of the bank during the last three years, it becomes desirable to shew why it is that the contraction of the circulation of the bank has affected private credit more than in 1832, when a similar loss of bullion and contraction of the bank's engagements were exhibited. The difference between the two periods appears to have been occasioned by the altered state of private banking in the interior of the country. In the first, there was no particular excitement either in England or Ireland, nor any excess in the issues of provincial paper. In the second, both countries teemed with competition created by the additional establishment, as previously stated, within the short space of two years, of not less than seventy-two joint stock banks in England and Wales, and ten in Ireland, with their innumerable branches in almost every town throughout the two kingdoms. It is needless to attempt to describe the competition that grew out of this excessive multiplication of banks : its effects were exhibited in a great and undue, and even rash extension of paper-money and credits, accompanied by an unusual reduction in the rate of interest in the interior of both countries, but particularly in Ireland : the commonest observer must have seen the gathering clouds, and dreaded the consequences.

" These circumstances at length attracted the attention of Parliament. The volume of evidence, taken before a Committee of the House of Commons, and published since the close of the last session, must satisfy every unprejudiced mind of the danger attending the continuance of such a system. Suffice it here to say, that the influence which should have attended the contraction of the Bank of England paper arising from the export of bullion, was counteracted by the imprudent facilities of credit and cheapness of money occasioned by the proceedings of the issuing banks in the interior of England and Ireland. Upon the publication in the Gazette of the issues of the joint stock and private banks of England and Wales in the early part of last July, an increase of 25 per cent. of their issues was exhibited above the amount existing in March 1834, while the circulation of the Bank of England had been diminished nearly to the same extent. The increase in the issues of the joint stock banks of Ireland, though not published, has since been ascertained to have greatly exceeded in proportion that exhibited in this country.

" The consideration of the joint stock system had been, for some time prior to the year 1825, forced upon public attention by the many failures which had taken place subsequently to 1810 in private banking establishments, amounting to more than one hundred and fifty : and as about eighty private banks suspended their payments in 1825, the government thought themselves then called upon without further delay to endeavour to change the system altogether—a sound system of banking being an object of the highest importance to the whole community. The view taken by government was strengthened by observing the little comparative derangement sustained by Scotland under the joint stock banks, by which the monetary concerns of that part of the kingdom have been almost exclusively conducted. Looking to that country as an example, it was perhaps natural to conclude that what afforded evidence of advantage in one part of the kingdom would be equally good for all the rest. There is no intention to criticise the Scotch system of banking, but were it narrowly examined, it might not appear so perfect in all its parts as its many warm advocates are inclined to believe. Suffice it to say, that it has produced great benefit to Scotland, which is a sufficient reason for leaving it untouched so long as it commands public confidence.

" In precipitating a change in England ministers seem not to have given sufficient attention to the real causes which occasioned the failures in this country, or the peculiar origin and state of the banking interest in Scotland. The evil of the system in England had grown up during the period of the restriction upon cash payments, and especially during the depreciation of the currency from 1810 to 1819, when the issues of paper-money were governed solely by the extent of the demand upon approved securities ; and as every bank not having more than six partners had the privilege of issuing notes without limit, it is not to be wondered, while such an unsound principle of issue was generally approved, that banking establishments should have multiplied in all parts of the country merely for the profit to be obtained from their respective paper mints, without paying much, if any, regard to security for the eventual payment of their notes either in paper of the Bank of England, or coin. As the period of return to cash payments approached, these ephemeral establishments began to disappear, and the banking business of the interior assumed a more substantial character : the principal evil suffered to remain was the continuance of the privilege to the country banks of issuing one and two-pound notes after they had been withdrawn by the Bank of England. This rendered coin the only means of upholding that description of circulation; and this coin, in the event of discredit, could only be obtained from the Bank in London.

" Such was the state of the provincial banking interest when overtaken by the universal panic of 1825. During that eventful period it is true, as already stated, that nearly eighty private banks suspended their payments ; but it is equally true, and perhaps no stronger proof could be afforded of the really substantial state of the country banks at that time, that a very small portion (it is believed not ten) proceeded to bankruptcy. If, therefore, due attention had been given by Lord Liverpool's administration to the causes which occasioned the insolvencies prior to the resumption of cash payments, and a little more time had been taken to inquire into the real state of the country banks in 1825, it is probable that the discredit so unjustly thrown upon the system of private banking in the annexed correspondence would never have been heard of. So far as the opinions then expressed were based upon the example of Scotland, it is maintained that they were founded in error. The two systems were different in origin and principle. That of England had been formed upon the Bank of England and private establishments precluded by parliament from embracing more than six partners, while the system of joint stock banks had ever been the main support of the circulation of Scotland. Both systems existed with equal advantage to the several districts where established—a change in either could only be accomplished by competition endangering the credit and currency of the country.

" In making these observations upon what appears to have been an injudicious encouragement given to the formation of joint stock banks in England, where adequate banking institutions already existed, there is no intention of questioning the propriety of sanctioning such establishments in a country differently situated. Banking is one of the principal means of promoting the prosperity of a nation, and it must consequently always command the vigilant attention of a government anxious to forward the welfare of the various branches of the community. As a general principle, it may be stated, that joint stock societies are only deserving of encouragement when individual capital and enterprise are found deficient. They are peculiarly applicable to banking business in an early stage of accumulation of property, and before private credit is extensively created. Such was the case in Scotland at the time when joint stock banks began to be established in it; such was also the situation of America, and such too, is now the situation of the Canadas. In the interior of Ireland the first attempt was made to conduct the banking business by private capital, supported by the Bank of Ireland, in the same way as in England. The situation of the two countries was however, widely different, and consequently the private banks of Ireland almost totally failed; which, leaving the field open to other agency, occasioned the formation of joint stock banks in their place. In all the instances here alluded to, those institutions, if their issues of paper be duly regulated, without which their respective currencies cannot fail to be in a frequent state of inconvenient and even dangerous fluctuation, will continue to prosper; and with their own prosperity will tend to promote the public and private interests dependent upon them.

" Adverting, therefore, to the mischief which appears to have attended the uncalled-for encouragement given to joint stock banks in England, while the advantage of those bodies is admitted in countries differently situated, it becomes the duty of government to bring the subject under the consideration of parliament, and to propose such regulations as may check the unlimited formation of such institutions hereafter, in places where banks already exist, affording every security and accommodation which the district may require. And further, to regulate the future management of those now in existence, in order to guard against a recurrence of that excess in the circulating medium, which on the late

occasion neutralized the influence of the contraction of the circulation of
the Bank of England, and occasioned a serious, it may be said ruinous,
pressure upon the money market.   Unless measures, having those objects in view, be adopted with firmness on the part of the government,
a repetition of the pressure will no doubt recur with increased violence.
Earl Spencer, when Chancellor of the Exchequer, was fully aware of
the danger to be apprehended from the present system ; and the
attempt made by his Lordship at the time of the renewal of the bank
charter to establish regulations for the conduct of joint stock banks of
issue, sufficiently proves that at least one member of government was
convinced of the necessity of protection being afforded to the public
against its abuse.   So dangerous does the system appear, as it now
stands, that it becomes questionable whether the Bank of England and
the bodies in question can permanently exist together."

In reply to this, we may observe,

1. The amount of the country circulation is not
sufficient to shew that the issues were carried to excess.

And here it may be proper to notice two important
principles with regard to the currency.   The first
is, that the amount of notes in circulation is in itself
no decisive proof either of excess or otherwise ; for
certain circumstances may require an increased
amount of notes to carry on the same extent of
operations.   Such, for instance, as an advance of
prices, arising either from scarcity or speculation, an
increase in the production of commercial commodities,
or a want of confidence that may cause the circulation
to be hoarded to meet contingencies.   In consequence
of this principle having been overlooked, the Bank
of England has sometimes been unjustly censured.
Writers have imagined that because the amount of
notes in circulation has increased, that money has become more abundant, and the exchanges must become
less favourable.   But it is always necessary to take
into account the circumstances under which these
increased issues have been made.   If, throughout the
year, the same amount of notes were kept in circulation, the currency would sometimes be deficient, and
sometimes be excessive.

The second principle is, that an increase in the
amount of the country circulation would not necessarily

have any effect upon the foreign exchanges, even if the Bank of England did not exercise any controlling influence; for that increase may have arisen from an increase in the internal trade of the country. If there is a greater production of commodities, or a greater number of transfers, arising from increased trade, then more money will be required to circulate these commodities. And if this money be not issued to an extent that shall cause an alteration of prices, it is impossible that it should affect the foreign exchanges.*

" The joint stock banks," says Mr. Ricardo, " might extend their issues to places which had been before occupied by the Bank of England, and displace the notes of the latter, and this has certainly occurred in Lancashire. An increase of trade in the provinces might acquire a larger comparative amount of circulation; it is likely, that this has been the case in the last year. The improving commerce of Liverpool and Manchester, the capital employed in the establishment of banks, and the formation of railways, the greater part of which capital has been furnished by the country districts, and the dealings in the shares of these undertakings, may have required such an increase of paper, as materially to alter the proportion that before subsisted between the country and bank circulation."

That the country circulation was not excessive seems evident from two circumstances: first, from the small amount of increase, when compared with the extended trade and the increased prices; secondly, from the fact that it has not declined. It will hardly be contended that the amount was excessive in the last quarter of 1836; yet then it had declined only £246,500 from the quarter ending June 1836, and was superior to any other quarter.

It will also be seen that the country circulation sustained but little increase until the quarter ending December, 1835, after the speculative spirit had commenced; a proof that the notes had not been the cause of the speculations, but that the speculations had drawn out the notes.

Mr. Palmer states—" Upon the publication in the

---

* See the History and Principles of Banking.

Gazette, of the issues of the joint stock and private banks of England and Wales, in the early part of last July, an increase of 25 per cent. of their issues was exhibited above the amount existing in March, 1834; while the circulation of the Bank of England had been diminished nearly to the same extent."

This language conveys the impression that the country circulation had increased between the periods mentioned 25 per cent., and the circulation of the Bank of England had diminished nearly 25 per cent. From the table at page 133, we find the facts are these :—

	March, 1834.	June, 1836.	
Country Circulation	10,191,827	12,202,196	2,010,369 increase.
Bank of England do.	19,000,000	17,900,000	1,100,000 decrease.

It will be seen that the increase of the country circulation is £2,010,369 upon £10,191,827, which is less than 20 per cent. With regard to the decrease of the Bank of England circulation, we presume Mr. Palmer did not mean that £1,100,000 was 25 per cent., that is, one-fourth of £19,000,000 : he could mean only, that £1,100,000 is nearly £2,010,369.

2. The joint stock banks formed last year could not be the cause of the alleged excessive issue.

Mr. Palmer has stated that forty-two banks were formed last year, but he has not stated at what time in the year they were established. As the demand for gold commenced in the middle of April, any excessive issue that produced that demand must have existed for some time previously. Now previous to the 30th of April, only four joint stock banks were registered in 1836. One of these was a private bank, that became a joint stock bank by increasing its partners to fifteen ; and another does not issue notes. It will hardly be contended, that the other two banks, one registered the 11th January, and the other the 27th February, issued so many notes as to render the exchanges unfavourable by the middle of April.

It is obvious from this statement, that the increase of joint stock banks last year was not the cause but the effect of the speculative spirit that existed in the country. Money was abundant, and sought employment; interest was low, and hence a mode of investment that promised a higher rate of interest was eagerly embraced. The private bankers too became convinced that it would be their interest to merge their establishments in joint stock banks. The fact that so many of the new banks were formed upon the basis of respectable private banks, is of itself a proof that these new companies were not speculative undertakings, but were built upon a rational expectation of success.

I have placed in the Appendix, a list of 113 country banking establishments that have been merged in joint stock banks. The materials of this list were supplied by various managers of joint stock banks in the country, and it was arranged by Mr. Henderson, the sub-manager of the London and Westminster Bank. Possibly there may be other instances, which are not included in this list. The following table will shew the number of private establishments that have been merged in the joint stock banks formed in each year respectively, from 1826:

1826	15
1827	—
1828	—
1829	2
1830	—
1831	11
1832	2
1833	14
1834	16
1835	4
1836	49
Total	113

It will hence appear that the forty-two joint stock banks, which were formed in 1836, have absorbed forty-nine country banks.

While it is admitted that some of these banks were the effect of the spirit of speculation that then existed, it is not admitted that this is any reflection upon those banks. In seasons of excitement both good and bad projects are brought forward: and when the excitement has subsided, the good projects are carried on, while the bad ones are abandoned. Is it any objection to the Provincial Bank of Ireland, that it was nurtured amid the speculations of 1825? And can it be an objection to any of the English joint stock banks that they were brought before the public in 1836? A proof of the solidity of the banks that were formed last year, is found in the circumstance, that they have not been abandoned. All of them have stood the recent pressure, without seeking the *assistance* of the Bank of England.

3. Mr. Palmer has virtually acquitted the joint stock banks of the charge of excessive issue, by stating distinctly, that the commercial exchanges have never been unfavourable, and that the exportations of gold since June 1833, have been produced by causes over which the joint stock banks had no control; viz. the foreign loans, and the demand from America.

" In order to establish the position that the commercial exchanges were not against England, it may be right to refer to the increase or decrease of gold at the Bank, from which alone any correct inferences are to be drawn as to the state of our currency in comparison with that of foreign countries.

" The first period may be taken from October 1833, to April 1835, during almost the whole of which time there was a continued purchase of gold by the bank, at £3 : 17 : 9 per oz.; the exchange on Paris never fell below 25.35 for short paper, and the premium upon gold remained in Paris at about 9 per mille; thus shewing that during that period there was no demand upon the bank for bar-gold, and no profit upon the export of that metal or the gold coin of the realm.

" The second period was from April 1835, to April 1836, during the whole of which time the foreign exchanges were considerably higher than during the preceding eighteen months, and consequently the influx of gold correspondingly increased at the bank.

" The third and last period is that from April to December of the past year, during the whole of which time the foreign exchange on Paris was seldom under 25.35; the premium upon gold, however, was for a short time as high as 13 and 14 per mille, which occasioned a loss of about £100,000 of the bank's stock of gold bullion, an amount too trifling to establish the fact of an unfavourable commercial rate of exchange."

4. The Bank of England has the means of effectually controlling the country circulation, and is therefore chargeable with any excess that may have existed.

The amount of gold that can be demanded from the Bank of England must depend upon the amount of its own notes in circulation. The holder of the note of a joint stock bank cannot demand gold for it of the Bank of England : he may demand payment of the joint stock bank, who may give him in exchange a Bank of England note, for which he may get gold. But the joint stock banks have no means of drawing out notes from the Bank of England, they can only procure those previously in circulation ; these notes may be obtained by the sale of stock or exchequer bills, but as they were previously in circulation, the amount of the Bank of England circulation is not thereby increased, while that of the country banks who pay away the Bank of England notes in payment of their own is to that extent diminished. The bank then can always limit its liability to be called upon for gold, by limiting its issues. In 1826, when it was a question how far a small note circulation in Scotland and Ireland was compatible with a gold circulation in England, two directors of the Bank of England were examined upon the subject ; they stated that the Bank of England could not be affected, because the Scotch banks could not get gold from the Bank of England, unless they first got possession of its notes.

The following is the evidence of J. B. Richards, Esq.

" Although the paper circulation of Scotland was confined within its own limits, if a sudden demand should arise there for gold, what would be its effect in England, and particularly on the Bank of England ?—It could only reach the Bank of England, I apprehend, by getting possession of Bank of England paper ; and by that means, or by discounting bills, or by some other process, arriving at the gold of the Bank of England ; their own notes would never bring it out, because they are not convertible at the Bank."

If the Bank of England has the power of controlling the country circulation, and has not exercised

that power, she has no right to complain of the
excessive issues of the joint stock banks ; and the bank
has no right to assert that she does not possess that
power, unless she has tried to exercise it, and has
failed. It must be admitted, that the Bank of England has no control over the country circulation but
by controlling her own issues. But we contend that
every contraction or expansion of the circulation of
the Bank of England will be always certainly, and
generally immediately, followed by a corresponding
contraction or expansion of the country circulation.
As I have referred to this subject in the preceding
section, I will now only quote the language of Colonel
Torrens:

" Were it true, that the paper of the provincial banks flows into the
channels of circulation as the paper of the Bank of England is withdrawn, and thus prevents the currency from contracting under the influence of an adverse exchange, then there would be no narrowing of
mercantile accommodation, and no pressure upon the money market,
requiring advances from the Bank of England in support of commercial credit. On the other hand, the fact, so frequently and so fatally
experienced, that a contraction of the issues of the Bank of England
inflicts immediate pressure on the money market, is a practical demon-
stration, that the paper of the provincial banks does not flow into the
channels of circulation as the paper of the Bank of England is withdrawn ; and that the operations of the provincial banks do not counteract the efforts of the directors to regulate the currency upon sound
principles, and to preserve the medium of exchange from any deeper
fluctuations than those to which it would be occasionally liable were
the circulation purely metallic. In 1825, the Bank of England nar-
rowed its issues by upwards of £3,000,000 ; but the provincial banks,
instead of being able to counteract the operation, by increasing their
issues to a corresponding amount, were crushed and extinguished under
the calamitous pressure which it occasioned. And, in the present year,
when the directors of the Bank of England resorted to measures for
contracting the currency, the provincial banks of issue, instead of being
able to throw increased supplies of paper into the channels of circulation,
were crippled and paralysed, and compelled to resort to the Bank of
England for assistance.
" Now, if the bank directors were to regulate their issues by the
foreign exchanges, the paper circulation of the metropolis would be
exactly equal, both with respect to amount and value, to a metallic
circulation ; and consequently, every excess of provincial paper would
raise prices in the markets of the provinces, without raising them in the
markets of London ; would turn the balance of payments against the
provinces ; cause the excess of provincial paper to be returned upon the
banks of issue, in exchange for bills upon London ; and, by creating an

increased demand for foreign bills, to pay the foreign debts incurred during the high range of provincial prices, would have a tendency to contract the currency of the metropolitan district, rather than to render it redundant. If the directors of the Bank of England were to regulate their issues upon sound principles, the over-issues of the provincial banks would be almost immediately returned upon them, and therefore could not, except for periods too brief to be important, have any sensible effect in increasing the amount, and reducing the value, of the general medium of exchange. While the Bank of England retains its exclusive privileges in the metropolitan district, no considerable or protracted derangement in the money market can take place, except in consequence of the failure of the directors to regulate their issues upon sound principles."

5. The contraction of the circulation of the Bank of England has not been sufficient to shew that she could not control the country circulation.

The table given at page 133, certainly shows a reduction, but the Bank of England could have had no great fear of the issues of the joint stock banks, if this was the whole extent of her efforts to control them. But if this reduction appears trifling, when compared with the object to be effected, it will appear with reference to the stock of bullion to be still more inconsiderable. Upon this subject I quote Colonel Torrens and Mr. Loyd :

COLONEL TORRENS.

" An inspection of this table will convince your Lordship of the correctness of my assertion, that the bank directors act in systematic violation of the principle of leaving the currency to contract and expand under the action of the exchanges. In December 1833, their circulation was £17,469,000, and their bullion £10,200,000 ; in March 1834, their bullion was reduced to £8,753,000 ; and if they had acted on the principle of leaving the currency to contract under the action of an adverse exchange, their circulation would have been reduced to £16,022,000. But what was the fact ? In utter disregard of the only sound principle upon which a paper currency can be regulated, the bank directors, while bullion was thus flowing from their coffers, increased their circulation to £18,544,000 ; and thus threw upon the money market an excess of circulating money to the amount of £2,522,000.

" In March 1835, the treasure in the coffers of the bank was reduced from £10,200,000, its amount in December 1833, to £6,295,000 ; and if the directors, during this continued adverse exchange, had allowed their issues to contract as their gold was withdrawn, their circulation would have been reduced from £17,469,000, its amount in December 1833, to £13,564,000. Yet, incredible as the fact may ap-

pear (and utterly incredible it would be, if not established by authentic
official returns,) the directors kept out a circulation of £18,152,000,
and thus created in the money market an excess of paper to the amount
of £4,588,000.

" The continuance of the adverse exchange, was the necessary result
of this excess in the circulation. The Gazette account of the quarterly averages of liabilities and assets of the Bank of England, from
the 23rd of August to the 14th of November, 1836, gives the following
results :—

LIABILITIES.		ASSETS.	
Circulation -	-£17,543,000	Securities	- £28,134,000
Deposits -	- 12,682,000	Bullion	- 4,933,000
	£30,225,000		£33,067,000

" Taking these figures as they stand, without troubling ourselves to
inquire how much the actual quantity of bullion, held by the bank
during the last week of the quarter, fell short of the average of the
whole quarter (which is all the return gives), we shall still have sufficient data to shew the monstrous extent to which principle has been departed from in the regulation, or rather in the no regulation, of the currency. Between December 1833, and November 1836, the treasures
in the coffers of the bank was reduced from £10,200,000 to
£4,933,000; while the issues of the Bank of England paper were
increased from £17,469,000 to £17,543,000! How did the directors
contrive to get out more paper while the adverse exchange was depriving them of gold ? Simply by violating the principle by which they
profess to be guided. While the adverse exchange was reducing their
treasure from £10,200,000 to £4,933,000 ; and while, on every
sound principle, they should have allowed their paper in circulation to
contract from £17,469,000 to £12,202,000, they increased their securities from £24,567,000, their amount in December, 1833, to
£28,134,000, their average amount for the quarter ending the 15th of
November, 1836 ; and by issuing paper on the increased amount of
securities, succeeded in causing the currency to expand, under the
action of a decided and protracted adverse exchange."

MR. LOYD.

" Is it possible for the joint stock banks to maintain an expansion
of their issues for any permanency in the face of a regular, steady,
and undeviating course of contraction on the part of the bank ; or will
such a course on the part of the bank bring the subordinate issuers into
such a situation that a corresponding change in their issues becomes
inevitable ? A correct determination of this question is a matter of
the greatest importance, and it is much to be regretted, with this view,
that Mr. Palmer has not furnished us with minute and detailed accounts of the action of the bank, from December, 1835, to the present
time. Such accounts when produced may possibly substantiate his case.
But the information to be derived from the very imperfect statements
given us, does not tend to this conclusion :—

Dec. 29, 1835......London circulation £13,800,000
Mar. 29, 1836...... Do. 14,400,000
June 28, 1836...... Do. 14,200,000

" This statement does not look like that steady and undeviating contraction of their issues which can justify the bank in complaining of any counteraction on the part of the joint stock banks as a thing entirely beyond their control, and so independent of them as to menace their existence.

" This view of the matter seems to gain additional strength when we look to the issues of the branch banks :—

Dec. 29, 1835......Branch banks £3,400,000
Mar. 29, 1836...... Do. 3,600,000
June 28, 1836...... Do. 3,700,000

By this statement, it appears that the country issues of the bank were themselves increasing at the period during which the bank complains so severely of the increased issues of its rivals.

" In the face of these statements we are not warranted in coming to the conclusion that the action of the joint stock banks is utterly beyond the control of the central issuer ; the bank must first prove that it has really tried the effect of a steady and uninterrupted course of contraction, and that in face of this the issues of the joint stock banks have as steadily increased. Such may be the case ; but Mr. Palmer's pamphlet has not furnished us with any evidence of it, and the information, imperfect and unsatisfactory as it is, which he does give us, directly tends to the opposite conclusion.

" But to return to the above table :* we would ask any reflecting person to look first to the column of bullion, and mark its regular and rapid decrease ; then to compare with this the column of circulation, terminating with a larger amount than that with which it commences, and having done so, to declare whether he discovers any evidence of the bank having made the amount of its circulation to fluctuate as it would have done had it been purely metallic ; or whether he can perceive, during the drain of bullion which commenced in April, or during the months which immediately preceded that event, any signs of that steady and undeviating contraction of circulation on the part of the bank, on which alone any just objection to the conduct of the joint stock banks can be founded? It is not a satisfactory reply to this question to say " that the diminution of bullion has been met by a diminished amount of deposits." If the joint stock banks see, by the published returns, that the circulation of the bank is maintained at its full amount, they are warranted in concluding that there is no real call for a diminution of their issues, notwithstanding that some of the depositors in the bank may have thought proper to draw from it a portion of their funds. Indeed, the bank is not entitled to calculate at all upon the long-sightedness

* This is a table of the circulation and the bullion from January 1836 to February 1837.—The reader will find this in the Appendix.

or prudence of the joint stock banks, but ought to rely solely upon the influence which a steady and continuous course of contraction on her part must exercise upon the proceedings of her subordinate rivals. This it is clear she has not done from January 1836 to February 1837, and therefore she appears to be without any sufficient ground for attributing the whole or the greater portion of the existing derangement to their misconduct. If they have done wrong, it appears to have been from the want of that controlling action on the part of the Bank of England which she might have exerted and has not."

One of the most effectual checks upon excessive issue, possessed by the Bank of England, is to maintain a high rate of interest. Had the rate of interest been advanced in 1834, that measure alone would have prevented the joint stock banks rediscounting in London to the extent they did, and have prevented many of those speculative schemes that were produced solely by the cheapness of money. If the price of money, that is, the rate of interest, be low, it proves that money is abundant, as compared with the demand, how low soever the circulation may appear to be from the bank books. And on the other hand, if the market rate of interest be high, it shows that money is scarce, whatever may be the amount of the outstanding notes of the bank. I think the bank should never charge less upon either loans or discounts than five per cent. If money was wanted for the purposes of trade that rate would be readily paid, and if it was not wanted, the bank ought not to issue. The bank having the power of making money, or what is equivalent to money, ought not to come into competition with other banks, especially as it is not subject to any check upon its issues, by daily or weekly exchanges with other establishments. The issues of the Bank of England are never known to be in excess, until they have turned the exchanges, and occasioned a demand for gold. But then the mischief has been done; a rapid contraction subsequently, only increases the distress; whereas, had this excessive issue never taken place, there would have been no speculation from an expansion of the currency, nor any distress from its subsequent contraction.

6. The Bank of England can control the issues of the joint stock, as effectually as she can control the issues of any other banks, in which the public have equal confidence.

Mr. Palmer intimates that the Bank of England cannot control the issues of the joint stock banks so effectively as it could control the issues of the private banks. In one respect this is true. When the private banks possessed the circulation of the country, the Bank of England had only to contract their own issues to a moderate extent, and some dozen of the private banks immediately stopped payment. A general run took place upon the others; prices immediately fell, and the exchanges became favourable. But now, even when there is a general clamour against joint stock banks; when the Bank of England rejects all their indorsements; when they are denounced by a parliamentary committee, still they most provokingly refuse to stop ; and the public, so far from running upon them for payment of their notes, actually circulate a larger amount. It must, therefore, be admitted, that the circulation of the joint stock banks is, *in this respect,* less under the control of the Bank of England than that of the private banks. But this fact shows the superior confidence placed in joint stock banks; and if the public placed the same confidence in private banks, they would be equal in this respect to joint stock banks. For the Bank of England holds as effective and as prompt a control over the circulation of the joint stock banks, as it would have over that of any other banks, in which the public have equal confidence.

We are informed by Mr. Palmer, that in 1825, above eighty private banks stopped payment. This occasioned of course a run for gold upon all the rest; prices consequently fell, and the exchanges became favourable. Had the same system existed in 1836, the same result would probably have followed : or had the measures adopted by the Bank of England in

1836, occasioned the stoppage of a proportionate number of joint stock banks, the exchanges would have become favourable. But is it a matter of regret that the country has banking institutions that deserve and enjoy the confidence of the public? Are we seriously advised to adopt a system of insecure banks, in order that the Bank of England may have the power of destroying them? And is it likely that the legislature will be disposed to follow such advice?

It must be recollected that up to June 1836, the country bankers had a circulation nearly double that of the joint stock banks, and there is no certain evidence to prove that the whole of the increased issues were not made by them. But could it be proved, that during the early part of last year the joint stock banks did issue to excess, that would be no argument against them, unless it were also proved that this excessive issue arose from the principles of joint stock banking. To justify the charge against the principles of joint stock banks, it must also be proved, that the private bankers would not have issued to the same extent. And how can this be proved? Was not the panic of 1825 attributed by Lord Liverpool and Mr. Robinson " to the rash spirit of speculation, supported, fostered, and encouraged by the country banks?" If then the private banks produced the panic of 1825, what reason is there to suppose that if they had been the exclusive issuers in 1836, that their issues would have been to a less amount than those of the joint stock banks? But if the panic of 1825, was produced by causes unconnected with the country circulation, is it not possible that the same causes which produced a panic in 1825 may have produced another in 1836 ? And what then becomes of the charge against the joint stock banks?

7. We may observe, that the difference between the years 1832 and 1836 may be accounted for without attaching any blame to the joint stock banks.

Mr. Palmer inquires why the system which worked well in 1832, should not work well in 1836 ; and Mr. Ricardo will supply us with an answer.

" The consequences of the events of 1825 were of too serious a nature to admit of a speedy recovery—a period of calm therefore succeeded; and from 1826 to 1828, the bank is found to be amassing treasure, which is not a state of things likely to induce speculation. In 1830, at the period of the French revolution, the bank had a circulation of notes of £22,500,000, and a reserve of bullion amounting to £12,000,000. The exchange being above par, this was a favourable position for a necessary diminution of the currency, of which that event was likely to be the forerunner. The demand for specie which then occurred for exportation, is ascribed by Mr. Palmer to the derangement between the currencies of this and other countries produced by the revolution in France : it is more likely to have arisen from the balance of trade being against this country, in consequence of the larger investments made, between 1830 and 1832, in the French and Dutch funds by English capitalists. Mr. Palmer states that from 1830 to 1832, the system upon which the bank acted " adjusted itself so satisfactorily;" but, upon a reference to the returns, it will be found that a very considerable diminution of the circulation then took place. From August 1830 to January 1832, there is a decrease in the bullion of about six millions, and also a decrease in the circulation to the same extent : that no derangement therefore took place in the currency, on this occasion, is clearly to be attributed to its gradual reduction, which in this case was allowed by the bank to be consequent on the exportation of the bullion. At this period the currency had righted itself, a reaction took place, bullion began to flow into the bank, and the circulation began to increase. This increase continued gradually till October, 1833, when the paper amounted to £19,823,000, and the bullion to £10,905,000. Evident signs of a redundant currency now began to manifest themselves; the exchanges were depressed, and gold disappeared from the coffers of the bank. From December, 1833, to May, 1835, there is an increase in the circulation, notwithstanding that the bullion had progressively diminished to the extent of £3,750,000 ! If, at this time, the same course had been adopted by the bank as in 1830 and 1831, would not the " speculative action" mentioned by Mr. Palmer have been materially checked ?"

We may further observe, that in 1832 the Bank of England did not advance the rate of interest, they did not solicit the government to raise the interest on exchequer bills—there was no wholesale rejection of bills on American houses—they did not raise an outcry against joint-stock banks—nor had they determined to reject all bills bearing their indorsement — hence there was no public alarm, and consequently no pressure.

8. Could it be proved that the joint stock banks were the cause of the speculative spirit that preceded the pressure, that would not prove that they were the cause of the pressure itself.

In discussing the causes of the pressure on the money market, Mr. Palmer has confined his attention to the cause of the speculation that preceded the pressure. Now when Mr. Clay stated, so late as May last, that there were no stocks on hand, and Mr. Palmer states that the commercial exchanges have never been unfavourable, it may be questioned, whether the degree of speculation has not been considerably overrated: but, admitting the existence of speculation to the full extent that has been represented, may it not then be asked, whether the subsequent pressure was the *necessary* consequence of that speculation. That seasons of excitement should be followed by seasons of repose is natural enough; but then the change is always gradual. A sudden change from a high point of excitement, to a low point of depression, is not the natural result of the operations of trade; it is the sole result of our monetary system; and the question is, who were the banks, whose safety required this sudden re-action?

That this sudden change is not attributable to the joint stock banks, will be admitted by their opponents; in fact, they were accused in the public papers of pursuing after the pressure had commenced the same reckless course they did before. It is quite certain, that their circulation went on increasing; and equally certain, that a currency perpetually increasing cannot produce distress.

In what way can the excessive issue of notes produce a pressure upon the money market? A pressure means a difficulty of getting money, in consequence of its scarcity. But how can excess of notes produce a scarcity? It is true, that if notes are issued to excess, and then suddenly withdrawn, distress may be produced. But in this case, it is not the excessive issue, but the contraction of the circulation that produces distress. Excess can never produce distress without a subsequent contraction. Now the circulation of joint stock banks has never been contracted : the circulation has got on increasing to the present time; and in what way a continually increasing currency can produce a scarcity of money it is not easy to explain.

"The fall in price," says Mr. Palmer, "of almost all the leading articles of raw produce (sugar, coffee, tea, silk, cotton, piece goods, metals, drugs, &c.) from the 1st July last, when the rate of interest was first advanced, has not been less than from twenty to thirty per cent."

Mr. Palmer has intimated here and elsewhere in his pamphlet, that this fall of prices was occasioned by the advance in the rate of interest by the Bank of England. The Bank of England may contend that this advance became necessary, in order to check the spirit of speculation, to depress prices, and thus to prevent the exportation of gold. But this defence, would amount to an admission, that the bank had the power of preventing the speculation altogether, and would consequently be an abandonment of all the charges against the joint stock banks. Those charges are founded upon the assumption, that the joint stock banks created these speculations, in opposition to the most strenuous exertions of the Bank of England; but if the Bank of England could suppress the speculations at their height, could it not have controlled them in their infancy ?

9. We observe, that the legislative enactments proposed by Mr. Palmer do not seem adapted to prevent the evil of which he complains.

He proposes first, that parliament shall adopt " such regulations as may check the unlimited formation of such institutions hereafter, in places

where banks already exist, affording every security
and accommodation which the district may require."
Mr. Palmer makes this recommendation, after having
twice asserted that the joint stock banks have " innumerable branches formed in almost every town in the
two kingdoms." Here we may inquire — In what
new place can joint stock banks be planted? And
secondly, what authority is to decide whether the
existing banks of any district do afford every security
and accommodation which the district may require?

Mr. Palmer proposes, secondly, " to regulate the
future management of those now in existence, in order
to guard against a recurrence of that excess in the
circulating medium, which on the late occasion
neutralized the influence of the contraction of the
circulation of the Bank of England, and occasioned
a serious, it may be said ruinous pressure upon the
money market." The only measure Mr. Palmer has
suggested is that at page 39.

" It is perfectly immaterial whether banks of issue retain their just
proportion of reserves in Bank of England notes or coin, but one or
the other it is submitted that they ought to be compelled to retain
with reference to their liabilities, or to abandon the issue of notes, the
upholding of which, under discredit, becomes a source of difficulty and
danger to the public at large, as well as to the Bank of England. In
the late instance the discredit fortunately extended no farther than
Ireland, but the apprehension of what might ensue in England occasioned a considerable abstraction of bank paper from London by the
issuing banks of the country, which to that extent so far increased the
pressure of contraction—and was the principal cause of the pressure
upon the money market, which is the first head of the present inquiry.
In such times it is not only the contraction of money which constitutes
the evil, but the consequence which invariably ensues of timidity on
the part of bankers generally, to grant their customary accommodation,
and of those situated in the more distant parts of the country accumu-
lating and locking up reserves three or four times greater than they
retain under ordinary circumstances."

It is not easy to see in what way this regulation
would be a check to over-issue. A bank that had a
large amount of gold, or Bank of England notes in
its vaults, would be not the less disposed to issue its
notes, nor would the public be the less disposed to take

them. Nor is it easy to see in what way it would guard against discredit. The property of the banks would not be increased; they would merely hold a larger amount of gold, or Bank of England notes; and a less amount of exchequer bills or other securities. As the profits of the banks would be thus reduced, they would be less worthy of confidence, and more open to discredit. But it is easy to see in what way this measure might increase the profits of the Bank of England:—they would have more notes in circulation, and the capital thus raised might be invested in government securities that would yield interest. Thus, there would be a transfer of a certain portion of the profits of the private and joint stock banks to the Bank of England.

The following is a summary of the charges that have been brought against the joint stock banks.

I. It has been asserted, that the joint stock banks have issued an excessive amount of their notes.

1. We do not admit the fact, that the country circulation was excessive. We assert, that the increased amount of notes in circulation, arose from the increased trade of the country.

2. Admitting the country circulation was excessive, there is no evidence that the excess arose from the joint stock banks; it might have arisen chiefly or entirely from increased issues by the private bankers.

3. Admitting even that the joint stock banks issued to excess, yet as the system of private banking affords no protection against excessive issue, this excessive issue is no argument against the system of joint stock banking.

4. Admitting that the country circulation was excessive, and that the whole excess was issued by the joint stock banks, then we contend, that the blame rests with the Bank of England, who by adopting in 1835 the measures she adopted in 1836, might have prevented this excess.

II. It has been asserted, that the excessive issues of the joint stock banks, have rendered the foreign exchanges unfavourable.

1. We state, upon the authority of Mr. Horsley Palmer, that the commercial exchanges have never been unfavourable, and that the demand for gold arose from causes wholly unconnected with joint stock banking.

2. We deny the possibility of the joint stock banks being able by any excessive issue, to render the foreign exchanges unfavourable, in opposition to the controlling power of the Bank of England.

3. Admitting both the facts, that the joint stock banks have issued to excess, and that this excessive issue have rendered the exchanges unfavourable, then we contend that the blame rests not with the joint stock banks, who are ready to pay off all their engagements, but with the Bank of England, in not providing ample means to meet her own engagements; the supplying of the foreign demand for gold being one of the conditions on which she holds her exclusive privileges.

III. It has been asserted, that the excessive issues of the joint stock banks, have been the cause of the recent pressure.

1. We do not admit the fact of excessive issue; but admitting the fact, we say, that there is no necessary connection between excessive issue and subsequent panic.

2. That the joint stock banks have not been the immediate cause of the pressure, is evident from the continued increase of their circulation: a pressure being always produced either by a contraction of the currency, or by the destruction of credit; to neither of which have the joint stock banks contributed.

3. That the sole necessity for the pressure arose from the small amount of gold in the Bank of England; that had the gold been three times the amount, the

foreign demand would have been supplied, and the speculative spirit would have expended itself without producing any disastrous results ; and that the low amount of gold in the Bank of England, cannot be charged as a crime upon the joint stock banks.

4. That the pressure upon the money market was rendered more severe by the clamour raised against the joint stock banks ; by rendering it necessary for the joint stock and private banks in the country, to keep larger reserves of cash, and thus diminished their means of giving accommodation to their customers ; that for this increased pressure, not the joint stock banks, but the enemies of joint stock banks, are answerable.

5. That the joint stock banks have considerably mitigated the pressure : the confidence placed in their stability, having delivered the public from the recurrence of a panic similar to 1825.

Secondly. The recent pressure upon the money market, has been ascribed to the mis-government of the Bank of England.

The plan upon which the Bank of England professes to be governed, was explained by J. Horsley Palmer, Esq. before the Bank Charter Committee, in the year 1832, in the following terms :—

" What is the principle, by which in ordinary times the bank is guided in the regulation of their issues ? The principle, with reference to the period of a full currency, and consequently a par of exchange, by which the bank is guided in the regulation of their issues (excepting under special circumstances,) is to invest and retain in securities, bearing interest, a given proportion of the deposits, and the value received for the notes in circulation, the remainder being held in coin and bullion ; the proportions which seem to be desirable, under existing circumstances, may be stated at about two-thirds in securities and one-third in bullion ; the circulation of the country, so far as the same may depend upon the bank, being subsequently regulated by the action of the foreign exchanges."

The following explanation of this principle was given by Lord Althorp in the House of Commons.

" The principle upon which the bank managed its affairs, had been correctly stated, and he believed fully approved, namely, to keep one-third of bullion in proportion to their liabilities, to allow the public to act on the currency, and not force it by any artificial means ; to allow their circulation gradually to diminish, as the exchanges were against us, and the drain of bullion became great; and when the exchanges turned in our favour, and the bullion came back, to let the circulation gradually extend in proportion."

Upon this subject, I shall content myself with transcribing the sentiments of other writers. But for the information of those who are not familiar with the subject, I may state, that the system of Mr. Horsley Palmer, as explained before the Bank Charter Committee, has been understood by different writers in three different senses.

First. It has been understood to mean, that the bank shall *at all times*, keep a stock of gold equal to one-third of its liabilities; that is, equal to one-third the amount of its notes and deposits added together ; and consequently, if any portion of its gold be withdrawn, the reduction in the amount of the liabilities shall be equal to *three times* the amount of the gold withdrawn.

Secondly. It has been understood to mean, that *at the time of a full currency*, the stock of gold shall be one-third the liabilities, and that if any portion of the gold be withdrawn, the reduction in the amount of *the notes in circulation alone* shall be equal to the amount of gold withdrawn. This is the sense in which it appears to have been understood by Lord Althorp, and this is the principle upon which Colonel Torrens contends the bank ought to be governed.

Thirdly. It has been understood to mean, that *at the time of a full currency*, the stock of gold shall be equal to one-third of the liabilities; and if any portion of its gold be withdrawn, the reduction in the amount of its liabilities, *that is, the deposits and notes together*, should be equal to the amount of gold withdrawn. This is the explanation given by Mr. Palmer himself, and it is the principle upon which the bank professes to be governed.

The object of the writers, who have replied to Mr. Palmer is, to shew, first, that the principle involved in the third explanation is erroneous, and that the bank ought to be regulated by the principle involved in the second explanation ; and secondly, presuming the principle in the third explanation to be sound, they contend, that the bank has not acted uniformly upon that principle. I quote in the following order, Mr. Palmer, Mr. Loyd, Colonel Torrens, Mr. Ricardo, Mr. Bennison, and Mr. Palmer's reply.

MR. HORSLEY PALMER.

" The conduct of the Bank of England from the year 1819 to the present time is before the public. The events which seemed to have led to the panic of 1825 were attempted to be explained by the author of this tract, in evidence given before the committee of the House of Commons upon the renewal of the bank charter in 1832; when he further endeavoured to shew that the almost total drain of coin from the Bank in December 1825, which endangered the credit of that establishment, was occasioned solely by the discredit of private paper-money, particularly of that part below the denomination of five pounds. It was also shewn in that evidence that the policy pursued by the bank subsequent to the withdrawal of the one pound and two pound notes in England and Wales, had been to maintain their securities as nearly as possible at a fixed amount, and to allow the contraction of the currency, effected by the return of bank notes for bullion, gradually to proceed until the value of the paper-money remaining in circulation was so far increased as to occasion the return of that specie to the bank which might have been exported, and thus to replace the currency upon a level with that of other countries. That system had appeared to work satisfactorily and without any forced action on the part of the bank in contracting its circulation. It was tried upon the change of government in France in July, 1830, when credit throughout that kingdom was shaken to its foundation. At that period the Bank of England was possessed of about twelve millions of bullion. Immediately upon the events referred to taking place, the currency of England exhibited an excess compared with that of France and other parts of Europe. The consequence of that derangement between the currencies of this and other countries was a continued diminution of the bullion held by the bank from July, 1830, to February or March, 1832, when the increased value of money in England and the gradual restoration of credit upon the Continent gave a favourable turn to the foreign exchanges ; which continued in our favour till the autumn of 1833, at which time the bullion in deposit at the bank amounted to nearly eleven millions. At this period an exportation of the precious metals again commenced, from causes that will hereafter be explained, as well as the reason why that system which happened to adjust itself so satisfactorily from 1830 to 1832 failed from 1833 to 1836; for although during the former period the bullion in the bank was diminished from twelve millions to five millions, yet in the progress of this reduction, as there was no excitement, and no undue credit given by the banks in the interior of the country, the interest of money gradually rose from $2\frac{1}{2}$ to 4 per cent. per annum for first-rate commercial paper; and then, without discredit or distrust of any kind, the bullion returned into the coffers of the bank, and money nearly resumed its former value, the rate of interest having gradually fallen from 4 to $2\frac{3}{4}$ per cent. in July, 1833.

" Adverting to the excess of the country issues, and looking to the race running with increased violence in Ireland as well as England, the bank was fully justified in attempting to arrest the evil which might attend a continuance of the export of bullion from the redundancy of money, by making an advance in the rate of interest in London and at the branch banks. In fact, the only question about which there can be any real difficulty is, whether she ought not to have taken this step somewhat earlier. To have acted, however, in anticipation of events likely to occur, would have been in direct violation of that principle upon which the bank professed to be guided, and which parliament had tacitly sanctioned. It would moreover have established a precedent and imposed future responsibilities upon the directors, which it is questionable whether they should ever incur, either upon their own account or that of the public. The bank acted precisely as any board of commissioners empowered solely to issue notes for bullion would have done, and can in no way be chargeable with the consequences.

" With reference to the past action of the bank there is no reason to doubt that the value of the currency would have been maintained without occasioning any severe pressure upon the money market had the countervailing issues by other bodies not occurred; still if there exist any well-founded reasons for supposing that the principle explained in the evidence of 1832, and acted upon by the bank, is not sound—or that the proportion of one-third of bullion with reference to the liabilities of the bank at the period of a full currency be not sufficient, it merely remains for parliament to express an opinion upon either of those points, and there can be no question but that the bank will immediately regulate its course accordingly. The principle referred to was never intended to apply under any extraordinary events that might arise. In such times it would become the duty of the bank to reduce their securities without delay, and thus to increase the relative proportion of bullion to their liabilities prior to the commencement of a demand, which in such altered state of circumstances might be expected to occur."

MR. SAMUEL JONES LOYD.

" The legislature, in ordering the publication of the accounts of the bank, had two objects in view: first, to enable the public to exercise some judgment upon the general course pursued by the bank directors, and thus to place their proceedings to a certain extent under the control of public opinion; and, secondly, by furnishing the public with a knowledge of the fluctuations which were taking place in the amount of bank notes in circulation or of specie in deposit, to enable them to foresee approaching pressure, and by timely precautions to diminish the intensity of its action and to mitigate its effects. Now, from the accounts as published, it appears that the bank has deviated from all the rules by which it professes to be guided, and which a regard to sound principle requires it to adhere to. By these accounts it appears that the amount of securities, so far from being kept at a fixed point, has fluctuated largely ; it also appears that the circulation has in some instances increased whilst the specie has been diminishing; and from the same accounts it will be very difficult to make out that steady and continual contraction of the circulation month by month during the diminution of specie in store, upon which alone any plausible ground of censure upon the proceedings of the joint stock banks can be founded. But we are told in a pamphlet, explanatory of the action of the bank, and written by one of the most influential of the directors of that establishment, that, upon the data furnished by the accounts as published, no safe conclusions can be founded ; that other explanatory circumstances and considerations, not officially laid before the public, must be taken into the account; and that, when due allowance has been made for these, conclusions will arise not only differing from, but diametrically the reverse of those to which every person must come upon the inspection merely of the published accounts.

" The principle upon which the bank professes to be guided in the regulation of the currency, is this ; to meet its outstanding liabilities consisting of circulation and deposits, it holds at its disposal securities and specie ; and its principle of action is, to keep the amount of its securities fixed, and to leave any variation in the amount of circulation and deposits to be balanced by a corresponding variation in the amount of specie. This principal was set forth by the bank directors in their evidence before the parliamentary committee previous to the last renewal of the charter, and was recommended principally upon the ground that the effect of it would be to render the bank a passive agent, and that all variations in the amount of specie would thus become the result not of any direct action on the part of the bank, but solely on that of the public. If they demanded specie, it could be obtained only by paying in notes or diminishing deposits; and if, on the other hand, the specie was increased, there must at the same time be a corresponding increase in the amount of circulation or deposits. Under this view of its probable action, the principle above stated met with a degree of acquiescence which a more close examination of the subject will hardly warrant.

" The bank, it must be observed, acts in two capacities ; as a manager of the circulation, and as a body performing the ordinary functions of a banking concern. The duties of these two characters though very often united in the same party, are in themselves perfectly distinct. In the principle laid down by the bank for its own guidance, the separate and distinct nature of these two characters has not been sufficiently attended to. The rules applicable to its conduct as a manager of the currency are mixed with the rules applicable to its conduct as a simple banker, and the rule or principle under discussion is the result of this mixture. As a manager of the currency it is undoubtedly a sound rule by which to guide itself, that against the amount of notes out it shall hold at its disposal securities and specie ; that the amount of securities shall be invariable, and that consequently all fluctuations in the amount of notes out shall be met by a corresponding fluctuation in the amount of specie in deposit; thus the public and not the bank will be made the regulators of the amount of the circulation, and that amount will by this principle be made to fluctuate precisely as it would have fluctuated had the currency been purely metallic.

" For the regulation of the conduct of the bank as a manager of the currency, this rule is perfectly unobjectionable, and rests indeed upon the soundest principles.

" But when the same rule is further applied to the regulation of its conduct as a banking concern, it is necessarily found to be wholly impracticable. It is in the nature of banking business that the amount of its deposits should vary with a variety of circumstances; and as its amount of deposits varies, the amount of that in which those deposits are invested (viz. the securities) must vary also. It is therefore quite absurd to talk of the bank, in its character of a banking concern, keeping the amount of its securities invariable. The reverse must necessarily be the case.

" The rule is, " that the securities being kept equal, any diminution in the amount of specie may be met by a corresponding decrease in the aggregate amount of circulation and deposits." The possible consequence is, that a large diminution of specie may take place, and be met not by a corresponding decrease of circulation, but solely by a decrease of deposits. Thus a heavy drain upon the treasure of the bank might take place under this rule without any contraction of the currency by which that drain is to be checked or the bank to be protected.

" If these views be correct, it follows that the rule now adopted by the bank is incorrect, and cannot be safely relied upon in the management of the currency. The rule ought to be, that the variations in the amount of circulation shall correspond to the variations in the amount of bullion, and the adherence of the bank to this rule ought to be obvious upon the face of the published accounts. By this means, and by this means only, can we obtain " a paper circulation varying in amount exactly as the circulation would have varied had it been metallic ;" and in addition to the establishment of this only sound principle of currency, we shall obtain a simple and intelligible account, requiring no further explanations nor the production of any information not at the command of the public, to enable them to come to a correct understanding of it."

COLONEL TORRENS.

" It is universally admitted by persons acquainted with monetary science, that paper-money should be so regulated as to keep the medium of exchange, of which it may form a part, in the same state, with respect to amount and to value, in which the medium of exchange would exist, were the circulating portion of it purely metallic. Now it is self-evident, that if the circulating currency were purely metallic, an adverse exchange, causing an exportation of the metals to any given amount, would occasion a contraction of the circulating currency to the same amount; and that a favourable exchange, causing an importation of the metals to any given amount, would cause an expansion of the circulating currency to the same amount. Therefore, when the directors of the Bank of England allow, not their circulation, but their deposits, to contract and expand under the influence of the foreign exchanges, they depart from the only sound principle upon which paper money can be regulated. If the circulating currency of the metropolis consisted of gold, an adverse exchange, causing an exportation of gold to the amount of £1,000,000 would withdraw from circulation one million of sovereigns; and therefore, as the circulating currency of the metropolis consists of Bank of England notes, an adverse exchange, causing one million in bullion to be withdrawn from the bank, would require to have £1,000,000 of bank notes withdrawn from circulation. As often as an adverse exchange abstracts any given amount of treasure from the bank, without a withdrawal to the same amount of Bank of England notes from circulation, so often do the directors of the Bank of England exhibit a practical proof of their incompetency to perform the important function of regulating our monetary system. To say that their rule is to keep their securities even, and to allow the exchanges to act upon their whole liabilities, is not a defence, it is an admission that they do not understand their business.

" When an excessive issue of bank paper has rendered our currency redundant, in relation to foreign currencies, the exchanges turn against us, and gold is demanded for exportation; and when, at the same time, the bank directors, disregarding the only sound principle upon which a paper circulation can be regulated, do not draw in their notes, as their treasure is withdrawn, the drain upon their coffers is continued until the bank is in danger of stopping payment. To avert this danger, the bank directors resort to a late and violent action on the circulation; they disregard the rule of keeping their securities even; they raise the rate of interest; they refuse bills of unquestionable character; they sell exchequer bills; and thus create alarm and distrust, until that credit currency, by means of which the far greater number of our commercial transactions are effected, begins to give way. The directors now find that danger approaches from another quarter. The banks throughout the kingdom, whether of deposit or of issue, feel more or less of pressure, and become desirous of contracting their liabilities, and of increasing their reserve of cash; in proportion as confidence is shaken, gold is preferred to paper, and sovereigns are held rather than the notes of the Bank of England; and a domestic drain, more sudden and more serious than the foreign, threatens to exhaust its coffers.

" These are the only circumstances under which it can be necessary that the bank should exercise its vaunted function of sustaining commercial credit. When the directors have neglected to any considerable extent, to draw in their notes as an adverse exchange draws out their

N

gold, their establishment becomes exposed to two opposite dangers; and they cannot avoid the one, without approaching the other. If they do not contract their issues, their treasure may be exhausted by the continual action of the foreign exchange; and if they do not increase their issues, their coffers may be emptied by the immediate action of a domestic panic. Of the two dangers, that of having their coffers emptied by domestic panic, is the most serious and the most pressing; and therefore, in an emergency, having only a choice of evils, the bank directors are justified in disregarding the principle of regulating their issues by the foreign exchanges, and in making such advances as may be necessary to restore commercial credit. But does the necessity under which the bank directors are occasionally placed, of resorting to extraordinary measures for the purpose of mitigating a pressing mischief, afford a justification of the previous deviations from principle by which that mischief was created? Could a surgeon, who had wounded an artery, instead of having opened a vein, vindicate his professional reputation, by showing that he had secured the blood-vessel before his patient bled to death? Could an incendiary escape condemnation, by proving that he had laboured at the engine by which the conflagration which he had kindled was at length subdued?

" When, in 1826, the bank directors restored commercial credit, by making extensive issues, regardless of the state of the foreign exchanges, their conduct received, as it deserved, the highest praise; but this conduct, however praiseworthy in itself, cannot be referred to, in justification of the previous mismanagement of the circulation of the Bank of England, by which the frightful panic of 1826 was occasioned. In like manner, though the conduct of the present directors, in making liberal advances upon mercantile securities, and in affording assistance to the provincial banks, without waiting for an influx of the precious metals, is laudable and wise, yet this conduct, however calculated to avert a more serious crisis, cannot remove the responsibility they have incurred by that earlier departure from principle, which has led to the mitigated panic of the present year. The only disturbances in the money market, which the directors of the Bank of England have any power to correct, are those which their own mismanagement of the currency creates. If they could be prevailed upon to attend with strictness to their essential duty, of regulating their issues by the course of the foreign exchanges, they would never be called upon to perform the superfluous duty, of watching over and supporting commercial credit. When they cease to inflict disease, they will no longer be required to administer remedies."

MR. SAMSON RICARDO.

" It is a curious fact that, from 1831 to 1836, there is no one period, except for four or five months in 1833, in which this proportion of one-third and two-thirds has been preserved, and it must then indeed have been a very full currency, for it was speedily followed by a continued reduction of the bullion. There is no case, even during these four months, where the bullion, except to a very trifling amount, has ever exceeded one-third, so that the bank has never been in a position to increase its issues agreeably to its own rule.

" The great error of the bank has been to confound the deposits and the circulation, whereas they are totally different in their character. A demand for gold for exportation should be allowed to act on the currency only in order to correct its excess; a withdrawal of deposits should be met by a realization of securities—it is the neglect of this principle that has occasioned much of the mischief which has occurred. When the rate of interest is low, that portion of the deposits which belongs to private individuals is generally larger; that which consists of monied capital waiting for employment, is likely to be the first withdrawn upon a rise in the rate of interest, the usual consequence of high prices, and the exportation of the precious metals.

" If a sum of gold be taken from the coffers of the bank to be sent abroad, and this same amount be withdrawn from the bank notes in circulation, prices will be affected and the equilibrium restored; but if it be taken from the deposits, it can in no manner possibly relieve the currency—the gold will have disappeared, and the effect of its abstraction be neutralized. In this part of the subject it has been necessary to re-state some of the facts and reiterate some of the arguments so ably adduced by Colonel Torrens in the pamphlet before alluded to, the correctness of which has in no way been disproved in Mr. Palmer's work."

MR. BENNISON.

" The system of classing together their circulation and deposits as liabilities, and likewise classing together securities and bullion as assets, resting satisfied that all is going right, when the reduction in their liabilities is equal in amount to the reduction in their assets, may easily lead to lamentable consequences, whilst they adhere to the plan of keeping up their securities to a given amount, whether their deposits be increased or diminished, and whether there be a drain for bullion proceeding from ordinary or extraordinary circumstances. To make my argument more clear, I will suppose a case. The bank affairs may stand thus :—

Circulation	-	£19,000,000	Securities	-	£24,000,000
Deposits	-	13,000,000	Bullion	-	10,000,000
		32,000,000			34,000,000

" The exchanges are exactly balanced; there is neither importation nor exportation of bullion, and the circulation is adequate but not redundant. Now suppose the government or individuals draw out deposits to the amount of three millions, the bank will be quite easy, because they have not increased their liabilities: but the account will then stand thus.

Circulation	-	£22,000,000	Securities	-	£24,000,000
Deposits	-	10,000,000	Bullion	-	10,000,000
		32,000,000			34,000,000

"But this operation has disturbed the balance of the money-market; the circulation of twenty-two millions is redundant, as will soon be proved by the exportation of bullion to the amount of excess, and the return of notes to the bank in payment for it: the account will then stand:—

Circulation	-	£19,000,000	Securities	-	£24,000,000
Deposits	-	10,000,000	Bullion	-	7,000,000
		29,000,000			31,000,000

Thus they cancel the notes paid in for bullion, and reduce the circulation and liabilities in the same proportion as the assets have been reduced, which is quite satisfactory to the bank managers, although they have lost three millions of their bullion, and are liable to lose all the remainder by a similar process, without perceiving any derangement in the relative proportions of liabilities and assets.

" It is evident, after this process has gone on to some extent, they must take the alarm, and endeavour to retrieve themselves by desperate and violent means, before they come to actual stoppage; and this is the grand evil and cause of our dangerous checks and panics in the midst of the greatest prosperity.

" Let us now examine what the bank ought to do under the circumstances stated above. Like all other banking establishments, when deposits are paid in, she ought to employ them on good securities; (bills of exchange or exchequer bills in preference to all others;) and on the contrary, so fast as notes are withdrawn by depositors, she ought to realize her securities to bring back the notes abstracted; thus keeping the amount of securities always fluctuating in like proportion with the amount of deposits.

" It is evident this plan would effectually guard against any excess or diminution of the circulation by her deposit business. Now for the circulation business:—We have supposed in the preceding statement, that £19,000,000 is a fair circulation, neither redundant nor deficient, consequently things will remain at rest; but if circumstances alter, and the nineteen millions of circulation should then be redundant, an exportation of bullion would commence, and notes would flow into the bank in exchange for her gold. By cancelling all notes sent in for bullion, the excessive circulation would soon be corrected; and as the evil could not be prolonged by again drawing the notes into circulation through deposit accounts, all further mischief would be stopped."

MR PALMER'S REPLY.

" The objection to such an action on the part of the bank, so long as it is the depositary of the surplus or unemployed money of the capital, seems to be this:—The value of money in London affects the value throughout the country, and any measure which might tend unduly to reduce the rate of interest would so far be prejudicial, by increasing the oscillations in the money market. If the bank were continually throwing back upon the public the surplus money deposited by the bankers of London and others in times of influx of bullion, such conduct would, it is submitted, unduly lower the rate of interest; whereas, under the course hitherto pursued, such deposits being considered purely as part of the circulation of notes, and held as such in bullion, no disturbance arises, and the currency is left freely to find its level with reference to that of other countries. It is admitted that a change in the number or character of the customers' accounts, tending to a permanent alteration of the amount of the deposits, would necessarily occasion a corresponding change in the amount of securities, but so long as the former continue unchanged in character, there does not appear any necessity for varying the latter if there be one-third of their amount retained in bullion prior to the commencement of the drain. If Mr. Loyd's notion were adopted of forming two bodies—one for issuing notes, and the other for managing the general banking business, the Bank of England would be not unlikely to become a great joint stock bank. The advantages expected from the separation seem to be

" 1st. That the circulation would fluctuate exactly as if purely metallic.

" 2nd. That the knowledge on the part of the public of the fluctuation of the amount of paper money would induce all parties to govern themselves accordingly.

" That the first advantage would be obtained may be conceded. Respecting the second, it is believed that ninety-nine persons out of a hundred will pay no attention to the information thus afforded them. The true guide for the public at present is the fluctuation in the stock of bullion held by the bank, and if attention be not paid to that, we may be assured that all other statements will be useless. If therefore the present joint action can be maintained under proper management, and the fluctuations of bullion be made known, it is questionable whether any advantage will be obtained by the change proposed by Mr. Loyd. Upon that point, however, the writer begs to be understood as offering no decided opinion.

" The opinion thus expressed is intended to apply to the working of the bank in its joint character under ordinary circumstances. The real difficulty of conveying accurate information as to the issues under the existing form of publication in the Gazette is correctly stated by Mr. Loyd, and was represented to the government at the time of its being determined upon, while it was at the same time maintained, that there was no accurate conclusion to be drawn by the public, except from the increase or decrease of the stock of bullion : to a publication of that simple nature the government objected, and finally resolved upon adopting the plan now acted on with all its admitted defects. For these therefore the bank is not blameable."

———

Thirdly. The recent pressure on the money market has been ascribed to the transactions between the government and the bank respecting the West India

loan in the year 1835.   This sentiment is advanced
by Mr. Salomons.

" A better founded cause for the derangement of the currency than
the issues of the joint stock banks may be shewn to be the transaction
between the government, the public, and the Bank of England, connected with the West India loan.   This measure, which required very
skilful treatment, was managed with a most reckless haste.   At first,
the bank seemed determined not to interfere, but, either not proof
against the solicitations of the government, or having unfortunately
listened to evil advisers, they permitted themselves to lend money on
all descriptions of securities, and thus themselves gave the impulse to
those speculations of which they and the public are now the victims.
Joint stock banks were multiplied all over the country ; rail-road and
other schemes covered the land ; the means for setting these projects
on foot, in many cases, came from the proceeds of the West India
loan, and although it was not yet assigned to the various claimants, the
funds paid in for that loan on account of the government, were poured
out in masses from the coffers of the Bank of England, who advanced
money to all applicants, both on the deposit of that loan and all other
government securities.   Whether the government stimulated the bank
to act thus, I do not inquire ; my business is with the facts of the
case, and with these I must deal.
" Believing, as I do, that the first impulse to speculation came from
London, and not from the country, I am inclined to assert, that if the
joint stock banks had not been in existence throughout the country,
and by the instrumentality of the shareholders dispersed in all di-
rections, who were both individually and collectively interested in the
support of public and private credit, we should have had as severe a
bank and commercial crisis in 1836 as we had in 1825, and in both
instances produced by excessive speculations fostered by the improvident conduct of the Bank of England."

It may be objected, that the amount of Bank of England notes in circulation in 1835 was not greater than
that of 1834.   Mr. Salomons anticipates this objection,
and contends, that an alteration in the channels of
the circulation would have as great an effect in stimulating speculation as an increase in the amount.   This
is a very important principle, and one that had not previously been urged upon public attention.

" The writer of these observations, impressed with the parallel that
exists between the period of 1825 and 1836, is inclined to attribute
the difficulties of both periods to the same causes, viz. the derangement
of the currency caused by the assistance given by the bank to the
government in order to enable them more easily to carry into effect
financial measures.   At the former period they aided the government
to pay off the four per cents., and at the latter they advanced money

on the West India loan, and on other government securities. Although it may be asserted that no great permanent addition to the circulation took place since the bank did contrive to keep its securities even, yet the ordinary channels of the circulation being changed, a derangement of the currency must be produced ; and the consequences that have followed the interference of the bank on several occasions, might be quoted to prove the correctness of these remarks, were not the facts themselves sufficiently obvious.

" It concerns the public as much that the channels through which the circulation is supplied, should not be suddenly and frequently changed, as that its amount should not be frequently and hastily augmented. Let us suppose the Bank of England suddenly to change the channels through which its notes circulate, and instead of a definite part of its issue representing an advance in the ordinary course of public business, as the fountain from which the circulation of the country is supplied, the bank should change the nature of its investments by issuing a similar amount upon government stock : although the securities may remain even, yet the change of them must have an immediate effect on the circulation of the country, by supplying in masses to a more active class of persons, that money which was formerly distributed throughout the community, and performing the duties of a necessary and healthy circulation.

" If the Bank of England, as the chief circulator of paper, were to augment its issues to any great extent in the country, through their branches, and were to diminish, in the same proportion, their circulation in London; although the total amount of circulation would be the same, and the amount of securities representing that circulation, and held by the bank, be also the same ; would not the effect be, at least for a time, to make money plentiful in the country and scarce in London ?

" If we suppose the converse proposition, money would become scarce in the country, and plentiful in London.

" An operation, producing equally important results, may be carried on in London itself, without any great variation either in the amount of nominal circulation, or in the amount of securities. For let us suppose that an agreement be made with the government, in reference to some pending loan-transaction, that the bank shall either lend or issue on some particular class of securities, a part of its circulation, which would otherwise be employed in the ordinary course of their transactions. Would not that also, " pro tanto," have its effect upon the price of money, by changing the channel through which the circulation of the bank flows for the supply of public wants ?

" It then appears evident that the public are interested, as much in preventing the changes which affect the channel as those which affect the quantity. Whenever the bank lends money to the government out of the usual course, it affects the channel of the circulation. The assistance afforded by the bank in the West India loan, must have affected the channels of the circulation as well as the quantity. As regards the quantity, perhaps the bank may have been enabled, after a time, to reduce the quantity so as to keep their securities and the circulation to their ordinary level. But the bad effects resulting from a change in the channel are not so easily remedied.

" The means for all the mischief of the last year, were abundantly supplied by the advances of the Bank of England to the public on account of the West India loan in 1835. These advances increased the circulation as well as directed it into new channels, and laid the foundation of much future difficulty and distress.

" It is thus clearly proved, that although on a three months' average, the bank may get both its circulation and its securities within their ordinary limits, its account with the public is not so easily made up : for large sums of money issued in masses, cheapen the rate of interest, alter the price of commodities, and give the grand impulse to every kind of speculation."

Fourthly. The recent " pressure" has been ascribed " to the exportation of bullion required by the payments on foreign loans and the purchases of foreign stock."

MR. HORSLEY PALMER.

" The speculative action here alluded to, and pertaining to the present inquiry, originated in the loans to Don Pedro upon his first attempt to recover the throne of Portugal. The money advanced effected the overthrow of Don Miguel, and upon that overthrow followed the speculative mania in the foreign stock market. More loans were contracted in aid of Donna Maria, and provided the contractors could only secure their agency and commission, the public were left to take care of themselves. The rage for speculation being further excited by the popular idea of overthrowing absolutism and establishing liberal governments throughout the Peninsula, Spain came in for her share of the plunder obtained through English credulity. These loans were going forward from July, 1833, until towards the end of 1834, when the profit realized upon the daily extending engagements in the foreign stock market engendered a further spirit of speculation in almost every kind of previously neglected South American, Spanish, and Portuguese bonds, causing an enormous advance in all, and in some nearly 100 per cent. In short, until the spring of 1835 hardly a packet arrived from the Continent which did not come loaded with every sort of foreign securities for realization upon our foreign stock exchange. During that period, and through the means here referred to, the bullion and coin held by the bank in October, 1833, was reduced by the sum of £5,100,000, effected by £2,900,000 silver sold, and £3,200,000 sovereigns exported. It may perhaps be maintained that the sale of silver by the bank was the means of preventing a further export of gold than otherwise would have taken place, and that there is no proof of the export of bullion having been occasioned by the operations upon the foreign stock market. In reply it may be stated, that not only the demand for the silver and export of the sovereigns originated and continued during the mania alluded to, but further, that that demand ceased the moment the reaction took place in May, 1835, when a panic seized the dealers in foreign securities, causing their prices to fall with far greater rapidity than they had risen.

" In the progress of the contraction, which ensued upon the diminution of the bullion held by the bank, the market rate of interest gradually advanced for first-rate commercial paper from 2½ to 3½ per cent. per annum, which may be quoted as having been its value in May, 1835; at that time there was no material increase in the paper money circulation of the interior, consequently, immediately upon the discredit taking place, the export of gold ceased and the foreign exchanges further advanced, bringing back the major part of the gold which had been exported in the preceding eighteen months, thereby clearly shewing that the currency was not redundant."

MR. RICARDO.

" Foreign stock is a commodity, the dealings in which with other countries operate precisely in the same manner as would the dealings in any other article of commerce. Whether the stock imported be for investment or speculation, the effect on the currency will be precisely the same. If, at any one period, a larger portion of these securities be purchased in the markets abroad than can be paid for in commodities, the balance will be sent in bullion; but this would also be the case if the excess were cotton, or silk, or wool. The only difference is, that foreign stocks are transmitted and paid for more promptly; and with an exchange apparently not unfavourable, it may not be practicable to obtain bills, without creating a depression which renders it equally advantageous to export the precious metals. It may also happen that, in the engagements attendant on a foreign loan, when payments are fixed at certain periods, shipments of bullion may be made to particular places upon which bills cannot be obtained, without the exchanges being generally below par; but this cannot be carried to any considerable extent, (it certainly has not occurred since 1825,) and in most cases the bullion will come back through other channels.

" The "speculative action," which is animadverted upon by Mr. Palmer, is rather the effect than the cause of a derangement in the currency, which derangement is likely to have been first occasioned by a redundant circulation of the Bank of England. When money is abundant, the rate of interest low, and the prices of English securities high, a disposition to speculate uniformly arises, and this will expend itself on any objects which may present themselves. In 1824 and 1825, it took an extensive range: numerous were the foreign loans and foreign undertakings entered into, and to these were added a variety of internal enterprises; hence the wide-spread ruin occasioned by the bursting of all those schemes, in consequence of the sudden contraction of the currency towards the end of 1825. The mischief was greater than it ever has been since; and at that period, there were no joint stock banks upon whose shoulders to lay the blame.

" At the beginning of 1834, money became very abundant, and the price of the English funds improving, the " speculative action" again exhibited itself. Attention was chiefly attracted, in the absence of other schemes, towards Portuguese and Spanish securities; in addition to these, a large amount of Dutch stock was imported; and the extent to which these operations were carried, brought about the evils of May, 1835, the mischief of which was entirely confined to the stock market.

" In 1836, the " speculative action" arising out of the low rate of interest once more raised its head; but in this instance it vented itself in railways and joint stock banks. These undertakings have already experienced a very severe check: the ultimate result remains to be seen.

" If the artificial abundance of money, which gave rise to the various " speculative actions" above alluded to, can be traced to have arisen out of the mismanagement of the circulation by the Bank of England, then will the blame sought to be attached to others fall more justly on the directors of that establishment.

" To subject every transaction in foreign stocks to a stamp duty, must be very difficult, if not impracticable. A tax of this kind on bonds that pass from hand to hand, would be so easily evaded, that it is not likely the legislature would impose it. With regard to rendering time bargains illegal, the example of this law applied to the English funds shows that such a law is not effectual in checking speculation."

MR. SALOMONS.

" To attempt to limit the freedom of trade, by interfering with the unrestricted transfer of foreign funds, seems to me most imprudent; and, notwithstanding the opinion of Mr. Horsley Palmer, whose sentiments are entitled to very great attention, I have no hesitation in saying, that he is quite mistaken in his views regarding the effect which the foreign stock transactions have on the country. I will not go into the question of the policy either of the introduction of foreign stock into England, or of the investments that may have been made in them, but I will venture to assert, and I speak advisedly, that the country has gained enormously by the investments, that have up to the present time been made, in the debts of the various solvent European governments; nay, I go still further, and assert that their transmission has on the whole been favourable to commerce, that they have tended to regulate the exchanges, instead of having had an injurious effect on them; and many most important payments could not have been made, without the powerful assistance derived from the export of foreign stock, as the most ready means of payment. It will be, indeed, difficult to shew how such descriptions of foreign funds, for which a ready market exists on the Continent as well as in London, could at all injuriously affect the exchanges. Such funds are, in truth, a universal currency, and payments either at home or abroad, can be made, by their transmission, and the balance of trade as readily adjusted, as by an import or export of the precious metals.

" It should be anticipated, that whenever the interest of money becomes reduced to a low rate in this country, some individuals will then look to foreign funds, as a mode of investment paying a higher rate of interest than can be obtained at home; and an export of bullion may in consequence take place to pay for such foreign funds. But after all, this ought to be regarded only a symptom of an overflowing currency, and should also exhibit an excess of bullion in the coffers of the Bank of England. Whenever an opposite state of things arises, and money becomes more valuable in this country than abroad, an export of foreign funds usually takes place, and essentially contributes to set the exchanges right.

How were the large importations of corn in the years 1829 and 1830 paid for, except by the means provided by the export of foreign funds? During those years the sales of French stock by English holders amounted to a most enormous sum. The unfortunate events that preceded the change of government in France were in progress ; they had, however, no bad effect upon the price of the public funds of the European States. Whether the English holders of French Stock were alarmed at the pertinacity of the Polignac administration, or whether they were contented with the great advance in the price of the French funds, which in those years had attained their maximum, sales of securities were made to an extensive amount ; and notwithstanding the very large importation of corn which took place at that period, it seems by the high rates of exchange which were then current, that the proceeds of those sales paid for the importation of corn, and also increased the bullion in the coffers of the Bank of England. I may also say with confidence that during the whole of the year 1836, the amount of export of foreign European funds, and remittances to this country for the dividends due on them, greatly exceeded the import of such securities, and thus assisted the exchanges at a most important and eventful period."

Fifthly. The pressure has been ascribed to " the recent demand for gold for the United States, arising out of the operations adopted relative to the currency of that country."

MR. PALMER.

" The reduction which took place in the bullion of the bank from April to September last is that to which it is now necessary to advert. The diminution amounted to £2,600,000, and was effected in the following manner :—

£200,000 amount of Silver sold.
  100,000   „   Gold do.
2,300,000   „   Sovereigns supposed to have been exported to America.

" In order to explain the cause and origin of the American demand, it may be proper to advert to the proceedings in America for the two precedi 'g years. The avowed hostility of the President, Jackson, to the renewal of the Charter of the Bank of the United States terminated, after a violent struggle, in compelling that institution to prepare for closing all its transactions in 1836, and for repaying that portion of its capital that belonged to government. In order, however, to increase the embarrassment of the bank, measures were taken for removing from its custody the deposits of public money, and for placing them in the hands of various States' banks, under condition that they should be prepared to pay a given portion of all demands upon them in gold coin. To facilitate this object, Congress passed a law reducing the quantity of fine gold in the Eagle, the equivalent of ten dollars, from 246 to 232 grains. This depreciation of the American gold coin had the effect of raising the current value of the English sovereign from 4.44 dollars to 4.87$\frac{1}{2}$, or 8$\frac{1}{2}$ per cent. above its previous current value. Simulta-· neously with and in aid of these measures several of the States were persuaded to prohibit the circulation of notes of less amount than five dollars. In taking these measures it was an avowed object on the part of the President to endeavour to establish a gold currency in conjunction with silver throughout the union. The hostility evinced towards the Bank of the United States, and the refusal to renew its charter, caused an immediate contraction of the usual accommodation granted at the numerous branches of that establishment, and further, entailed upon the favoured States' banks the necessity of procuring an additional supply of gold to enable them to fulfil the conditions under which they received the deposits of government money. This combination of circumstances, having no relation to the ordinary commercial transactions existing between this country and America, materially reduced the rate of exchanges with Europe, so much as to afford a profit upon the importation both of gold and silver from England and other parts of Europe. The President, too, in order further to aid his favourite project of increasing the metallic currency throughout the States, directed, in the early part of last year, his agents in Europe to remit in gold to America the whole of the indemnity money to be received from France and Naples. About the time of that remittance having been made, a loan for a million or twelve hundred thousand pounds was negotiated in London on account of the United States' bank, to facilitate the settlements upon the expiration of the charter. The effect of that loan upon the currency of this country was further increased by a much larger amount than usual of American securities, or of States' stock ; bank and canal stock, &c. having been sent to Europe for sale, and upon which credit had been given by some of the principal houses in England in anticipation of the sums they were expected to realize, thus throwing an inordinate amount of American paper upon our markets. If all these circumstances be adverted to, together with the very large amount of produce imported from America, the surprize will be, not that some, but that so small a portion of bullion should have been abstracted from England as that already stated. Since the 1st September last the demand has entirely ceased, and notwithstanding the desire of the American President to retain the bullion acquired from this country, it is not improbable that we may soon see it return from that quarter of the world."

MR. RICARDO.

" The demand for gold for America was one of a peculiar nature, and could be attended with no disadvantage to this country, if the currency had been in a sound and wholesome state : it was accompanied with a great depression of prices in the United States, and must have been largely paid for in commodities. An alteration had been made in the value of the gold coin of America, and other measures adopted with regard to her currency, which compelled her immediately to seek for a supply of the precious metals ; this her want of circulating medium obliged her to obtain at any cost. England and France were the two countries with which America was in most intimate relations, and which were best able to administer to her immediate wants; in addition to the £2,300,000 supposed to have been taken from England, a large quantity was also obtained from France, which was furnished by the Bank of France, as stated in the report of that association.

" Fortunately for America there was a considerable debt due to her from France which was then paid ; fortunately also England took off a large amount of the local stocks of the different States, otherwise the fall in her produce and the distress consequent on the diminution of prices would have been infinitely increased.

" The consideration of this question shows the difference which there is between an import or export of gold, arising out of the ordinary transactions of commerce, which may either occasion a balance of trade in favour of or against a country, and that which is caused by a forced contraction or augmentation of the circulation. In the one case gold is the most profitable article which can be received or paid—it is either added to, or abstracted from, the circulation, and the equilibrium of prices is shortly restored. In the other case, prices are forced by a contraction of the currency much below the level of those of other countries, or raised by an increase of it considerably above that level ; thus on the import of gold a large amount of commodities is given in exchange, and on its export a lesser amount of commodities received : such have at times been the consequences of the forced action on the currency under the system adopted by the Bank of England, subjecting the public to severe loss, and inflicting serious injury on individuals, in their commercial relations with one another."

<hr />

Sixthly. The following articles, published April 7, 1837, ascribe the recent pressure to the improvident conduct of some of the American houses, and to the facilities they obtained from the bill brokers. I insert these articles, chiefly because they are supposed to have had their origin in the bank parlour, and to express the sentiments of at least some of the directors.

FROM THE COURIER.

" The Bank of England has been again compelled to come forward with a fresh loan to sustain the falling credit of certain parties engaged in the American trade. The extraordinary circumstances under which the houses engaged in that trade have been placed by the non-arrival of packets from America, would seem to justify and warrant an interference of this sort on the part of the bank, though we must say, speaking generally, that this continued tinkering and bolstering cannot be too much deprecated, particularly when it is recollected that the Bank of England has not at this moment the third part of the treasure she ought to possess ; and when the fact, that not a single ounce of bullion has returned to us from the Continent, to which we exported during the adverse exchange of the past year above two millions sterling, shows conclusively that the currency is still in excess and ought to be diminished. It is not enough, in vindication of the relief afforded to embarrassed houses, to say, that their transactions have been fair and honourable. Nothing can justify the bank in coming forward to bolster them up, that is, in doing what in her present situation is obviously inconsistent with all sound principle, but the injury that would arise to the public interests by her resolutely adhering to the strict line of duty. If this injury be great and imminent, the bank will be justified, but not otherwise. However honourable the transactions of the American houses, it is certain that the majority, for there are exceptions, have conducted their business with the most reckless improvidence, and in such a way as called forth at a distant period, from parties acquainted with the facts, the most confident predictions of their ruin. It is certain, indeed, that they could not have gone so very far beyond their means as they have done, but for the support and encouragement given them by the money-dealers. The latter are, in fact, by far the greatest culprits, and have evinced the most stupendous infatuation and ignorance in their transactions with the American houses of which any example is to be found in the history of commerce. They first gave them unlimited credit, and could not get too many of their bills ; and when the natural course of events (for they never could have discovered it themselves) made them aware of the consequences of their conduct, and of the extreme risk they were running, they instantly got upon the opposite tack—from unhesitating confidence they went to the extreme of suspicion and distrust, and totally rejected the paper of which a little while before they could not get too much !

" What may be the *denouement* of this affair no individual can at present foresee ; but, however it may end, it is certain that it will ever form one of the most discreditable chapters in the history of British commerce. Nothing of any kind has occurred to interrupt the intercourse between this country and America ; nor has any thing occurred in either country to lessen its resources or to diminish its power of meeting its engagemnets. There has not, in fact, been any more room or real ground for derangement in the intercourse between Liverpool and New York, than in that between Liverpool and Manchester, or between London and Hampstead. Instead of being involved in the greatest difficulties, and threatened with total ruin, the parties engaged in the trade, had they displayed the most ordinary prudence or sagacity, would have been conducting a secure business, and realizing handsome profits. But they would not be satisfied with this. Parties with £100,000, or £200,000 must needs carry on a business for which a capital of one or two millions would hardly have been adequate ; in consequence, they had to depend wholly on discounts, became gamblers instead of merchants, and are now reaping the natural and legitimate fruits of their conduct ! We believe Jonathan has managed his part of the business with infinitely more sense and discretion, than has been displayed on this side the water. Unless he has done so, there will be a frightful extent of bankruptcy."

FROM THE MORNING POST.

" The directors of the Bank of England, after much anxious deliberation, have adopted, at a very late hour this evening, a resolution of great importance to the commercial world at the present crisis. We announce the decision of the bank with great satisfaction, because we know that it will dispel much of the alarm, which has for some days existed in a very extensive and important department of commerce, and avert an impending calamity, the consequences of which must have been deeply and widely felt, and this without exposing the bank to any considerable danger of eventual loss. The circumstances which called for the interference of the bank in this instance were, as will presently be seen, so urgent and extraordinary, as to require and justify a deviation from the rules which have generally governed the conduct of that corporation.

" The case we are about to state is that of a commercial house of the first rank, whose transactions have been principally with America ; and, important as this case is in itself, the decision of the bank with respect to it acquires additional importance, from the fact, that it has been regarded by that corporation as one of a considerable class ; and from the probability that the extraordinary intervention which it has required and obtained, will not be withheld in other cases, in respect to which claims equally valid, and explanations equally satisfactory, can be brought forward.

" The house in question has shown that it possesses a capital of between £300,000 and £400,000 of its own, and that its commercial friends and connexions in this country have come forward to its aid, and subscribed an additional capital of equal amount. It has shown that all its transactions have been in the fair and honourable course of commercial dealing. It has shown that its debtors, chiefly in America, are persons who have hitherto been considered affluent and honourable men, and that there is at this moment, no ground to suspect either their integrity or solvency. It has shown that all its transactions have been in the strictest commercial sense, legitimate and prudent, free from the imputation of any other error, than that of their excessive magnitude in proportion to the not inconsiderable capital by which they were to be sustained.

" This house was, however, one of those which, in the recent pressure, was compelled to apply to the bank for assistance, and obtained it, upon the ordinary securities, to an extent supposed to be sufficient to carry it over every difficulty—to an extent which there is no doubt would have been sufficient for this purpose, but for the extraordinary circumstances which have since arisen. It will at once be perceived that we allude to the non-arrival of the American packets, several of which have been overdue for a considerable period. To houses in such a situation as we have described, the consequences of an extraordinary and unexpected delay in the arrival of large remittances need not be explained. The calamity, to avert which so much has already been done, seemed this morning to be inevitable, together with its necessary consequences, the discredit and ruin of other houses to an indefinite and appalling extent. In these circumstances another application was made to the Bank of England, and the result, as we have already stated, was a resolution of that body to give assistance to the full extent of the exigency, without insisting upon what would have been an impossible condition—the actual possession of tangible securities. The bank will enable the house to which we have referred to meet all its outstanding obligations, with the proviso that it shall not enter into any new engagements until the advances of the bank are fully repaid.

" In the facts we have thus detailed we see another very striking example of the advantages which the commercial world derives from the existence of such a body as the Bank of England, possessing, in its own boundless credit, the ample means of arresting the fatal progress of discredit in the mercantile community, and unfettered by any rules of conduct so strict and absolute as to prevent the prompt and efficacious application of those means in whatever manner may be best adapted to the existing emergency. It is plain that no power analogous to this could be confided to any government establishment, or be acquired by any banking institution of recent origin.

" It may not be improper on this occasion to advert to one of the causes which have mainly contributed to involve mercantile houses of considerable capital, of great credit, and of unblemished reputation, in the kind of embarrassment from which the firm in question has been so seasonably and generously rescued. This cause is the system, the imprudent and vicious system, which we understand to be very generally pursued by the bill-brokers of the city of London. These persons have at their disposal a large proportion of the unemployed capital of the metropolis, which is entrusted to them for the purpose of being invested in good bills of exchange. The bills which bear the names of certain houses are deemed preferable to any other; and with respect to this class of bills, the brokers act as if it were impossible for them to have too many. They grasp at them with an eagerness which would seem to imply that they hold them to be not merely as good as money, but much better. Hence it not unfrequently happens, that the houses enjoying this extreme facility of obtaining money, are led progressively into an extension of their transactions beyond what the amount of their capital, independent of this resource of unstinted discount can sustain. But the moment it happens to be remarked that the paper of a particular house, or of a particular class of houses, or of a particular branch of trade, is unusually abundant, the inference is drawn that trading in excess, as compared with capital, is going on ; and the commercial money market, that is, the general body of bill-brokers, immediately take the alarm, and, instead of gradually and gently diminishing the amount of their transactions in the paper supposed to be redundant, they at once cast it off altogether. Thus the commercial money market first tempts merchants of high credit to trade beyond the extent of their independent resources, and then, when they are least prepared for such a reverse, suddenly throws them back upon their own independent resources. Some of the houses whose position has recently occasioned so much anxiety have, we believe, experienced this vicissitude in its most aggravated form. The example should teach merchants, in the most palmy state of their credit, the necessity of apportioning the extent of their transactions to the amount of their capital, instead of placing too implicit a reliance upon the precarious resources of credit, which are generally least available when most required."

Although the distress in America is not attributed to any misconduct on the part of the banks, yet it has led, in the States of New York, to some proposals for a modification of the law. The following articles are taken from the Times ; but it does not appear that the regulations mentioned have yet been adopted.

" The attempt making in the United States to procure the repeal of the restraining law, by which all private banks, and discounts by private individuals are prohibited, has been attended with some circumstances well worthy of general notice. The aim has been on the part of the corporate banks to prevent altogether the introduction of any act to repeal the restraining law ; but not having succeeded in this, their next object has been to annex such conditions to the repeal as would render it of little avail, and leave to them the same ascendancy still in the money transactions of the union. Hence it has assumed all the characters of a bill drawn up to protect the corporate banking interest, instead of giving increased facilities to the merchants ; and much indignant feeling has in consequence been vented against the measure. The second section of the bill, for example, establishes an invidious distinction between this and any other department of business, by requiring the person who opens an office of discount and deposit to report to the clerk of the city or county his name, residence, and the amount of capital he intends to employ. The third section places a still stronger impediment to free action, by forbidding him to issue or circulate any other notes than those of the safety fund banks of the State. According to this provision, the private banker cannot accommodate the customer about to travel with any of the notes of the States through which he is to pass; and any infringement of the law is made punishable with fine and imprisonment. The private banker, or the keeper of an office of discount and deposit, is further prohibited from resorting for accommodation to any banks already established; and it is even made penal in such banks to afford him accommodation. They are also to be restrained from buying land, dealing in goods, or trading in stock, and their business confined exclusively to receiving deposits, lending money, and taking paper on personal, instead of landed security, for the loans made. These, and other clauses, had so far perverted the original intention of those who had urged on the measure for establishing discount and deposit banks, that they felt little interest in carrying it through, and characterized the bill as only meant, in effect, to increase the power of the chartered banks."

" The legislature of New York (Feb. 7.) had introduced a bill " to improve the currency of that State, by compelling the safety fund banks to keep their bills at par. To accomplish such object, it proposed to provide that every bank should, as often as once a week, cause to be entered upon its books the amount of specie on hand, and the amount of notes in circulation; and that the bank commissioners should be empowered to examine the books. At the quarterly examination, any bank whose average circulation of bills should exceed twice the amount of specie on hand, should be deemed guilty of violating the law, and the bank commissioners were to report them to the legislature. The law was not to apply to such banks as should keep their bills at par in New York. No bank was to be allowed to charge a greater premium on the sale of any draught on Albany or New York than one half per cent."

In his farewell address to the people of America, the late President, General Jackson, thus refers to the Bank of the United States:

" In reviewing the conflicts which have taken place between the different interests in the United States, and the policy pursued since the adoption of our present form of government, we find nothing that has produced such deep-seated evil as the course of legislation in relation to the currency. The constitution of the United States unquestionably intended to secure to the people a circulating medium of gold and silver. But the establishment of a national bank by Congress, with the privilege of issuing paper-money receivable in the payment of the public dues, and the unfortunate course of legislation in the several states upon the same subject, drove from general circulation the constitutional currency, and substituted one of paper in its place.

" It was not easy for men engaged in the ordinary pursuits of business, whose attention had not been particularly drawn to the subject, to foresee all the consequences of a currency exclusively of paper, and we ought not, on that account, to be surprised at the facility with which laws were obtained to carry into effect the paper system. Honest, and even enlightened men, are sometimes misled by the specious and plausible statements of the designing. But experience has now proved the mischiefs and dangers of a paper currency, and it rests with you to determine whether the proper remedy shall be applied.

" The paper system being founded on public confidence, and having of itself no intrinsic value, it is liable to great and sudden fluctuations, thereby rendering property insecure, and the wages of labour unsteady and uncertain. The corporations which create the paper-money cannot be relied upon to keep the circulating medium uniform in amount. In time of prosperity, when confidence is high, they are tempted, by the prospect of gain, or by the influence of those who hope to profit by it, to extend their issues of paper beyond the bounds of discretion and the reasonable demands of business. And when these issues have been pushed on from day to day, until public confidence is at length shaken, then a reaction takes place, and they immediately withdraw the credits they have given, suddenly curtail their issues, and produce an unexpected and ruinous contraction of the circulating medium, which is felt by the whole community. The banks by this means save themselves, and the mischievous consequences of their imprudence or cupidity are visited upon the public. Nor does the evil stop here. These ebbs and flows in the currency, and these indiscreet extensions of credit, naturally engender a spirit of speculation injurious to the habits and character of the people. We have already seen its effects in the wild spirit of speculation in the public lands, and various kinds of stock, which within the last year or two seized upon such a multitude of our citizens, and threatened to pervade all classes of society, and to withdraw their attention from the sober pursuits of honest industry. It is not by encouraging this spirit that we shall best preserve public virtue and promote the true interests of our country. But if your currency continues as exclusively paper as it now is, it will foster this eager desire to amass wealth without labour ; it will multiply the number of dependants on bank accommodations and bank favours ; the temptation to obtain money at any sacrifice will become stronger and stronger, and inevitably lead to corruption, which will find its way into your public councils, and destroy, at no distant day, the purity of your government. Some of the evils which arise from this system of paper press with peculiar hardship upon the class of society least able to bear it. A portion of this currency frequently becomes depreciated or worthless, and all of it is easily counterfeited, in such a manner as to require peculiar skill and much experience to distinguish the counterfeit from the genuine note. These frauds are most generally perpetrated in the smaller notes, which are used in the daily transactions of ordinary business ; and the losses occasioned by them are commonly thrown upon the labouring classes of society, whose situation and pursuit puts it out of their power to guard themselves from these impositions, and whose daily wages are necessary for their subsistence. It is the duty of every government so to regulate its currency as to protect this numerous class as far as practicable from the impositions of avarice and fraud. It is more especially the duty of the United States, where the government is emphatically the government of the people, and where this respectable portion of our citizens are so proudly distinguished from the labouring classes of all other nations, by their independent spirit, their love of liberty, their intelligence, and their high tone of moral character. Their industry, in peace, is the source of our wealth; and their bravery in war has covered us with glory; and the government of the United States will but ill discharge its duties if it leaves them a prey to such dishonest impositions. Yet it is evident that their interests cannot be effectually protected unless silver and gold are restored to circulation.

" These views alone of the paper currency are sufficient to call for immediate reform; but there is another consideration which should still more strongly press it upon your attention.

" Recent events have proved that the paper money system of this country may be used as an engine to undermine your free institutions; and that those who desire to engross all power in the hands of the few, and to govern by corruption or force, are aware of its power, and prepared to employ it. Your banks now furnish your only circulating medium, and money is plenty or scarce, according to the quantity of notes issued by them. While they have capitals not greatly disproportioned to each other, they are competitors in business, and no one of them can exercise dominion over the rest; and although, in the present state of the currency, these banks may and do operate injuriously upon the habits of business, the pecuniary concerns and the moral tone of society, yet, from their number and dispersed situation, they cannot combine for the purposes of political influence; and whatever may be the dispositions of some of them, their power of mischief must necessarily be confined to a narrow space, and felt only in their immediate neighbourhoods.

" But when the charter of the Bank of the United States was obtained from Congress, it perfected the schemes of the paper system, and gave to its advocates the position they have struggled to obtain, from the commencement of the federal government down to the present hour. The immense capital and peculiar privileges bestowed upon it, enabled it to exercise despotic sway over other banks in every part of the country. From its superior strength it could seriously injure, if not destroy, the business of any one of them which might incur its resentment; and it openly claimed for itself the power of regulating the currency throughout the United States. In other words, it asserted (and it undoubtedly possessed) the power to make money plenty or scarce at its pleasure, at any time, and in any quarter of the union, by controlling the issues of other banks, and permitting an expansion, or compelling a general contraction, of the circulating medium, according to its own will. The other banking institutions were sensible of its strength, and they soon generally became its obedient instruments, ready at all times to execute its mandates; and with the banks necessarily went, also, that numerous class of persons in our commercial cities who depend altogether on bank credits for their solvency and means of business, and who are therefore obliged for their own safety to propitiate the favour of the money power by distinguished zeal and devotion in its service. The result of the ill-advised legislation which established this great monopoly was, to concentrate the whole money power of the union, with its boundless means of corruption and its numerous dependants, under the direction and command of one acknowledged head ; thus organizing this particular interest as one body, and securing to it unity and concert of action throughout the United States, and enabling it to bring forward, upon any occasion, its entire and undivided strength to support or defeat any measure of the government. In the hands of this formidable power, thus perfectly organized, was also placed unlimited dominion over the amount of the circulating medium, giving it the power to regulate the value of property and the fruits of labour in every quarter of the union ; and to bestow prosperity, or bring ruin, upon any city or section of the country, as might best comport with its own interest or policy.

" We are not left to conjecture how the monied power, thus organized, and with such a weapon in its hands, would be likely to use its The distress and alarm which pervaded and agitated the whole country when the Bank of the United States waged war upon the people, in order to compel them to submit to its demands, cannot yet be forgotten. The ruthless and unsparing temper with which whole cities and communities were impoverished and ruined, and a scene of cheerful prosperity suddenly changed into one of gloom and despondency, ought to be indelibly impressed on the memory of the people of the United States. If such was its power in a time of peace, what would it not have been in a season of war, with an enemy at your doors ? No nation but the freemen of the United States could have come out victorious from such a contest; yet, if you had not conquered, the government would have passed from the hands of the many to the few ; and this organized money power, from its secret conclave, would have dictated the choice of your highest officers, and compelled you to make peace or war as best suited their wishes. The forms of your government might for a time have remained, but its living spirit would have departed from it.

" The distress and sufferings inflicted on the people by the bank are some of the fruits of that system of policy which is continually striving to enlarge the authority of the federal government beyond the limits fixed by the constitution. The powers enumerated in that instrument do not confer on Congress the right to establish such a corporation as the Bank of the United States, and the evil consequences which followed may warn us of the danger of departing from the true rule of construction, and of permitting temporary circumstances, or the hope of better promoting the public welfare, to influence, in any degree, our decisions upon the extent of the authority of the general government. Let us abide by the constitution as it is written, or amend it in the constitutional mode, if it is found to be defective.

" The severe lessons of experience will, I doubt not, be sufficient to prevent Congress from again chartering such a monopoly, even if the constitution did not present an insuperable objection to it. But you must remember, my fellow-citizens, that eternal vigilance by the people is the price of liberty ; and that you must pay the price if you wish to secure the blessing. It behoves you, therefore, to be watchful in your states, as well as in the federal government. The power which the monied interest can exercise, when concentrated under a single head, and with our present system of currency, was sufficiently demonstrated in the struggle made by the Bank of the United States. Defeated in the general government, the same class of intriguers and politicians will now resort to the States, and endeavour to obtain there the same organization which they failed to perpetuate in the union ; and with specious and deceitful plans of public advantages, and state interest and state pride, they will endeavour to establish, in the different states, one monied institution with overgrown capital, and exclusive privileges sufficient to enable it to control the operations of the other banks. Such an institution will be pregnant with the same evils produced by the Bank of the United Sates, although its sphere of action is more confined ; and in the state in which it is chartered, the money power will be able to embody its own strength, and to move together with undivided force, to accomplish any object it may wish to attain. You have already had abundant evidence of its power to inflict injury upon the agricultural, mechanical, and labouring classes of society ; and over those whose engagements in trade or speculation render them dependent on bank facilities, the dominion of the state monopoly will be absolute, and their obedience unlimited. With such a bank and paper currency, the money power would, in a few years, govern the state and control its measures ; and if a sufficient number of states can be induced to create such establishments, the time will soon come when it will again take the field against the United States, and succeed in perfecting and perpetuating its organization by a charter from Congress.

" It is one of the serious evils of our present system of banking, that it enables one class of society, and that by no means a numerous one, by its control over the currency, to act injuriously upon the interests of all the others, and to exercise more than its just proportion of influence in political affairs. The agricultural, the mechanical, and the labouring classes, have little or no share in the direction of the great monied corporations ; and from their habits and the nature of their pursuits, they are incapable of forming extensive combinations to act together with united force. Such concert of action may sometimes be produced in a single city, or in a small district of country, by means of personal communication with each other ; but they have no regular or active correspondence with those who are engaged in similar pursuits in distant places ; they have but little patronage to give to the press, and exercise but a small share of influence over it ; they have no crowd of dependants about them, who grow rich without labour, by their countenance and favour, and who are, therefore, always ready to execute their wishes. The planter, the farmer, the mechanic, and the labourer, all know that their success depends upon their own industry and economy, and that they must not expect to become suddenly rich by the fruits of their toil. Yet these classes of society form the great body of the people of the United States ; they are the bone and sinew of the country, men who love liberty, and desire nothing but equal right and equal laws, and who moreover hold the great mass of our national wealth, although it is distributed in moderate amounts among the millions of freemen who possess it. But, with overwhelming numbers and wealth on their sides, they are in constant danger of losing their fair influence in the government, and with difficulty maintain their just rights against the incessant efforts daily made to encroach upon them. The mischief springs from the power which the monied interest derives from a paper currency, which they are able to control ; from the multitude of corporations, with exclusive privileges, which they have succeeded in obtaining in the different states, and which are employed altogether for their benefit ; and unless you become more watchful in your states, and check this spirit of monopoly, and thirst for exclusive privileges, you will, in the end, find that the most important powers of government have been given or bartered away, and the control over your dearest interests has passed into the hands of these corporations."

The latest packet from America brings intelligence that the Bank of the United States have consented to assist the merchants in making their remittances to England. The following correspondence has passed between the President, Mr. Biddle, and some of the mercantile houses in New York.

" TO MR. N. BIDDLE, PRESIDENT OF THE BANK OF THE UNITED STATES.

" NEW YORK, MARCH 28, 1837.

" Sir,

" In consequence of the peculiar position in which the commercial community is placed, it was resolved at a meeting of the merchants held this day, that the Bank of the United States be invited to interpose at this conjuncture by a shipment of coin, and by the use of their credit, so as to meet the exigencies of the occasion, and by the sale of bills of exchange on Europe, by the issue of post notes, payable at Philadelphia, and of bonds payable at some distant day in London, Paris, and Amsterdam, to facilitate negociations at home, and furnish safe remittances abroad, and thus, not only be of service to this city, but to the United States at large.

" By order of the meeting,

" J. A. STEVENS, *Chairman.*
" C. A. HEKSCHER, *Secretary.*
(Signed by 101 houses.)

" NEW YORK, MARCH 29.

" Sir,

" I had this day the honor of receiving your communications of the 28th instant, accompanied by the signatures of many highly respectable citizens of New York, requesting the interposition of the Bank of the United States to assist in removing the existing embarrassments of the commercial community. The board of directors, on learning from a committee of your fellow-citizens the existence of these difficulties, directed me to visit New York for the purpose of ascertaining their nature and the most effectual mode by which the bank could be useful. All the suggestions for that purpose contained in your letter will accordingly be presented to the board of directors, from whom they will receive the most respectful and early attention. In the mean time what my own observation suggests as the cause of these troubles is, that recent events in the South and in Europe have, in concurrence with reasons of an earlier date, produced a paralysis of private credit, which deranges the whole system of our foreign and domestic exchanges. For this the appropriate remedy seems to be to substitute for the private credit of individuals the more known and established credit of the bank, until public confidence in private stability has time to revive. To the foreign exchanges I would apply that restorative, by issuing the engagements of the bank, payable in London, Paris, and Amsterdam, to be remitted in lieu of private bills. These will be ready by the next packet, and they will enable the country to make, without injury, an early provision for the adjustment of the foreign exchanges, by the natural operation of remitting its produce and its coin. A similar operation I shall recommend to the board in respect to the domestic exchanges, by an enlarged and immediate purchase of bills of exchange on the distant sections of the union.

" These are the two measures which seem to be the best adapted for the present emergency. They are proposed with the sincerest desire that they may be useful, and with a clear conviction that, aided by the spirit and intelligence which belong to this community, they will carry it triumphantly through its present difficulties. The surest ground of confidence for others is confidence in ourselves ; and I have seen this community bear up against calamities which would have broken the spirit of a less free and generous people.

" N. BIDDLE,

" President of the Bank of the United States."

The following communication upon the subject, is from a correspondent of the Times :

" NEW YORK, APRIL 2, 1837.

" For several days past the money market has been in a most agitated and alarming state. When the packet of the 24th ult. sailed from this place, public confidence was greatly shaken, and the commercial men of the country appeared to be tottering on the brink of ruin. Through the instrumentality of the United States Bank light is again breaking in upon the mercantile community. At no period since the war of 1812 have the capitalists experienced greater apprehension, or the rate of interest been so high, as during the past week. An arrangement has been effected with Mr. Biddle, in pursuance of which he has agreed to issue the bonds of the United States Bank for a specified amount, payable 12 months after date, in London, Paris, or Amsterdam, at the option of the purchaser. For these bonds he receives mercantile notes at a rate which will bring the bonds a fraction below the cash price of first-rate private bills of exchange; thus enabling the merchant, by extending the time of payment a few months, to continue his remittances, in bills or paper of solidity equal to any which can be made in Europe or America. The American merchants, as a class, are men of great enterprise and industry; many of them are opulent; but the injudicious interference of the government in attempting to regulate the currency has produced such a scene of speculation and such a transfer of specie to the interior, as to embarrass all the regular business of the country. It may not be uninteresting to retrospect.

" Immediately on the removal of the public deposits from the late Bank of the United States, speculations in its stock on a fall to a large amount ensued. Here the mania commenced. New local banks were thereupon chartered by the several states, and their stocks became the object of speculation. Paper money being abundant in the hands of a favoured few, these gentlemen turned their attention to the national domain. The disease had now become contagious, and consequently almost universal. Every description of property, foreign or domestic, personal or landed, was greatly enhanced in price; but more especially lands. In the height of this mania, the President directed the Secretary of the Treasury, under the date of the 11th of July, 1836, to instruct the receivers of public money in the Western and South Western States, to take nothing in payment of the public lands but gold or silver, or the notes of banks in their vicinity that would be redeemed forthwith in specie.

" The effect of this order was twofold. It compelled the Western and South Western banks to contract their loans, and thus gradually withdraw from circulation a portion of their paper, lest they should subject themselves to a run. At the same time it compelled both the speculator and the actual settler, who wished to purchase the public land, to provide himself in the Atlantic States with specie, and transport it to the place where his payment was to be made.

" By these anti-commercial regulations, the gold and silver was withdrawn from the marts of commerce, where it ought to have been left, as the means of regulating and balancing the accounts between the United States and foreign countries; and it was thrown into a district of territory, where it remains unemployed in the vaults of certain banks, in the form of deposits, to the credit of the government. This is an unnatural state of things, and has tended incalculably to embarrass the merchants on the seaboard. It may be asked, in what manner have these merchants been so much embarrassed, if they have not entered into these land speculations? it is due to them to give the explanation.

" I have already remarked, that the Western and South Western banks were compelled to restrict their loans. The effect of this was to prevent, to a limited extent, the merchants in those states from remitting the amount they owed in the Atlantic cities. But this was not the greatest evil. Many of the interior merchants, allured by the brilliant prospects of realizing fortunes, sold the goods which they had purchased on credit in New York, Philadelphia, &c., and invested the proceeds in the public lands, and thus deprived themselves of the means of paying their debts, although they might be perfectly solvent. These operations have been in progress for the last twelve or thirteen months. Their ultimate effect every thinking man ought to have anticipated. Under such circumstances, the money market became sorely pressed, and it was utterly impossible for the merchants to have continued their payments much longer, either at home or abroad, without some relief. That relief, for foreign purposes, could not be had in the form of metal, because the great bulk of it is in the interior of the country, and cannot be transported to the trading cities while the rivers are closed, but at great hazard, great expense, and a tedious journey. The relief could not be granted in the form of discounts, by the local or state banks, because the proceeds of such discounts, it was apprehended, would be drawn in specie for the payment of foreign debts. In such a crisis, what was to be done?

" A committee of merchants from this city, invited Mr. Biddle to New York. They submitted to him their case. He became satisfied that without relief they could not promptly meet their engagements. At the same time he was equally well satisfied, that the great body of them were not only solvent, but in many instances opulent, and that all they required was time to collect their debts. The Bank of the United States was in a condition to grant the requisite relief. Its board of directors had hoarded, with the caution of the miser, the credit of the institution. That credit is placed on a foundation so deep and so broad that it cannot be shaken. The bank has finally settled with the government for the seven millions of stock, which it owned in the late United States Bank. It had just received a decision of the Pennsylvania legislature, (a majority of which was elected as its opponents) by a vote of sixty-one to thirty-one, declaratory in substance that the state had no right to interfere with its charter. In short, in every point of view, in the language of a sailor, the bank was sailing before the wind with a free sheet.

" Under such circumstances, Mr. Biddle has agreed to exchange the credit of the bank for the credit of the American merchants. This evinces his confidence in their stability, and it affords them time for the collection of their Western and South-Western debts, which collection, in many instances, will be made in specie. This specie, if found necessary, will be shipped to England by the United States Bank, to meet the payment of its bonds, and thus the balance, if any be due by this country, will be liquidated, and trade flow in its accustomed channels.

" The scarcity of money is already operating, both upon the price of produce and real estate. It will continue thus to operate, until things have found their proper level. Every species of property is falling, and a strong disposition pervades the trading community to limit its business. The rage for speculation is at an end ; and in the midst of all the present agitation and turmoil, to my view, the prospects are more cheering than they have been at any period for some months past. I do not mean to be understood that there will be no more failures—I wish I could think so. What I mean to say is, that the relief, in my opinion, which has now been granted, will not only facilitate remittances, and thus sustain the character and credit of many commercial houses, which, without it, must have suspended payment; but that it also made certain, during the present year, the exportation of sufficient specie to balance any debts or obligations due, or to become due, from American citizens; and this specie will be drawn from a section of the country where it is of no use, and shipped, without producing injury, or creating inconvenience to any other section of the country.

" I have extended my remarks on this subject, because I consider it of vital importance to both Great Britain and the United States, and because I have long apprehended and prognosticated the most disastrous consequences in the money market. I frankly confess, that I could not discover the source from whence the necessary relief was to be derived. But the Bank of the United States has generously, and I think wisely, stepped in, and done for the American merchants, what the British Government most providently does for the same class of men—loaned its credit. The British Government grants exchequer bills; Mr. Biddle in like manner has granted the bonds of the bank; and although he may, and probably will, sustain some loss by the transaction, yet he will have earned for the institution so much good will, and such kind feeling, that it must ultimately prove advantageous.

" Exchange from 11 to 12 per cent., say $11\frac{1}{4}$ or $11\frac{1}{2}$. Southern bills, endorsed in New York, from $9\frac{1}{2}$ to $10\frac{1}{2}$, according to the degree of confidence in the endorser.

" A GENEVESE TRAVELLER."

APPENDIX.

No. I.

An Average Quarterly Account of the Liabilities and Assets of the Bank of England.

	Circulation.	Deposits.	Total Liabilities.	Securities.	Bullion.	Total Assets.
1833.						
Oct. - - -	19,800,000	13,000,000	23,000,000	24,200,000	10,900,000	34,200,000
1834.						
Jan. 1 - -	18,216,000	13,101,000	31,317,000	23,596,000	9,948,000	33,524,000
Feb. 4 - -	18,377,000	14,086,000	32,463,000	24,762,000	9,954,000	34,716,000
March 4 -	18,700,000	14,418,000	13,118,000	25,547,000	9,829,000	35,376,000
April 1 -	19,097,000	14,011,000	33,108,000	25,970,000	9,431,000	35,401,000
May 6 -	18,978,000	14,081,000	33,059,000	26,691,000	8,884,000	35,575,000
June 3 -	18,922,000	14,539,000	33,461,000	27,312,000	8,645,000	35,957,000
July 1 -	18,895,000	15,096,000	33,991,000	27,593,000	8,695,000	36,252,000
July 29 -	19,110,000	15,675,000	34,785,000	28,502,000	8,598,000	37,100,000
Aug. 26 -	19,147,000	15,384,000	34,531,000	28,679,000	8,272,000	36,951,000
Sept. 23 -	19,126,000	14,754,000	33,880,000	28,691,000	7,695,000	36,386,000
Oct. 21 -	18,914,000	13,514,000	32,428,000	27,840,000	7,123,000	34,963,000
Nov. 18 -	18,694,000	12,669,000	31,363,000	27,138,000	6,781,000	33,919,000
Dec. 18 -	18,304,000	12,256,000	30,560,000	26,362,000	6,720,000	33,082,000
1835.						
Jan. 15 -	18,012,000	12,585,000	30,597,000	26,390,000	6,741,000	33,131,000
Feb. 10 -	18,099,000	12,535,000	30,634,000	26,482,000	6,693,000	33,175,000
Mar. 10 -	18,311,000	12,281,000	30,592,000	26,657,900	6,536,000	33,193,000
April 7 -	18,591,000	11,289,000	29,880,000	26,328,000	6,329,000	32,557,000
May 5 -	8,542,000	10,726,000	29,268,000	25,764,000	6,197,000	31,961,000
June 2 -	18,460,000	10,558,000	29,028,000	25,562,000	6,150,000	31,712,000
June 30 -	18,315,000	10,954,000	29,269,000	25,678,000	6,219,000	31,897,000

	Circulation.	Deposits.	Total Liabilities.	Securities.	Bullion.	Total Assets.
July 28 -	18,322,000	11,561,000	29,883,000	26,244,000	6,283,000	32,527,000
Aug. 25 -	18,340,000	12,308,000	30,648,000	26,964,000	6,326,000	33,290,000
Sept 22 -	18,240,000	13,230,000	31,470,000	27,888,000	6,261,000	34,149,000
Oct. 20 -	17,930,000	14,227,000	32,157,000	28,661,000	6,186,000	34,847,000
Nov. 17 -	17,549,000	16,180,000	33,729,000	30,069,000	6,305,000	36,374,000
Dec. 15 -	17,821,000	17,729,000	35,050,000	31,048,000	6,626,000	37,674,000
1836.						
Jan. 12 -	17,262,000	19,169,000	36,431,000	31,954,000	7,076,000	39,030,000
Feb. 9 -	17,427,000	18,366,000	35,793,000	31,022,000	7,471,000	38,493,000
March 8 -	17,739,000	16,966,000	33,705,000	29,806,000	7,701,000	37,507,000
April 5-	18,063,000	14,751,000	32,814,000	27,927,000	7,801,000	35,728,000
May 3 -	18,154,000	13,747,000	31,901,000	27,042,000	7,782,000	34,824,000
May 31 -	18,051,000	13,273,000	31,324,000	26,534,000	7,663,000	34,197,000
July 1 -	17,899,000	13,810,000	31,709,000	27,153,000	7,362,000	34,515,000
July 28 -	17,940,000	14,495,000	32,435,000	28,315,000	6,926,000	35,241,000
Aug. 25 -	18,061,000	14,796,000	32,857,000	29,345,000	6,325,000	35,670,000
Sept. 22 -	18,147,000	14,118,000	32,265,000	29,406,000	5,719,000	35,125,000
Oct. 21 -	17,936,000	13,324,000	31,260,000	28,845,000	5,257,000	34,102,000
Nov. 17 -	17,543,000	12,682,000	30,225,000	28,134,000	4,933,000	33,067,000
Dec. 15 -	17,361,000	13,330,000	30,691,000	28,971,000	4,545,000	33,516,000
1837.						
Jan. 14 -	17,422,000	14,354,000	31,776,000	30,565,000	4,287,000	34,652,000
Feb. 12 -	17,868,000	14,230,000	32,098,000	31,085,000	4,032,000	35,117,000
Mar. 7-	18,178,000	13,260,000	31,438,000	30,579,000	4,048,000	34,627,000
April 6-	18,432,000	11,192,000	29,624,000	28,813,000	4,071,000	32,884,000

No. II.

A List of Private Banking Establishments, which have been merged into Joint Stock Banks : arranged by Mr. W. T. HENDERSON, *Sub-Manager to the London and Westminster Bank.*

Place.	Firm of Private Bank.	Joint Stock Bank.	When first estab.
1 Abergavenny	Jones and Davis ...	Monmouths. & Glamorgans. Bkg. C.	1836
2 Aberystwith	Benson and Co.	North and South Wales Bank	1836
3 Ashton under Line	Buckley and Co......	Saddleworth Banking Co.	1833
4 Atherstone	Chapman and Co. ...	Coventry Union Banking Co.	1836
5 Barnard Castle ...	Skinner and Co......	National Provincial Bank of England	1833
6 Barnstaple	Pyke and Co..........	Ditto...................................... .	1833
7 Bedale...............	Hutton and Co.......	Swaledale & Wensleydale Bkg. Co.	1836
8 Birmingham	Rotton and Co.	National Provincial Bank of England	1833
9 Bridgwater	Stuckeys&Woodlands	Stuckey's Banking Co.	1826
10 Bristol.	Stuckey, Lean & Co.	Ditto	1826
11 Ditto	Elton, Baillie & Co.	Bristol Old Bank........................	1826
12 Ditto	Cave, Ames and Co.	Ditto......................................	1826
13 Ditto	Haythorne & Wright	National Provincial Bank of England	1833
14 Bruton.............	Stuckey Nephew&Co	Stuckey's Banking Co................--.	1826
15 Burford	Pitt and Co.	County of Gloucester Banking Co ..	1836
16 Bury	Grundy and Wood .	Bury Banking Co.	1836
17 Cardiff	Towgood and Co. ...	Monmouths. & Glamorgans. Bkg. C.	1836
18 Carlisle	Wakefield and Co....	Carlisle Banking Co.	1836
19 Cheltenham	Hartlands and Co....	Gloucestershire Banking Co.	1831
20 Ditto	Pitt and Co.	County of Gloster Banking Co.......	1834
21 Chepstow	Jones and Blewitt ...	Monmouths. & Glamorgans. Bkg. C.	1836
22 Chippenham	Gundry and Co......	Wilts and Dorset Banking Co.	1836
23 Cirencester	Pitt and Co.	County of Gloster Banking Co.	1834
24 Colebrooke Dale .	Darby and Co.	Shropshire Banking Co.	1836
25 Collumpton........	Hurley and Co.......	Devon and Cornwall Banking Co...	1831
26 Coventry...........	Beck and Prime.... .	Coventry and Warwicks. Bkg. Co. .	1835
27 Ditto	Bunney and Co......	Ditto......................................	1835
28 Crewkerne	Payne and Co.........	Stuckey's Banking Co.............. ...	1826
29 Darlington	Skinner and Co......	National Provincial Bank of England	1833
30 Daventry...........	Watkins and Co.....	Northamptonshire Banking Co.......	1836
31 Ditto	Perceval and Co. .. .	Northampton Union Banking Co....	1836
32 Denbigh	R. Sankey	North and South Wales Bank.........	1836
33 Dewsbury	Hagues and Co......	West Riding Union Banking Co......	1832
34 Dobcross...........	Buckley and Co......	Saddlesworth Banking Co.	1833
35 Dursley	Vizard and Co.	County of Gloucester Banking Co ..	1834
36 Ditto	Wood, Pitt and Co....	Ditto........	1834
37 Ditto	Bloxsome and Co. . .	National Provincial Bank of England	1833
38 Evesham...........	Hartlands and Co...	Gloucestershire Banking Co.	1831
39 Exeter..............	Sparkes and Co......	Devon and Cornwall Banking Co....	1831
40 Falmouth	Carne and Co.	Western District Banking Co.........	1836
41 Farringdon	Pitt and Co....	County of Gloucester Banking Co. .	1834
42 Frome	Waldron and Co. ...	Stuckey's Banking Co.	1826
43 Glastonbury	Reeves and Co.	Ditto......................................	1826
44 Gloucester	Russell and Co.	Gloucestershire Banking Co..	1831
45 Gloucester	T. Turner	National Provincial Bank of England	1833
46 Gainsborough......	Skinner and Co.......	Ditto......................................	1833
47 Halifax	Rawdon Briggs & Co.	Halifax Commercial Bank............	1836
48 Ditto	Rawson and Co......	Halifax & Huddersfield Union Bank	1836
49 Hereford	Jones and Co.........	Herefordshire Banking Co.	1836
50 Huddersfield	Rawson and Co......	Halifax & Huddersfield Union Bank	1836
51 Ditto	Wilson, Sons & Co.	West Riding Union Bank	1832
52 Ilfracombe	Vye and Co.	National Provincial Bank of England	1833
53 Ilminster	Stuckeys and Co.... .	Stuckey's Banking Co.	1826
54 Kingsbridge	Nicholson and Co....	Devon and Cornwall Banking Co....	1831
55 Knaresborough ...	Coates and Co.	Yorkshire District Bank...............	1834
56 Langport	Stuckeys and Co. ...	Stuckey's Banking Co.	1826

Place.	Firm of Private Bank.	Joint Stock Bank.	When first estab.
57 Leamington............	Tomes and Co.	Warwick & Leamington Bankg. Co.	1834
58 Leeds	Perfects and Co......	Yorkshire District Bank	1834
59 Ditto	George Smith & Co.	Leeds and West Riding Banking Co.	1835
60 Leeds	Bywater and Co......	Leeds Commercial Bank............ ...	1836
61 Leicester.......... .	Pares and Co.........	Pares' Leicestershire Banking Co. ...	1836
62 Leyburn	Hutton and Co.	Swaledale & Wensleydale Bnkg. Co.	1836
63 Liverpool	Aspinal and Co......	Liverpool Central Bank	1836
64 Ditto	Hope and Co........	Liverpool Borough Bank	1836
65 Lymington	John West............	Wilts and Dorset Banking Co.	1836
66 Malmesbury	Robins and Co.	Ditto.......................	1836
67 Melksham	Moule and Co.	North Wilts Banking Co.	1835
68 Monmouth	Jones and Davis......	Monmouths. & Glamorgans. Bkg. C.	1836
69 Nantwich ....∙ ...	Mare and Eaton......	Northern & Central Bk. of England	1834
70 Neath	Rowland and Co. ...	Glamorganshire Bank..................	1836
71 Newcastle up.Tyne	Backhouse and Co...	Northumberland & Durham Bkg. C.	1836
72 Ditto	Chapman and Co. ...	Newcastle Union Banking Co.	1836
73 Newport............	Jones and Blewitt ...	Monmouths. & Glamorgans. Bkg. Co.	1836
74 Ditto (Salop)......	Horden and Co......	Shropshire Banking Co.	1836
75 Northampton	Perceval and Co. ...	Northamptonshire Union Bankg. Co.	1836
76 Ditto ....∙....	Watkins and Co......	Ditto.......................................	1836
77 Nottingham	Moore and Robinson	Moore & Robinson's Nottingh. B. C.	1836
78 Oldham	Buckley and Co......	Saddleworth Banking Co.	1833
79 Penzance.	Boase and Co.........	Western District Banking Co.........	1836
80 Plymouth	Hingston & Prideaux	Devon and Cornwall Banking Co...	1831
81 Pontefract	Perfect and Co.	Yorkshire District Bank...............	1834
82 Pontypool	Jones and Blewitt ...	Monmouths. & Glamorgans. Bkg. C.	1836
83 Richmond, Yorks.	Hutton and Co......	Swaledale & Wensleydale Bkg. Co.	1836
84 Rotherham........	Walkers and Co......	Sheffield and Rotherham Bank.... .	1836
85 Saddleworth	Buckley and Co......	Saddleworth Banking Co.	1833
86 Sheffield	Walkers and Co......	Sheffield and Rotherham Bank	1836
87 Shepton Mallet ...	Reeves and Co.	Stuckey's Banking Co................	1826
88 Shields	Backhouse and Co...	Northumberland & Durham Dist. B.	1836
89 Ditto	Chapman and Co. ...	Newcastle Union Banking Co........	1836
90 Shiffnal	Biddle and Co.	Shropshire Banking Co.	1836
91 Stokesley	Skinner and Co......	National Provincial Bank of England	1833
92 St. Columb.........	Magor and Co.	Western District Banking Co.	1836
93 Stockport	Christy and Co......	Manchester & Liverpool District Bk.	1829
94 Stockton	Skinner and Co......	National Provincial Bank of England	1833
95 Stratford on Avon.	Tomes and Co.	Stourbridge & Kidderminster Bk. C.	1834
96 Sunderland........	Backhouse and Co...	Northumberland & Durham Distr. B.	1836
97 Swansea	Eaton and Co.........	Glamorganshire Banking Co.	1836
98 Taunton	Stuckeys and Co. ...	Stuckey's Banking Co................	1826
99 Tetbury	Pitt and Co............	County of Gloucester Banking Co....	1834
100 Ditto	Wood and Co.	Gloucestershire Banking Co.........	1831
101 Tewkesbury	Hartlands and Co.	Ditto..	1831
102 Thirsk...............	Dresser and Co......	Yorkshire District Bank	1834
103 Totness	Prideaux and Co. ...	Devon and Cornwall Banking Co...	1831
104 Truro	Magor, Turner & Co.	Western District Bank	1836
105 Usk	Jones and Blewitt ...	Monmouths. & Glamorgans. Bkg. C.	1836
106 Warwick..........	Tomes and Co.	Warwick and Leamington Bank......	1834 .
107 Wellington	Reynolds and Co. ...	Shropshire Banking Co................	1836
108 Wells	Stuckeys and Co. ...	Stuckey's Banking Co................	1826
109 Wells	Reeves and Co.	Ditto.	1826
110 Whitchurch	Corser and Co.	Northern & Central Bank of England	1834
111 Whitehaven	Hartley and Co......	Bank of Whitehaven	1829
112 Wolverhampton ...	Hordern and Co. ...	Wolverhampton & Staffords. Bkg. C.	1831
113 Yeovil..........	Whitmarsh and Co. .	Stuckey's Banking Co................	1826

FINIS.

E. JUSTINS AND SON, PRINTERS, MARK LANE.

ERRATA.

Page 117, Line 6, for eleven, read *twelve*.
— 118, — 38, for contracted, read *counteracted*.